Solidarity Between the Sexes and the Generations

GLOBALIZATION AND WELFARE

Series Editors: Denis Bouget, *MSH Ange Guépin, France,* Jane Lewis, *Barnett Professor of Social Policy, University of Oxford, UK and* Peter Taylor-Gooby, *Darwin College, University of Kent, Canterbury, UK*

This important series is designed to make a significant contribution to the principles and practice of comparative social policy. It includes both theoretical and empirical work. International in scope, it addresses issues of current and future concern in both East and West, and in developed and developing countries.

The main purpose of this series is to create a forum for the publication of high quality work to help understand the impact of globalization on the provision of social welfare. It offers state-of-the-art thinking and research on important areas such as privatisation, employment, work, finance, gender, and poverty. It will include some of the best theoretical and empirical work from both well established researchers and the new generation of scholars.

Titles in the series include:

Social Exclusion and European Welfare States
Edited by Ruud J.A. Muffels, Panos Tsakloglou and David G. Mayes

Restructuring the Welfare State
Globalization and Social Policy Reform in Finland and Sweden
Virpi Timonen

The Young, the Old and the State
Social Care Systems in Five Industrial Nations
Edited by Anneli Anttonen, John Baldock and Jorma Sipilä

Solidarity Between the Sexes and the Generations
Transformations in Europe
Edited by Trudie Knijn and Aafke Komter

Solidarity Between the Sexes and the Generations

Transformations in Europe

Edited by

Trudie Knijn,
Professor of Social Science, Utrecht University,
The Netherlands

Aafke Komter,
Professor of Social Science, University College, Utrecht,
The Netherlands.

GLOBALIZATION AND WELFARE

Edward Elgar
Cheltenham, UK . Northampton, MA, USA

Published by
Edward Elgar Publishing Limited
Glensanda House
Montpellier Parade
Cheltenham
Glos GL50 1UA
UK

Edward Elgar Publishing, Inc.
136 West Street
Suite 202
Northampton
Massachusetts 01060
USA

A catalogue record for this book is available from the British Library

ISBN   1 84376 358 3

Printed and bound in Great Britain by MPG Books Ltd, Bodmin, Cornwall

Contents

Figures and Tables

FIGURES

TABLES

Contributors

Pearl A. Dykstra is a senior researcher at the Netherlands Interdisciplinary Demographic Institute (NIDI), and holds a chair in Family Demography at the University of Utrecht. Her publications focus on late life families, aging and the life course, family demography, social networks and loneliness. At present she is the coordinator of the Netherlands Kinship Panel Study (NKPS), a longitudinal study of 10,000 individuals and their families funded by the Netherlands Organization for Scientific Research (NWO). In 2000 she and her colleague Aart Liefbroer wrote a book (in Dutch) on the changing life courses of Dutch adults. Currently she and Gunhild Hagestad are working on a book on childless older adults, which is to be published by Greenwood Press.

Trudie Knijn is a Professor of Social Science at the University of Utrecht. She is a research member of the Inter-University Center for Social Science Theory and Methodology and one of the NKPS researchers. She founded the European Network 'Women, Welfare State and Citizenship' and has coordinated it since 1991. Her publications in English include: 'The Rationalized Marginalization of Care', in B. Hobson (ed.), *Gender and Citizenship in Transition* (2000); 'Careful or Lenient: Welfare Reforms for Lone Mothers in the Netherlands' (with Frits van Wel), *Journal of European Policy* (2001); 'Commodification and De-commodification' (with Ilona Ostner) and 'Contractualization' (with Ute Gerhard and Jane Lewis), both in B. Hobson, J. Lewis and B. Siim, *Contested Concepts in Gender and Social Politics* (2002).

Aafke Komter holds the endowed Comparative Studies of Social Solidarity chair at the University of Utrecht and is an Associate Professor at the Department of Interdisciplinary Social Science. She is Head of the Department of Social Science at Utrecht University College, the University's Honors College. She participates in the NKPS, the multi-actor and multi-method survey on family solidarity. She has conducted research on gift giving, reciprocity and social bonding. Some of her main publications are *The Gift. An Interdisciplinary Perspective* (1996) (ed.) and 'Reciprocity as a Principle of Exclusion', *Sociology* (1996). With Wilma Vollebergh she published 'Gift Giving and the Emotional Significance of Family and Friends', *Journal of*

Marriage and the Family (1997), and 'Solidarity in Dutch Families', *Journal of Family Issues* (2002).

Irena E. Kotowska is a Professor at Warsaw School of Economics and Head of the Demographic Unit at the Institute of Statistics and Demography, Warsaw School of Economics – SGH. She was appointed Vice-Chairman of the Social Sciences Section at the Polish Academy of Sciences in 1999 - 2002 and 2002 - 2005 and is an editor of *Studia Demograficzne*, the demographic journal of the Committee of Demographic Sciences, Polish Academy of Sciences Warsaw School of Economics – SGH. She recently published 'Labour Market Developments in Europe and Challenges for Poland' in *Europas Arbeitswelt von Morgen* (2000); 'Demographic and Labor Market Developments in the 1990s', in M. Ingham, H. Ingham and H. Domański (eds), *Women on the Polish Labor Market* (2001), and 'Poland Demographic Changes since 1989', *Der Donauraum: Geburtenrückgang in Mittel-und Osteuropa* (2001).

Arnlaug Leira is a Professor of Sociology at the Department of Sociology and Human Geography, University of Oslo, Norway and a Senior Research Fellow at the Institute for Social Research. Recent publications include *Working Parents and the Welfare State. Family Change and Policy Reform in Scandinavia*, Cambridge University Press (2002); (with T. P. Boje) *Gender, Welfare State and the Market* (2000); Editor of *Family Change: Practices, Policies and Values* (1999); 'Updating the Gender Contract?' *NORA*, (2002) and 'Care: Actors, Relationships', (with C. Saraceno), in B. Hobson, J. Lewis and B. Siim (eds), *Contested Concepts in Gender and Social Politics* (2002).

Jane Lewis is Barnett Professor of Social Policy at the University of Oxford. She works on gender and social policies, family policies, the history of social provision, social care and the role of the third sector. Her most recent books include: *The End of Marriage? Individualism and Intimate Relations* (2001); with K. Kiernan and H. Land, *Lone Motherhood in Twentieth-Century Britain* (1998), and (ed. with B. Hobson and B. Siim) *Contested Concepts in Gender and Social Politics* (2002).

Ruth Lister is a Professor of Social Policy at Loughborough University. She is a former Director of the Child Poverty Action Group and served on the Commission on Social Justice, the Opsahl Commission into the Future of Northern Ireland and the Commission on Poverty, Participation and Power. She is a founding Academician of the Academy for Learned Societies for the Social Sciences and a Trustee of the Community Development Foundation. She has published widely around poverty, income maintenance and women's citizenship. Her latest book is *Citizenship: Feminist Perspectives* (2003). Recent journal articles have appeared in *Citizenship Studies, Economy and Society, Theory, Culture and Society* and *Critical Social Policy*.

Claude Martin is a senior research fellow at the CNRS (National Center of Scientific Research) and a member of the Centre de recherches sur l'action politique en Europe (Institut d'études politiques and University of Rennes 1). He is director of the Laboratory of Social and Health Policy Analysis (Laboratoire d'analyse des politiques sociales et sanitaires) of the National School of Public Health in Rennes. His field of research is social policy and the restructuring of welfare states in Europe, the evolution of the family and policies towards the frail elderly. His publications in English include (with A. Math and E. Renaudat) 'Caring for Very Young Children and Dependent Elderly People in France: Towards a commodification of social care', in J. Lewis (ed.), *Gender, Social Care and Welfare State Restructuring in Europe* (1998); 'Marriage, Cohabitation and the PACS in France', *International Journal of Law, Policy and the Family* (2001) and (with C. Chambaz) 'Lone Parents, Employment and Social Policy in France: Lessons from a Family-Friendly Policy', in J. Millar and K. Rowlingson (eds), *Lone Parents, Employment and Social Policy* (2001).

Ilona Ostner is a sociologist and Professor of Social Policy at the Georg-August University, Goettingen, Germany. She is the author of numerous comparative articles on gender, family employment and social policy and co-editor (with Stephan Lessenich) of *Drei Welten des Wohlfahrtskapitalismus. Der Sozialstaat in vergleichender perspective* (1998), co-editor of the *Zeitschrift fur Soziologie* (Journal of Sociology) and (with T. Knijn) 'Commodification and De-commodification' in B. Hobson, J. Lewis and B. Siim (eds), *Contested Concepts in Gender and Social Politics* (2002).

Chiara Saraceno is a Professor of Sociology at the University of Turin, Italy and chairs the Interdisciplinary Center on Gender and Women's Studies (CIRSDe) there. She has published extensively on gender and the family, social policies and poverty and social exclusion. Her publications include *Social Assistance Dynamics in Europe. National and local welfare regimes* (2002); *Mutamenti della Famiglia e Politiche Sociali* (2003); (with Manuela Naldini) *Sociologia della famiglia* (2001); (with Marzio Barbagli) *Separarsi in Italia* (1998); 'Changing Gender and Family Models: Their Impact on the Social Contract in European Welfare States', in O. Zunz, L. Schoppa and N. Hiwatari (eds*), Social Contracts under Stress* (2002).

Constanza Tobío is a Professor of Sociology at Universidad Carlos III de Madrid and Vice-Dean in charge of the Sociology degree. Her main areas of research are urban sociology and the family - employment relationship, space and gender, lone parent families and women's strategies for combining employment and motherhood. She has published *Las Familias Monoparentaleles en España* (with Juan Antonio Fernández Cordón) and articles in several national and international journals. She is currently conducting research on Spanish women's strategies for coping with family responsibilities and paid work, a subject on which she has published several articles in *European Societies, Cahiers du Genre* and *Revista Española de Investigaciones Sociológicas*. She is currently a member of the RTN European Research Network 'Grandparenthood and Inter-generational Relationships in Aging European Populations'.

Fiona Williams is a Professor of Social Policy and Director of the ESRC Research Group on Care, Values and the Future of Welfare at the University of Leeds. She has published on gender, 'race', class and their relation to welfare, and on the experiences of people with learning difficulties. Her present research is focused on the empirical, conceptual and ethical dimensions of care practices. Recent publications include 'In and Beyond New Labour: Towards a New Political Ethics of Care', *Critical Social Policy* (2001); 'The Presence of Feminism in the Future of Welfare', *Economy and Society* (2002) and 'Contesting "Race" and Gender in the European Union: A multi-layered recognition struggle' in B. Hobson (ed.), *Recognition Struggles and Social Movements: Contested Identities, Power and Agency* (2003).

Introduction

Trudie Knijn and Aafke Komter

After almost a century, the theme of social solidarity is back on the academic and political agenda. As was the case at the end of the nineteenth century when classical sociologists like Durkheim and Weber reflected upon the effects industrialization and modernization would have on interpersonal ties, the final decades of the twentieth century bear witness to increasing concern about the development of social solidarity. How do the multifarious socio-economic, cultural and political transformations in western welfare states since the 1960s and 1970s affect patterns of solidarity, for instance between men and women or between various generations? And how do patterns of solidarity influence collectively organized welfare arrangements and public family welfare policy?

Transformations in family solidarity and in welfare states are interdependent and influence each other. Processes of restructuring labour, care and income between the sexes and generations question traditional family roles and positions. It is no longer self-evident there who cares for whom, who provides the income, how it will be distributed among the family members, and whether and how long children and elderly family members have a claim to familial resources to help and support them. Comparable questions arise at the social and political level. How effective is the social security system in the face of demographic changes in intergenerational relations? Who cares for the elderly and for young children now that women increasingly go out to work? How do the increasing income gaps among households affect social solidarity?

Individualization impacts the level of people's concern for each other and their willingness to help and care for those in need, for instance in their own family. But family solidarity cannot be studied without examining the changes in social policy as reflected in collectively organized forms of solidarity. There has been increasing academic interest in recent years in how demographic developments and changes in gender relations are linked to welfare state care arrangements. One of the major questions is: Which structures of care, labour and income (social security, care for the elderly, working hours) are needed to keep up with the changing relations between sexes and generations? In turn these changing relations affect how solidarity arrangements emerge collectively as well as in the family context.

Macro- and Micro-Solidarity

In collectively organized macro-solidarity as well as in family micro-solidarity, the horizontal axis of gender relations and the vertical axis of generation relations are of crucial importance. Macro- and micro-solidarity are mutually dependent and the nature of their interrelationship is subject to change based on contemporary social and cultural transformations. For instance, the individual decision to delay childbearing does not only depend on factors in the micro-context of the family, it is also affected by societal processes like women working more. In turn this decision has macro-sociological effects, for instance in terms of the provision of and access to care for the elderly and other forms of care. Similarly women's and men's decisions to share paid and unpaid work affect their work patterns and careers and their availability to provide informal care for members of the coming and going generations. Studying the interdependence between familial micro-solidarity and collective macro-solidarity will thus benefit from a focus on the interrelated horizontal and vertical dimensions of the family system: sexes and generations.

Various academic traditions exhibit an increasing awareness of the links between macro- and micro-solidarity. First, there seems to be a revival of theoretical and reflective studies in the field of family solidarity by a variety of authors such as Beck and Beck-Gernsheim (1990), Cheal (1991) and Giddens (1995). They share a theoretical interest in the interconnection between large-scale cultural transformations (individualization, globalization and reflexivity), social-structural dilemmas (e.g. between family and occupational life, social security and mobility on the labour market) and individual and relational issues (identity, dependence and mutual concern).

In addition, there is a growing body of internationally comparative research on social policy and family relations. It focuses, for instance, on the assumptions embodied in national social policy related to family life. Socio-political assumptions on family life and relations between the sexes and generations may have a stronger impact on financial support and care arrangements for the elderly, taxation policy and social security than economic developments. Research has addressed the effects of social policy on family formation and the division of labour within families. Moreover, how institutional arrangements within the welfare states themselves affect family life has been an important research topic (Lesemann and Martin, 1993; Sainsbury,

1994, 1996; Lewis, 1993; Hantrais and Letablier, 1996; Saraceno, 1996; Esping-Andersen, 1999). These studies show that social policy supports certain forms of family life more than others, thus creating unequal conditions for family solidarity. In recent years, the inequality between various family forms has been studied from a comparative perspective (Lewis, 1997; Kaufmann et al., 2002).

The nature of the welfare state – whether social democratic, corporatist or liberal oriented – appears to be related to patterns of family formation and solidarity. Oddly enough, the welfare states said to be the most family-oriented prove to be the least generous where a financial contribution to the costs of family life is concerned. This results in inequality between families with and without children, a lower birth rate and an increase in the age when women have their first pregnancies (Esping-Andersen, 1999; European Commission, 2000). Compared to the family-oriented countries of southern Europe, social democratic welfare states have a higher birth rate, less inequality between different family types, a smaller income gap between the sexes and a larger one between the generations (European Commission, 2000).

This brief sketch of the possible links between transformations in collective solidarity and family solidarity will have to remain very general. More detailed questions and more precise answers are needed to clarify the interdependence between macro- and micro-solidarity. We hope this book can contribute to the ongoing analysis of the links between transformations in family relations and the transformation of social policy by combining a theoretical and empirical cross-national perspective. Family relations in this book include gender as well as generational ones and family members are approached as active agents and as objects of transformations of welfare states. We focus on relations between partners, parents, fathers, mothers, children and grandchildren of both sexes in order to understand which patterns of interdependence still exist, what kind of changes take place and how they are supported or impeded by developments in European welfare states.

The authors have all participated in the colloquium *Solidarity between the Sexes and the Generations: Transformations in Europe.*[1] They share an interest in empirical studies on family relations and in more theoretical reflection on the meaning and implications of social policy for the position of individuals as family members. Dependence and interdependence, commitment and autonomy, individualization, familialization and de-familialization are the main concepts that inspire them. The concept of 'de-familialization' introduced by Lister (1994) and later adopted by McLaughlin and Glendinning (1994), Saraceno (1996) and Esping-Andersen (1999) appears to be very useful in analysing the changing assumptions underlying social policy as well as the norms and expectations of family members themselves. Another key concept in this book is 'solidarity'. We are challenged by the idea that family relations can no longer be taken for granted. This is why we propose examining the give and take in the family or between the sexes and generations from the perspective of solidarity. Some of the authors explicitly address the notion of family solidarity to find out why it is attracting new attention and whether it deserves a place in the social science vocabulary side by side with the concept of social solidarity.

Broad claims about changes in the relations between public and macro- and micro-solidarity are obviously in need of empirical substantiation. This volume includes detailed empirical studies as well as more theoretical approaches to the links between macro- and micro-solidarity. We hope this combination will stimulate future academic interest and further scientific research in the field. The book addresses three main issues that can combine to clarify the complex subject matter. Part I focuses on transformations in the relations between the public and the private, or macro- and micro-solidarity. Part II highlights some of the demographic trends and investigates the links between macro-sociological trends and family formation. Part III focuses on the micro-level of family solidarity, the changes in reciprocity and solidarity between family members, and how the rights and obligations of family members are defined in social policy.

Summary of the Chapters

In Chapter 1, Claude Martin investigates the history of family solidarity and cites two main phases, the first from the early 1960s to the mid-1970s and the second from 1985 to 1995. During the first phase, the theoretical dispute on family solidarity was between the importance of kinship ties and the family network on the one hand and the idea that the industrialization process helped promote the nuclear family on the other. In the second phase the concept of family solidarity not only imposed itself in sociological research, it became an increasingly important issue in public and political discourse. This period was characterized by a gradual withdrawal of the welfare state and public expenditures cuts in many European countries. The protective role of the family and the potential dangers of an absence of family ties for individuals were both stressed. Nowadays it is widely acknowledged that in addition to the state, the services sector, and the market, the family plays an important role in the complex system of allocations between private and public protection.

The links between the micro-solidarity in the family and the larger social solidarity of the welfare state is the central theme of Chapter 2. Trudie Knijn examines the widely debated issue of whether the welfare state and its caring provisions act as a substitute for family solidarity – the 'substitution thesis' – or on the contrary as a factor supporting or even strengthening family solidarity. She discusses various alternatives to the substitution thesis. One of them, the 'packaging thesis', holds that families combine all kinds of welfare and income resources to make ends meet. Yet another one, the 'complementary thesis', states that a higher social solidarity level accompanies a higher level of family solidarity. According to the 'transmission thesis', financial transmissions between family members are facilitated by state-guaranteed income support. Knijn presents empirical data supporting her argument that the substitution thesis does not hold. Her conclusion is that social solidarity does not replace family solidarity; it complements and reinforces it. She adds a word of caution: the family may not be the best institution for realizing equality between the sexes or the generations.

In Chapter 3 Ruth Lister analyses how micro-solidarity is influenced by the changing patterns of macro-solidarity. She presents evidence on shifts in the boundaries of responsibility between the public and the private and illustrates how friction can arise between government policies and the beliefs of individual family members. Policies stressing the obligations of family members may not concur with the reality of the expectations and preferences of the family members themselves. Transformations in the relation between the public and the private can be understood in terms of the extent to which individuals depend on their family or the state in their efforts to uphold a socially acceptable standard of living. These transformations are reflected in processes of familialization or de-familialization occurring in western welfare states. To get a clearer picture of the changing solidarity between the sexes and generations, Lister advocates cross-national research on how individuals construct their own responsibilities for their welfare, and how they perceive and respond to transformations in the relation between the public and the private.

Changes at the level of macro-solidarity are perceived from the micro-level of family solidarity in Chapter 3, but Jane Lewis' focus in Chapter 4 is on the implications of the deeply gendered nature of the division of paid and unpaid work for macro-level social policy. In the post-war period, governments based their policies on a male breadwinner model, but policy-makers' assumptions on how the family works are now gradually shifting towards an individualized adult worker model, according to which women as well as men go out to work and are equally involved in the care of children.

In both respects, there are considerable differences between the reality of women's and men's contributions to their households in EU members states, and the pattern implied by the adult worker model. New forms of social solidarity need to be promoted to enable women and men to conform to this model. Collective care services for young children and the elderly can help women reduce their double workload. New policies are also needed to promote a more equal valuing and sharing of care work between men and women at home.

Chapter 5 compares trends in income-tested family benefits in various European countries and the degree to which they contribute towards reinforcing individual versus family entitlements. Chiara Saraceno argues that policies on households and families seem to oscillate between strengthening family solidarity and strengthening individualization. She does a comparative analysis of the assumptions on gender and intergenerational dependencies incorporated in family benefits, in particular income-tested benefits for spouses, in various European countries. Contemporary welfare reforms are indicative of a re-familialization as well as a de-familialization of entitlements. On the basis of her analysis, she develops a typology of patterns of familialization versus individualization according to how various countries take into account and define family dependencies in providing benefits and testing income. Saraceno concludes by stating that family benefits are not neutral as regards gender or class divisions. An excessive focus on family solidarity as main locus of family help and care may increase social inequality.

Chapter 6 focuses on trends over time and across Western European countries in patterns of family solidarity, in particular the work-care arrangements in households and families. Pearl Dykstra holds that these arrangements reflect and are shaped by how welfare regimes organize the production of personal and social service needs. There are clear differences in the family patterns that emerge between familialistic welfare regimes such as Spain and Italy, and countries with de-familialized welfare regimes such as the Scandinavian countries, Belgium and France. In addition, Dykstra presents data on the changing life courses of women in Italy, Germany and the Netherlands. In all these countries, the number of fulltime homemakers, though still a numerical majority, is decreasing and the number of working mothers is increasing. Clear country differences are also observed, for instance in the percentages of young women who live on their own before they get married. More and more people are deviating from the standard pattern with its fixed sequence of life phases and gender-specific division of activities.

In Chapter 7, Irena Kotowska reviews some demographic changes in Central and Eastern Europe (CEE). The CEE countries are exposed to processes related to the transition to a market economy and at the same time to large-scale structural and cultural transformation processes. These processes reflect intended as well as unintended changes in collective and family solidarity. The demographic response expressed in family-linked behaviour may be even stronger and more differentiated than in Western countries. The main processes underlying the demographic changes are discussed, including the reassignment of economic functions between the state, the market and the household, and the changing conditions of labour market participation. The labour market situation for women has deteriorated and the position of the family has weakened. During the transition, families have come to rely less and less on state support. The reduction of state support has imposed a greater responsibility on the household to provide for itself. At the same time families are facing increasing income diversification, economic inequality and poverty.

Family solidarity is not necessarily a positive experience for everyone, as is shown in Chapter 8. Aafke Komter addresses the issue of how the micro-level of informal care within the family interacts with the macro-level of welfare state provisions. Research data show that higher levels of formal care are accompanied by higher levels of informal care, supporting the complementarity thesis discussed in Chapter 2. A high level of intergenerational solidarity is still maintained in many Western European countries. However, this does not necessarily coincide with the psychological well-being of elderly family members and their caregivers. Family ties are a mixture of positive and more negative feelings, such as disappointment, anger or dependence. The recipients may experience care as a form of control, and the caregivers may act out of strong norms based on a sense of obligation; in particular working women may experience the obligation to give care as a burden. Another darker side of family solidarity is its selectivity. Informal care is given mainly to family members rather than to friends, putting people who do not have any close relatives at a disadvantage.

The response of welfare states to the new demands of care for young children and the elderly is the topic of Chapter 9. Constanza Tobío discusses the role of kinship support in Spain and France against the background of the state support provided there. Intergenerational relations are conceptualized in terms of reciprocity and solidarity, and care between the generations is studied in two situations, i.e. grandparents who take care of their grandchildren and adult children who take care of their elderly parents. In France kinship support for young children and the elderly complements the ample state services. In Spain, however, the care provided by grandparents compensates for the scarce social policies. With an increasing number of working mothers and low level of public childcare services, in Spain these intergenerational relations play a fundamental role. Working women are supported by their own mothers, who take care of their grandchildren so their daughters can go to work. With the growing demands for childcare and care for the elderly, it should be a matter of debate to what extent this kind of resource will remain desirable or acceptable in the future.

Reciprocity and solidarity between parents and children are again central to Chapter 10. Similar to Tobío, Ilona Ostner defines reciprocity as referring to the norms and practices of give and take, whereas solidarity goes beyond reciprocity because it does not necessarily include an obligation to give back. She observes that in the century of the child, as the twentieth century has been called, children are referred to in terms of the costs they impose on their parents' budgets and opportunities, as well as in terms of the human resources they bring to post-industrial societies. Ostner addresses the question of why people want to have children at all in this type of society by analysing the processes of give and take – or the meaning of reciprocity and solidarity – in the relationship between parents and children. Filial and parental obligations are still strongly felt, and there is still a lot of give and take between children and parents. However, the public contract between the generations as reflected in the state-based provision of childcare and care for the elderly may be gradually replacing the former expectations of give and take within families.

In Chapter 11, Arnlaug Leira studies how familial obligations in Western Europe have been formally defined in family and welfare legislation. In particular she focuses on certain characteristics of the state-family relationship in Scandinavia, where social rights have become individualized and collective solidarity has come to include social care and welfare services. The case of the Nordic welfare states is interesting because social reproduction in these states has been pictured as going public in the past few decades. Leira discusses the Scandinavian policy reforms of the 1990s in some detail. She notes a shift in orientation from the 1970s to the 1990s; in the 1970s support for the modernization of motherhood was at the forefront, and in the 1990s more attention was devoted to how to promote care by fathers. Moreover, parental choice and support for traditional family values are both more strongly propagated. Policies promoting the expansion of state-supported childcare and paid parental leave, earmarking a special leave period for fathers, and the cash benefit of childcare schemes have contributed to the transformation of parental obligations into social rights in the Nordic countries.

In Chapter 12, Fiona Williams examines some of the processes involved in the increased use of migrant domestic labour in countries whose welfare systems have traditionally sustained familial obligations to care, whether by nuclear or extended families, and where dual career families are on the rise. Working mothers who earn enough sustain family solidarity by hiring migrant women to perform caring and cleaning services for them. Implicit in this situation are the unresolved problems of an unequal division of care in the home, the continuing male model of working time and conditions, and the limited responses of changing welfare regimes. Does the use of privately hired domestic help contribute to solving these problems? Williams explores this question by going into the reasons for the increased use of migrant women's domestic labour in some of the major European cities. Global networks of interdependence becoming manifest in the use of migrant women's labour and reveal the challenge to Western family solidarity posed by women's increased paid labour and by men's stagnating involvement in household and emotional labour.

Two Sides of Family Solidarity

Several conclusions, some of them tentative and others more firm, can be drawn on the basis of the chapters in this volume. Firstly, empirical research data on how family solidarity and collective solidarity are related seem to confirm the complementarity thesis more than the substitution thesis, in particular in welfare states with relatively high levels of state support; however, the case of Spain reveals that with low state support, family care acts as a substitute.

Secondly, there are substantial discrepancies in various countries between the assumptions the macro-level social policy on family issues is based on and the reality of women's and men's contributions at home. It is obvious that as long as the policy aims do not coincide with the real-life possibilities and preferences of the policy subjects, family solidarity will not take shape to suit the needs and wishes of the individuals involved.

Thirdly, in countries where social policy relies on family solidarity as the main source of care and support, this may result in growing social inequality. This danger is most imminent in Central Eastern European countries where the transition to a market economy has harmed the position of women and weakened the role of the family.

Fourthly, the chapters reveal the crucial role of women in the transformation of family life and welfare state policy. Welfare states and supranational institutions stress the role of women as workers because of the ageing process in contemporary society and for reasons related to the maintenance of social security systems. However, they are also needed as caregivers for the coming and going generations and also have to have their own babies in time. In many European countries, the issue of being productive on the labour market and being fertile at home is still too often perceived as a woman's issue. It has not yet been solved, which has resulted in adaptive strategies on the part of women themselves and steady but slow changes in social policy.

The reappearance of the theme of family solidarity in the public discourse not only reflects a concern about changes in family care as a consequence of changing relations between the sexes and the generations, it is also indicative of the need for systematic academic (national and cross-national) research into the complex interplay between private and public care and protection. This book warrants the conclusion that family solidarity has two sides to it; on the one hand there are the aspects of life that most people want to protect against excessive state or capitalist market economy intervention. A world of individualized and atomized adult workers with no time for care or intimacy is hardly attractive to anyone. On the other hand, the concept obscures inequalities among family members, in particular gender and generational inequalities and may thus have conservative implications. This book reflects the authors' pursuit of a solution to the dilemma of how to maintain family solidarity without denying the individual family members' need for autonomy.

NOTE

1. This colloquium was organized by the European Network 'Women, Welfare State and Citizenship'. It was held in Amsterdam (28 – 29 June 2001) and was sponsored by the Royal Netherlands Academy of Arts and Sciences (KNAW) and by the Dutch Council of Scientific Research (NOW).

REFERENCES

Beck, U. and E. Beck-Gernsheim (1995), *The Normal Chaos of Love*, Cambridge: Polity Press.

Cheal, D. (1991), *Family and the State of Theory*, New York: Harvester Wheatsheaf.

Esping-Andersen, G. (1999), *Social Foundations of Postindustrial Economies*, Oxford: Oxford University Press.

European Commission (2000), *The Social Situation in the European Union*, Brussels: European Commission.

Giddens, A. (1995), *The Transformation of Intimacy. Sexuality, Love and Eroticism in Modern Societies*, Cambridge: Polity Press.

Hantrais, L. and M.T. Letablier (1996), *Families and Family Policies in Europe*, London: Longman.

Kaufmann, F.X., A. Kuijsten, H.J. Schulze and K.P. Strohmeier (eds) (2002), *Family Life and Family Policies in Europe*, vol. 2, Oxford: Oxford University Press.

Lesemann, F. and C. Martin (eds) (1993), *Home-based Care, the Elderly, the Family and the Welfare State: An International Comparison*, Ottawa: University of Ottawa Press.

Lewis, J. (ed.) (1993), *Women and Social Policies in Europe: Work, Family and the State*, Aldershot: Edward Elgar.

Lewis, J. (ed.) (1997), *Lone Mothers in European Welfare Regimes. Shifting Policy Logics*, London: Jessica Kingsley Publishers.

Lister, R. (1994), '"She has other duties" – women, citizenship and social security', in S. Baldwin and J. Falkingham (eds), *Social Security and Social Change*, Hemel Hempstead: Harvester Wheatsheaf, pp. 31 - 44.

McLaughlin, E. and C. Glendinning (1994), 'Paying for care in Europe: is there a feminist approach?', in L. Hantrais and S. Mangen (eds), *Family Policy and the Welfare of Women*, Loughborough: Cross-National Research Group, pp. 52 - 69.

Sainsbury, D. (ed.) (1994), *Gendering Welfare States*, London: Sage Publications.

Sainsbury, D. (1996), *Gender, Equality and Welfare States*, Cambridge: Cambridge University Press.

Saraceno, C. (1996), 'Family change, family policies and the restructuration of welfare', Paper presented at the OECD Conference Beyond 2000: *The New Social Policy Agenda*, Paris: OECD, 12 - 13 November.

PART ONE

Transformations in the Relationship Between
the Public and the Private

1. The Rediscovery of Family Solidarity

Claude Martin

The concept of solidarity is frequently used today to evoke practices of reciprocity and mutual assistance at the family and kinship level. This implies a break with the past when it was specifically used to refer to collective relationships at the level of society (Bourgeois, 1912; Durkheim, 1902). This double usage, 'micro' and 'macro', is, however, not without problems. Should we somewhat unconcernedly employ the term 'solidarity' both for what occurs in a family network on the occasion of an exchange of services or the donation of an amount in cash and for the situation where two persons are mutually associated through their affiliation to one and the same pension fund? Is solidarity the same when it originates in the collective or family environment? Are there any components of solidarity that may cause us to adopt a similar employment of the concept in both spheres?

One way of answering this question may consist in simply rejecting the expression 'family solidarity' and taking this to mean nothing more than a delusion (Messu, 2000). But it may also be held that recourse to the concept of solidarity both at the level of society and at the level of the family or kinship, allows us to establish a bond between these different levels. Use of the concept of solidarity then becomes a relevant tool for analysing contemporary societal problems.

One may, for instance, assume that these various forms of solidarity can compensate one another. When one of these forms is intensified, the other may decline and vice-versa. It is sometimes felt that the development of the welfare state has contributed to a weakening of the strong ties of the family together with the obligations and norms of mutual aid which it assumed in traditional society. This in turn called for a strengthening of family solidarity to compensate for the limitations of collective solidarity. The profile of a 'minimum state' or a 'weak state' would render it necessary to develop a 'welfare family' or 'family providence' and vice versa.

Sociologists have strongly contributed to this use of the concept of family solidarity. Many of them have sought to define the concept, particularly by distinguishing between, on the one hand, material, instrumental mutual aid (from monetary exchanges to the provision of services) and, on the other hand, social ties and inclusion in relational networks (Déchaux, 1994). The triple economic, domestic and social function of familial solidarity testifies of its complexity.

In this chapter, I will not propose a 'substantial' definition of family solidarity but rather attempt to trace the conditions that have allowed this concept to impose itself little by little, whether in scientific or in political discourse, or in everyday speech. I will pay special attention to the academic usage of the concept of family solidarity. This entails both an understanding of the context in which the concept has taken root and of the discussions or controversies that such academic usage has engendered, constantly interwoven as it is with political and media usages.

EMERGENCE OF THE CONCEPT

The origin of the concept of family solidarity in French contemporary socio-logical research is to be found in the course of two episodes relatively distinct from one another: the first goes from the early 1960s to the end of the 1970s during which the theme of family solidarity is linked with the analysis of kinship ties ; the second, more recent one, covers the period from 1985 to 1995, when the concept of family solidarity clearly imposed itself not only within sociological research but also within public debate.

The more recent rediscovery of familial solidarity comes in a very different context from the preceding one: that of the withdrawal or crisis of the welfare state with its consequences in terms of the risk of exclusion. Sensitivity to the concept of family solidarity is observable in both its positive and negative effects: both the protective role of the family as well as the devastating effects of the absence of family ties on individuals lacking social ties are examined. Concern for those without sufficient familial resources to cope with the difficulties of their existence serves to put a still stronger emphasis on the protective virtues of the family and the assistance that it provides. Thus, family solidarity becomes an additional resource to make up for the shortcomings of public solidarity.

The Kinship Network: Sociability and Mutual Assistance

From the early 1960s and up to the end of the 1970s, a certain number of anthropological and sociological researches were devoted to the study of the kinship network as a relational and mutual assistance network. The aim was to assess the density of social bonds within the kinship system and the presumed reduction of kinship networks to the nuclear family. These studies also purported to ascertain the effects of the organization of the kinship system, on socialization practices, norm production and mutual protection.

Anthropologists and ethnologists have never ceased to affirm the pertinence of the network concept to comprehend the familial environment or village community relationships. Rather than family, they preferred to speak of kinship to designate the grouping of individuals united by ties of blood and alliances, or 'parentèle' so as to include certain acquaintances with whom one feels in close relationship. The anthropological approach is not restricted to the study of traditional societies (Segalen, 1993). Most of these studies contest the thesis formulated by Parsons (1955), according to which the industrialization process has contributed to isolate the conjugal domestic group from its kinship network and to promote the nuclear family model. According to Parsons, the nucleus consists of a conjugal household based upon marriage and is composed of the father whose 'instrumental' role consists of assuring relations with the outside world, while the mother is entrusted with an 'expressive' role within the family nucleus and a small number of children.

As early as 1957, a study by Young and Willmott about Bethnal Green, a working quarter of London, describes the density of familial relations at the level of the urban area in question, the residential proximity, the frequency of encounters and exchanges and the role assumed by relatives in the creation of a friendly network. These writers stress the mother-daughter relationship as of particular importance for the choice of residence. Most of the couples actually live with/near the wife's relatives so as to enable the maintaining of ties, advice and mutual assistance. In a second study, carried out some years later, the same writers examined a section of the population of Bethnal Green relocated in Greenleigh (Young and Willmott, 1968). They noted that the physical removal of blood-relationships undermined the mother-daughter relations while at the same time consolidating the conjugal relationship thereby permitting a reduction in the clear-cut distribution of gender roles assumed by the couple.

The theory of family-linked social networks is principally associated with the name of Bott (1957). She examined how conjugal relations and the distribution of gender roles assumed by the couple are connected with the household's openness to the outside world and wider kinship network. She assumed that the division of roles is linked to the density of the network of relations of the couple outside the household. The more a sociability network has tightened around a familial nucleus and blood-relations with strong interconnections have been intensified by spatial proximity, the more pronounced the division and hierarchization of gender roles and the mutual social pressure will be – the typical working-class model. On the contrary, a more open, more flexible, less localized and kinship-focused network permits a certain normative flexibility and corresponds to more egalitarian gender roles, a model more characteristic of the middle classes. The network will therefore include friends and colleagues.

In France, some studies in the mid 1970s confirmed the permanence of the familial network beyond the strictly conjugal ties and the reduction in the size of households. Gokalp (1978), for instance, described the structure of this network restricting the investigation to relations with the more immediate kin (grandparents, parents, children, brothers and sisters, brothers-in-law and sisters-in-law). These studies assessed not only the residential proximity but also the contact frequency within the kinship network. Gokalp showed that 63% of her representative sample were living at a distance of less than 20 kilometres from their parents. In the light of these studies, the French family would appear to be heavily concentrated in very limited areas, with the children seeking to maintain proximity with their parents and, later in life, with their own children, thereby prolonging a sort of 'distant closeness' with the remainder of their kin network.

In France, the concept of family solidarity is primarily linked with the work of Pitrou (1978). She went beyond a description of 'familial geography' to broach not only the subject of the differential sociability of social classes in an urban environment, but also that of the level of reciprocation and family solidarity. Her study has once again clearly demonstrated the strength of kinship ties, their intensity and frequency, but above all the fact that they are vehicles of a great number of exchanges of services, goods, counselling and information. Reciprocations however appear to be structured differently, not only according to social class, but also to stages in the life cycle.

Pitrou stresses the substantial assistance provided by relatives in the event of socio-economic difficulties, particularly in poor neighbourhoods where people seem to depend more on assistance of this kind. The family plays a role both of daily assistance and protection in cases of 'great blows'. Although in the more affluent neighbourhoods solidarity of this kind may also be operative, it is achieved in a different way. On the one hand, families have a greater number of assets to exchange and, on the other, the aim is to enable the younger generations to accede as quickly as possible to a social condition which is at least equivalent to that of their parents. As against this, mutual assistance would appear to be more diffused, more concealed, and less explicit.

To sum up, in this first period, the main theoretical debate is between those who give priority to the kinship and network aspect and those who adopt a micro-sociological conjugal approach. It is noteworthy that, in the 1970s and 1980s, studies on the kinship network became relatively rare compared to the flood of studies on familial ties from the standpoint of the weakening of conjugal relationships. The subject of family solidarity was gradually making place for a concern about the supposed crisis of the family and an increasing focus on conjugal aspects.

The New 'Kinship Regime' and the Renewed Recognition of Family Solidarity

Only during the end of the 1980s and in the course of the 1990s, the subject of family solidarity really imposed itself both in public and political debate and in the forums of experts and decision-taking assemblies. The family now became to be seen as a real locus of solidarity. Numerous studies assessed the ties of kinship and stressed the role of family solidarity in terms of economic support, the transfer of goods, intergenerational solidarity, social support, assistance with domestic chores and caring, or gift giving and reciprocity (Déchaux, 1990a; Martin, 1992; Attias-Donfut, 1995).

The study of reciprocity in kinship relations became the subject matter of statistical enquiries both in France, Belgium, Switzerland and Canada, for the purpose of assessing the intensities and flows. Also public authorities expressed their wish to achieve a better understanding of family relationships. For France, we can refer to three main enquiries: one carried out by INED (National Institute of Demographic Studies) on relatives and parents (Bonvalet et al. 1993 and 1999); another one on familial assistance and relations (Fougeyrollas-Schwebel and Chabaud, 1993); and the last one by the Caisse Nationale d'Assurance Vieillesse (CNAV) on family solidarity among three successive generations (Attias-Donfut, 1995). In Switzerland, Belgium and Quebec, similar enquiries were implemented (Coenen-Huther et al., 1994; Godbout and Charbonneau, 1993).

Clearly, the subject of networks and kinship solidarity had again become topical. This is also exemplified in the work by Mendras (1988). He advances the hypothesis of the emergence of a new 'regime of kinship'. Mendras assumes a relationship between the size of the domestic group and the importance of the network; the more the domestic group is reduced, the more important the network becomes. This in turn implies a reorganization of kinship relationships. This new organization of relationships in the kinship derives from a phenomenon termed 'distant-closeness', that is not assumed to weaken the intensity or frequency of reciprocations. On the contrary, the author envisages the emergence of a new type of relationships that prioritize solidarity free of daily obligations. This provides flexibility to all the parties involved, in particular children, who can engage in complex strategies so as to utilize more advantageously these kinship networks. This approach however entails the risk of restricting reality to the emerging practices of the educated middle class.

Déchaux (1990a) discusses the patterns of reciprocation in these new kinship relationships, distinguishing, on the one hand, between the concentration of less affluent families on blood-relations as against institutional solidarity and, on the other, the 'logics of dissimulation of intentions', the new model associated with the wish for autonomy that prevails in the middle class. This dissimulation of material interests in reciprocation is based on an important norm whereby parents are solidary with their children and provide them with assistance without any need on the part of the latter to request it at any time. According to Déchaux, this dissimulation may be linked to a contradiction between aspiration to autonomy and the reality of dependence of the younger generation.

Finally, this author stresses the importance of ties of filiation when confronted with the vulnerability of couples. The solidarity of blood relations today keeps being freely granted and it is in a process of substituting that of the couple in respect of the provision of protection. The functioning of the couple seems increasingly comparable with other spheres of social and professional life: that of permanent negotiation, where nothing is definitively acquired. By comparison with the precarious nature of the conjugal relationship – the place of negotiation – kinship would become the place of permanence. Kinship would be on the way to becoming a network by now structured more by affinity and personal choice than by genealogy (Déchaux, 1990b).

The solidarity of kinship goes far beyond the way it was conceptualized in the narrow field of the sociology of the family. At stake is the role expected of and/or assumed by families in promoting a condition of health and in providing care to the elderly. Following a period of pronounced institutionalization of care, especially for elderly people, in the course of this period a recognition of familial production of care has developed, a 'non-professional health work' generated within the family circle, most frequently by women (Cresson, 1995).

From a social and political standpoint, the aim of such valorization of family solidarity is twofold: on the one hand, it may reduce the cost of institutional care and on the other, the persons concerned are expected to find some benefit in maintaining their environment and network. However, the family has probably never ceased to fulfil its central role, supplemented by available public and private services (Lesemann and Martin, 1993). In this way the connection between kinship as a mutual assistance network and the withdrawal of state-based solidarity is effectively established (Martin, 1995b). Segalen has put it this way:

> The renewal of sociological interest in the ties of kinship derives from the reversal of ideological positions and profound social and demographic changes that have produced an impact on the social body, and notably on its ageing process. Owing to the crisis that has arisen in the *Welfare State*, other forms of solidarity, in particular family solidarity between the generations has been recognized (Segalen, 1993, p. 233).

PRIVATE AND PUBLIC SOLIDARITY, INEQUALITY AND SOCIAL EXCLUSION

The comeback of the issue of family solidarity in the late 1980s was linked to the crisis occurring in the social protection system. Thus, on the occasion of the 1983 symposium entitled 'Recherches et familles' (Researches and Families), under the auspices of the French Presidency of the Republic, after the election of François Mitterrand, Giovanni Sgritta wrote:

> In the immediate aftermath of the war and up to the end of the 1960s, social research tended to reflect the crisis occurring in the institution of the family whereas at present it reflects rather the crisis in a certain social pattern, it is the crisis of the *Welfare State*, highlighting at one and the same time the maintaining and the function of the family in the implementation of important social responsibilities (Sgritta, 1983, p. 169).

Giovanni Sgritta's assumption of an analytical shift from the crisis in the institution of the family towards that of public solidarity has subsequently been largely verified in the sense that this context of the welfare state crisis has imposed new categories of reflection on those responsible for the implementation of social policies. Sociability, mutual assistance, relational support and concern on the part of relatives have thus become instrumental in the formulation of public policies.

The provision of care for elderly dependants is one of the sectors where the shift in perspective outlined above has become evident, quite often for the purpose of stressing the extent to which the family, and above all women, continue to be the cornerstone of the support provided (Lesemann and Martin, 1993; Martin, 1995a; Joël and Martin, 1998). Hence one is witnessing a recognition of family solidarity as an alternative to the shortcomings and limits of collective or public solidarity.

Public authorities have since then become aware of the irreplaceable character of the protective capacity on the part of parents and relatives. With the crisis of the welfare state, policy makers have acknowledged the impossibility of substituting the responsibilities inherent in domestic duties required of women in certain periods of their life-cycle with the development of public and institutional services whether at the level of the care of very young children or of elderly dependants. Since the cost for the society would seem less and less bearable, policy makers recognized and promoted these gratuitous services conceived as a moral obligation whereby certain tasks are assigned to private providers. In consequence of this,

> what was until then considered as a residual of past times, destined to disappear gradually thanks to the development of institutional relationships, has reappeared under a new form as

a network of basic social relationships that enables individual members of society to remain united and keep for themselves an area of social activities preserved from the market (Insel, 1993, p. 221).

Family support is, however, very unequally distributed among genders. The gender division of roles and responsibilities and even the recognition of domestic work as real work that should be remunerated are nowadays considered as highly important issues. Chadeau (1992) estimated on the basis of a 'time use enquiry' that the quantity of time devoted to non-remunerated domestic work (preparation of meals, shopping, washing, ironing, caring for babies, children and adults, household chores etc.) was in 1985 25% greater than the time devoted by French society as a whole to remunerated employment, allowing for the fact that the greater part of this work was performed by women which is still the case at the end of the 1990s (Barrère-Maurisson, 2001). Nevertheless this gratuitous work does not cover all the goods exchanged within the household and which to a considerable extent are not substitutable (the gift of life, affection, cultural enhancement, traditional gift-giving etc.). By adding this second circle of what might be termed 'the gift-circuit' and reciprocations between households (monetary gifts between households through the intermediary of associations, foundations, charitable societies, traditional gift-giving etc.), Insel proposed early in the 1990s an initial, 'very limited and very approximate assessment of donations in contemporary French society, that is to say a volume amounting to approximately three quarters of GDP' (Insel 1993, p. 234). Since then, family solidarity raises the evermore-complex question of the boundary between paid employment, remunerated or indemnified activities, the services sector, voluntary work and non-remunerated domestic activities.

Relational Vulnerability

In evaluating the weight of this domestic economy, consideration has also been given to what might cause its absence. This is the other side of the rediscovery of family solidarity; the impact of 'life without family', as Pitrou puts it, carries the risk of being excluded from the family circle and from the primary socialization patterns, the risk of isolation, solitude and dependence of public solidarity. Ever since the introduction in France of the Revenu Minimum d'Insertion (R.M.I., the law that guarantees income support) in 1988, the phenomenon of isolation has become increasingly important. The research work and assessments of this new scheme stressed that over 70% of beneficiaries were 'isolated', which means single and without family.

The profound ambiguity of this cover-all category of 'isolated' individuals is evident. In effect, to say that an adult has not created a partnership or had children does not mean that he or she is isolated, or without any social contacts. In any case, it gives the idea that poverty and insecurity go hand in hand with isolation or solitude. It was attempted to determine what the growth of the number of isolated individuals might signify: independence or an assertion of autonomy or, on the contrary, externally imposed conditions of isolation and instability. Although one should not allow oneself to be blinded by the phenomenon of isolation since the pattern of mutual assistance is not just a matter of living together, it is undeniable that a certain number of persons living alone are solitary, and are living in a situation of vulnerability.

The risk of isolation is linked to the issue that, in the mid-1980s, was termed the 'new poverty', a form of poverty affecting persons fit for employment but who, following a hitch in their trajectory, find themselves drawn into a situation of precariousness. Among these hitches, one finds first and foremost the loss of employment, but family breakdowns also appear to be a source of marginalization or exclusion. Moreover there is a clear relationship between unemployment and conjugal breakdown, insofar as one may contribute to the other thereby bringing about a situation of social exclusion (Paugam et al., 1993).

Castel (1991a, 1995) and Martin (1993) even put forward the hypothesis of a relational vulnerability by envisaging a dual form of the individual's fragility, corresponding on the one hand to exclusion from the labour market and, on the other, to the loss or absence of sociability and the support provided by the family. Castel proposes a concept designed to qualify this process: 'disaffiliation, a particular way of dissociation of the social ties' (1991a, p. 139). His argument runs as follows:

> In pre-industrial societies, social interventions always had a double aim: integration through employment, and integration in a community or a relational pattern. The present situation can be understood as a new episode in the struggle against the double instability in the organisation of employment and of sociability (ibid: 140).

Castel distinguishes four modes of existence in contemporary society: the 'integration zone' where permanent employment goes together with relational supports; the 'vulnerability zone' which associates employment instability with the fragility of social relations; the 'assistance zone', characterized by the absence of employment frequently linked to the impossibility of working and satisfactory social integration; and, finally, the 'disaffiliation zone' where the absence of employment goes hand in hand with isolation and absence of support.

The fragility of couples, the reduction in the size of families, the relational complexity of new unions, can be interpreted as indicative of the contemporary force of disaffiliation, but also as the result of interventions on the part of the welfare state.

> The undermining of the family structure may not be due to shortcomings on the part of the *Welfare State*. Rather, it might be an effect of its relative success. In warding off a certain number of social risks, the state has left the family face to face with its relational fragility (..) Consequently, what has been left to the management of the modern family is to an ever greater extent its own relational capital (Castel, 1991b, p. 31).

Single-parent families, prevalent among poorer households, are especially confronted with this new form of poverty (Martin, 1997). Although it is evident that disunion (the principal cause of single parenthood today) engenders a more or less drastic economic impoverishment of the custodial parents' household, it does not necessarily entail conditions of poverty but merely accelerates the process of destabilization of already vulnerable individuals. In 1997, little more than 20% of single parent families in France were considered as living in conditions of poverty (according to OECD) whereas in the United Kingdom nearly 60% of single mothers were classified as poor. The reason for this poverty resides not so much in the family structure as in whether or not the single mother is employed and whether she has a full-time job or not. Another important factor is whether or not the ex-companion contributes to the upkeep of the children and whether or not support is provided by relatives (Martin, 1997). When these different factors add up negatively the situation of instability becomes extremely delicate.

To sum up, if kinship provides protection against the risks and economic difficulties inherent in contemporary society, it is easy to understand the importance of being integrated in a network of this kind. Whether it is a matter of young persons in search of their first job and cohabiting for an increasingly longer period of time with their parents, couples who separate and avail themselves of the support of their relatives to surmount this critical period or elderly persons who must count on the presence and support of their daughters to cope with their increased dependence, it would seem evident that such family protection may be needed throughout all one's life. Without it, the individual has no alternative but to rely in one way or another on public solidarity.

Family Solidarity and Social Class

An important question is whether family solidarity shows any social stratification effects and social class differences. This is also a question of determining whether or not such primary solidarity succeeds in reducing social inequality and, if so, to what extent. But even more fundamentally the question arises as to the bases of such mutual assistance. Do they have the same meaning for members of the various social classes and the various generation categories?

In the light of available work it appears likely that the expression of relational support and also the feeling of mutual obligation vary considerably according to social status. In more traditional circles (whether among the less affluent categories or at the other extreme the particularly well-off), the duties of solidarity and mutual help within the familial network tend to predominate. On the other hand, however, this unconditional assistance rules out any contravention of the norms currently in force in these circles. This 'appropriate' behaviour sometimes gives rise not only to a feeling of limitation and social control of one's private life but also, on occasion, to a sense of loneliness.

In other, culturally more generously endowed, backgrounds where the networks are more frequently composed of friends and non-family relationships, a different type of solidarity seems to prevail. The rule from which one must not depart is rather that of autonomy. The integration norm is less the unconditional mutual obligation obtaining within the familial network than autonomy within the friendship network. In a situation of this kind, the important thing is to be able to decide for oneself whether or not to assume the obligations of the proposed relationship – an elective involvement, so to speak. Although kinship may be less central, it is nevertheless present and very frequently assumes silently a role of unconditional support. One may continue to be partially dependent on one's relatives while still preserving one's autonomy.

Research results point also to class differences in the level of help. The more affluent a social network, the more important is the mutual help (Déchaux, 1994; Martin, 1995b; Paugam and Zoyem, 1997). Those who are better off, in terms of material means, commit themselves more readily to providing help than those who have little, whether in respect of material or financial help or for 'subsistence' aid, 'lending a helping hand' by taking over everyday responsibilities such as caring for the children.

But support is not only a matter of available means. We have proposed another explanation to account for the differences in the level of help (Martin, 1997, p. 182): 'One more easily supports those who are less in need of support'. From the perspective of the triple obligation of donation envisaged by Marcel Mauss (give, receive and return), need involves the risk of dependence. It seems as though help is less easily granted by relatives and friends when the perceived need for assistance is greater. When support is synonymous with the development of a feeling of dependency, it tends to dissuade both giver and beneficiary since, on the one hand, there is a risk of not having any form of reciprocation and, on the other, of undergoing an excessively onerous social and relational disqualification.

To appreciate the meanings and bases of private solidarity, it would appear opportune to take into account the patterns of reciprocal exchanges, inasmuch as these are themselves dependent on social class and the type of network involved. It is likely that the old distinctions put forward by Pitrou (1978) will again surface: on the one hand, the resort on the part of the less affluent classes to blood-relations and, on the other, the friendship networks and the promotional pattern of family solidarity among the middle classes. In recognizing an increasingly important role for these informal types of support and in considering them capable of compensating for the limitations of collective solidarity, the public authorities refuse to take into account the very considerable divergences from the norm and make of the family a value in itself.

CONCLUSION

Although sociology has greatly contributed in popularizing the usage of the concept of family solidarity, it has not always done from the same perspective nor has it always had recourse to the same concepts or made explicit reference to the concept of solidarity. The kinship network, the primary form of sociability, social support, social care, domestic work, the distribution of the roles between genders are some of the related concepts that have been used. The theoretical stakes have also evolved, from the controversy between those academic researchers favouring the anthropological approach of kinship and those focusing on the conjugal dimension, to the debate on the way private and public forms of solidarity are related, and on how the balance between the two should look. The latter issue is becoming to an ever greater extent a political controversy that opposes a number of ideological trends regarding the future of collective protection.

Recently the 'family question' has made its appearance both in the French and the European public debate covering issues of solidarity, familial responsibilities and/or obligations and their connection with issues of poverty, insecurity, delinquency and incivility. The role of the family in respect of the protection of vulnerable individuals, whether it be children, adolescents, young adults, those facing social isolation or the loss of employment, chronically ill persons, the handicapped, elderly dependants, seems to become increasingly important in the context of the reduction of public expenditures and the consolidation of social inequality. Inclusion in family networks appears to an ever-greater extent to be a means to ensure social cohesion and to avoid social disintegration.

The 'family question' has thus become a component of the 'social question' and indeed occupies an increasingly important place in the debate on the crisis and evolution of social protection systems. Family issues can no longer be reduced to the allowances for family support and protection provided by the state and the social partners, but are connected to a more far-reaching question – that of allocations between private and public protection, or the respective roles of the state, the services sector, the market and the family in respect of the protection of individuals.

There seem to be two currents of opinion on this family question. The first argues that demographic and familial disruptions are largely the result of the development of the welfare state itself that, by substituting itself for the familial institution, has deprived it of its functions, thereby giving rise to an undesirable individualism, a diminished responsibility of citizens and their increased dependence on the state. The solution would consist in attempting to restore the obligations and responsibilities within the primary networks of family relationships.

The second view entails that the development of the welfare state and services rendered to families has only restored the balance of functions that had been very unequally fulfilled by the primary groups without having fully taken over such functions. Family solidarity can only continue to perform its role in conjunction with collective protection systems. From this perspective, such complementarity must be maintained at all costs so as to avoid the undermining of private solidarity and the disintegration of social ties.

Family solidarity is not only a relevant sociological concept, it also constitutes a pertinent category to analyse public policies because it renders meaning to mutual assistance practices within and between households, practices that have never ceased to exist.

REFERENCES

Attias-Donfut, C. (ed.) (1995), *Les solidarités entre générations: Vieillesse, familles, État*, Paris: Nathan.

Barrère-Maurisson, M.E. (ed.) (2001), *Partage des temps et des tâches dans les ménages*, Paris: La Documentation Française.

Bonvalet, C., D. Maison, H. Le Bras and L. Charles (1993), 'Proches et parents', *Population*, 1, 83 - 110.

Bonvalet, C., A. Gotman, Y. Grafmeyer (eds) (1999), *La famille et ses proches*, Paris: INED PUF.

Bott, E. (1957), *Family and Social Network*, London: Tavistock Publication.

Bourgeois, L. (1912), *Solidarité*, Paris: Armand Colin (réédition Presses universitaires du Septentrion, 1998).

Castel, R. (1991a), 'De l'indigence à l'exclusion, la désaffiliation. Précarité du travail et vulnérabilité relationnelle', in J. Donzelot (ed.), *Face à l'exclusion. Le modèle français*, Paris: Editions Esprit, pp. 137 - 68.

Castel, R. (1991b), 'L'État-providence et la famille: le partage précaire de la gestion des risques sociaux', in F. de Singly et F. Schultheis (eds), *Affaires de famille, affaires d'État*, Nancy: édition de l'Est, pp. 25 - 31.

Castel, R. (1995), *Les métamorphoses de la question sociale. Une chronique du salariat*, Paris: Fayard.

Chadeau, A. (1992), 'Que vaut la production non-marchande des ménages ?', *Revue économique de l'OCDE*, **18**, 221 - 34.

Coenen-Huther, J., J. Kellerhals and M. Von Allmen (eds) (1994), *Les réseaux de solidarité dans la famille*, Lausanne: Edition Réalités sociales.

Cresson G. (1995), *Le travail domestique de santé*, Paris: L'Harmattan.

Déchaux, J.-H. (1990a), 'Les échanges économiques au sein de la parentèle', *Sociologie du travail*, **1**, 73 - 94.

Déchaux, J.-H. (1990b), 'Des relations de parenté inédites?', *Esprit*, Juillet-Août, 101 - 05.

Déchaux, J.-H. (1994), 'Les échanges dans la parenté accentuent-ils les inégalités?', *Sociétés contemporaines*, **17**, 75 - 90.

Durkheim, E. (1902), *De la division du travail social*, 2nd édition, Paris: Alcan.

Fougeyrollas-Schwebel, D. and B. Chabaud (1993), Groupe familial et parenté: les circuits d'échanges de travaux domestiques. Note de synthèse, CNRS-INSEE.

Godbout, J. and J. Charbonneau (1993), 'La dette positive dans le lien familial', in M.a.u.s.s., *Ce que donner veut dire. Don et intérêt*, Paris: La Découverte, pp. 235 - 56.

Gokalp, C. (1978), 'Le réseau familial', *Population*, **6**, 1077 - 94.

Insel, A. (1993), 'La part du don. Esquisse d'une estimation quantitative', in M.a.u.s.s., *Ce que donner veut dire. Don et intérêt*. Paris: La découverte, pp. 221 - 34.

Joël, M.-E and C. Martin (1998), *Aider les personnes âgées dépendantes. Arbitrages économiques et familiaux*, Rennes: Editions de l'ENSP.

Lesemann, F. and C. Martin (eds) (1993), *Les personnes âgées. Dépendance, soins et solidarités familiales. Comparaisons internationales*, Paris: La Documentation Française (English version F. Lesemann and C. Martin (eds) (1993), *Home-based Care, the Elderly, the Family and the Welfare State: An International Comparison*, Ottawa: University of Ottawa Press.

Martin, C. (1992), 'Support et affection. Logiques d'échange et solidarités familiales après la désunion', *Revue internationale d'action communautaire*, Montréal, **27/67**, 89 - 99.

Martin, C. (1993), 'Risque solitude. Divorces et vulnérabilité relationnelle', *Revue internationale d'action communautaire*, Montréal, **29/69**, 69 - 83.

Martin, C. (1995a), 'Vieillissement, dépendance et solidarités en Europe: Redécouvertes des solidarités informelles et enjeu normatif', in C. Attias-Donfut (ed.), *Les solidarités entre générations. Vieillesse, familles, État*, Paris: Nathan, pp. 223 - 42.

Martin, C. (1995b), 'Les solidarités familiales: débat scientifique, enjeu politique', in J.C. Kaufmann (ed.), *Faire ou faire-faire. Familles et services*, Rennes: Presses universitaires de Rennes, pp. 55 - 73.

Martin, C. (1997), *L'après-divorce. Lien familial et vulnérabilité*, Rennes: Presses universitaires de Rennes.

Mendras, H. (1988), *La seconde révolution française. 1965 - 1984*, Paris: NRF, Gallimard.

Messu, M. (2000), 'Famille et société: quelles solidarités?', in M. Chauvière, M. Sassier, B. Bouquet, R. Allard and B. Ribes (eds), *Les implicites des politiques familiales*, Paris: Dunod, pp. 123 - 32.

Parsons, T. (1955), 'The Kinship System of the Contemporary United States', in F. Bourricaud, *Eléments pour une sociologie de l'action*, Paris: Plon, pp. 129 - 50.

Paugam, S. and J.-P. Zoyem (1997), 'Le soutien financier de la famille: une forme essentielle de la solidarité', *Economie et statistique*, 308 - 10, 187 - 210.

Paugam, S., J.-P. Zoyem and J.-M. Charbonnel (1993), *Précarité et risques d'exclusion en France*, Centre d'études des revenus et des coûts (CERC), Paris: La Documentation Française, 102.

Pitrou, A. (1978), *Vivre sans famille*, Toulouse: Privat.

Segalen, M. (1993), *Sociologie de la famille*, Paris: Armand Colin, (3ème édition revue et augmentée).

Sgritta, G. (1983), 'Recherches et familles dans la crise de l'État providence, le cas italien', *Revue française des affaires sociales*, 37 (4), 167 - 72.

Young, M. and P. Willmott (1957), *Family and Kinship in East London*, London: Routledge and Kegan.

Young, M. and P. Willmott (1968), *Family and Class in a London Suburb*, London: Routledge and Kegan.

2. Family Solidarity and Social Solidarity: Substitutes or Complements?

Trudie Knijn

The basic dilemma that welfare programs face is an inherent and long-noted one in public policy: What is subsidized is likely to increase, and what is taxed is likely to decrease. [..] Yet in welfare programs the economic incentive for couples to stay together is diminished and, if and when couples break up, the negative economic consequences of the action are rendered relatively benign through public subsidies. Over time, as the family economic partnership is gradually replaced by dependence on government, the interdependencies and reciprocal obligations of family life diminish (Popenoe, 1996, p. 221).

In this chapter I focus on the relation between family solidarity and larger social solidarity. Much like Popenoe, politicians and some social scientists assume a negative relation between family and larger solidarity. Critics of the welfare state take it for granted that post-war welfare states emerged at the expense of family solidarity; they fear atomization, fragmentation and a loss of social cohesion. This *substitution thesis* holds that when state provisions develop, family solidarity declines. Some welfare state supporters acknowledge this thesis, but welcome the reduction of unequal private familial dependencies. The substitution thesis is however contested. Balbo (1987), Arber and Attias-Donfut (2000), Komter et al. (2000) and Kohli (1999) have shown that the development of the welfare state did not replace family solidarity; it only gave it a different shape, direction or content.

In the first section of this chapter I elaborate on the concept of familial solidarity. Who is included in 'the family' and which kin relationships are referred to? I present empirically based comments on the *substitution thesis* and a few alternatives for it such as the *packaging thesis*, the *complementary thesis* and the *transmission thesis*. In the final sections I develop a critique on family solidarity from the perspective of equal treatment, citizenship and social inclusion.

WHO BELONGS TO THE FAMILY?

David Popenoe is quite concerned as he focuses on the disruption of the nuclear family consisting of a male breadwinner and a dependent housewife by the welfare state. Interestingly enough, he uses a very restrictive definition of the family; in his view there can only be one form of nuclear family, whereas the first circle of family relations actually has many faces today. He is at odds with current developments when he denies that one-parent families, cohabiting couples, same-sex couples or parents are all forms of primary families (Stacey, 1991). In addition Popenoe proves to be a solid successor of Talcott Parsons in his exclusion of the second circle of family relations, i. e. relatives who do not belong to the household (Parsons and Bales, 1956). This circle of relatives may be of increasing importance to family life. They function as supporters or kin keepers while gender relations are reshaped and collective solidarity declines. These shifts in primary and secondary family relations are not only acknowledged by family theorists, in daily life people also define and redefine family relations by applying kinship terminology to people they want to include as family members, or as Cheal says:

> Naming people as family members is one important way of drawing family boundaries [..] learning how to name family members involves more than just giving the correct personal name to an individual. It also involves the correct use of kinship terminology. Words such as 'sister' or 'uncle' are used to classify different family members according to their kinship relationships' (Cheal, 2002, p. 3).

Family boundaries are partly drawn by using proper kinship terminology[1] for biological or legal members of the family. People who are not blood relatives – stepchildren, a new partner of a widowed or divorced grandmother – can also be included by calling them 'my child', 'my second father' or 'co-grandfather'. The opposite is the case when biological relatives are excluded or no longer recognized as family members because of conflicts or a lack of interaction. Family solidarity thus structurally pertains to both circles of the family – the nuclear and the extended family – but it is not certain that everyone in either of these circles is actually involved in family solidarity, nor will everyone participate in this process to the same degree.

GIVING AND RECEIVING CASH AND CARE

In the previous quote from the work of Popenoe, the focus is on individuals who do not receive family support and thus depend on social solidarity. Like many other critics of the welfare state, Popenoe only focuses on one side of the relation between the state and its citizens and views the state (social solidarity) as a donor to greedy citizens who refuse to support each other by more direct means (family solidarity). Functionalist scholars seldom examine the interaction among family members in reaching a balance of giving and receiving in the relation between the state and individual members of families. Emphasizing this balance and drawing a distinction between categories of relatives such as children, young adults, parents, the elderly, men and women of different ages in families can help determine solidarity patterns in families. Janet Finch (1989) shows that unequal solidarity patterns within families may result from gendered normative claims; it is often the daughter who is expected to care for elderly parents and the mother who is expected to stay home when a child is sick.[2] In addition, not every family member is in a position to give or receive support to the same extent. The elderly do not need childcare and youngsters often cannot give financial support. The balance of giving and receiving should be viewed from the perspective of what can be expected from family members on the basis of their resources, and in relation to what support the welfare state offers or expects.

In Popenoe's critique of the welfare state, family solidarity is confined to cash payments. Indeed, the post-war welfare states have mainly based their collective or social solidarity systems upon social security and tax redistribution. This is how poverty is reduced and individuals are protected from income loss due to unemployment, chronic illness or the loss of a breadwinner (de-commodification). Income redistribution between individuals, families and households has taken place in much the same way. De-commodification and redistribution are still the main objectives of welfare states and they result in interdependency or, to put it negatively, in state dependency for whoever cannot earn a living on the labour market. Redistribution of care however is a less developed aspect of welfare states in terms of GDP as well as time. Walker (1996) even distinguishes between macro-social solidarity mainly consisting of the redistribution of cash, and micro-level solidarity consisting of the exchange of care:

> This macrosocial policy contract (cash transfers) mirrors a micro-level one between kin, whereby, for various reasons including reciprocity and affection, adult children provide care for ageing parents. This intergenerational duty of care may be traced back to the biblical precept to 'honour' one's parents and the expectation of filial piety maybe found in a wide range of religions....(ibid., p. 3).

However macro and micro solidarity cannot be differentiated that simply along the lines of cash or care, since the two are interconnected. Feminist scholars have pointed out that cash and care are linked because care takes time that can reduce an individual's earning capacity, and care costs money if it has to be paid for by an individual or family. To some extent welfare states provide care services that are paid for by the taxpayer, whose earning capacity is improved if his wife is 'free' to provide care. The cash and care nexus of the relation between family and state solidarity is thus a complicated one, if only because cash flows are often based upon rights whereas care flows are mainly based upon normative claims and internalized duties.

COMMENTING ON THE SUBSTITUTION THESIS: SOME ALTERNATIVES

So far I argue that in determining the complex relation between family and social solidarity, new forms of primary as well as extended family relations should be included: who counts as a family member, what is expected from different family members on the basis of family and gender norms, and what is the inner familial balance of giving and receiving? The same argument holds true for the relation between social and familial solidarity. Not only do family members define certain people as part of the family, the state defines family boundaries and assumes that some people are responsible for others based on family membership whereas others are excluded. In addition, the state defines people's rights to cash and care in relation to their familial duties whereas other family relations are denied as basis for entitlement (Millar and Warman, 1996; see also Saraceno in this volume). In the following sections an overview is presented of some empirically based alternatives for the substitution thesis.

Packaging and Patchworking

The first alternative to the substitution thesis is the *packaging thesis*, which states that families, especially the women in families, combine resources from all kinds of welfare and income suppliers (state, market, voluntary organizations and family members) to make ends meet. Rainwater et al. (1986) introduced the concept of 'income packaging' to study the combination of economic resources that families, especially poor families, combine in order to survive. They show that the combination of informal income sources via gifts and loans with formal income sources helps poor families bridge periods of unemployment, illness and education. Empirical evidence for this packaging thesis with respect to family incomes is also given in studies on lone mother families. Heidi Hartmann shows that of all the AFDC (Aid for Families with Dependent Children) recipients in the USA, 19.5% are 'work/welfare packagers' due to inadequate wages and job instability in the low-wage service occupations (Spalter-Roth and Hartmann, 1994; Hartmann and Hsiao-ye Yi, 2001). In the Netherlands as well, income packaging is an important strategy of lone mothers. In a variety of ways they combine their income from the labour market (wages and benefits), from the state (social assistance) and from private resources (alimony or family support) (Hooghiemstra and Knijn, 1997; van Wel and Knijn, 2000). Cross-national studies also show that state intervention for lone mothers does not necessarily result in the fathers' withdrawal from their financial responsibilities. Countries like Sweden, Germany and Great Britain intervene to force fathers to pay alimony and thus oblige them to continue to bear responsibility for their former families and keep them from state benefits (Lewis, 1997). In a study among lone mothers in the Netherlands van Wel and Knijn (2000) find that the highest income category of lone mothers receives the highest percentage of alimony in addition to income from paid work and social benefits while many of these mothers could stay out of welfare by combining a wage with alimony.

Rainwater, et al. (1986) stress that, due to the specific institutional nature of the welfare state, not all the parts of the income package come as rights. Some of the parts have to be claimed on the basis of moral rules derived from reciprocity or solidarity. Social solidarity and familial solidarity result in different kinds of dependency; dependence on social solidarity means dependence as a citizen, which, aside from the need to cope with the discretionary power of social officers, guarantees equal treatment and prescribed rights and duties. Dependence on family solidarity is quite a different issue as the case of alimony illustrates. Most familial relationships are based upon moral rules and reciprocity is not guaranteed. Exclusion and lack of support are as widespread as inclusion and support.

The same applies to cash as to care; like cash, care is given and received in packages and some care resources come as rights whereas others result from pleas and bids or efforts to convince alternative care providers to provide care. Whatever family members claim or get depends on social conventions or their own ideas about good care and is embedded in systems of legal and customary entitlements and collective institutions that do or do not take into account the needs of family members. Claims are indicative of what people want, hope for and get. The problem however is that the nature of cash and care claims presupposes that the support is stable, secure and that not too much of a demand is made for support. Knijn, et al. (2003) show how mothers of young children package sources of childcare in Sweden, the Netherlands and Germany. They elaborate on the relation between public and private sources of care and on how rights and claims play a role; they conclude that childcare is mainly a mixed economy of welfare. In none of the countries under study, and probably nowhere else either, is it exclusively provided by one institutional level. All four levels of the welfare regime – the state, the market, voluntary organizations and the family – are involved, and there is considerable national variation in the responsibility the institutional levels take for childcare. The state is the main provider and purchaser of childcare and after-school care in Sweden and Germany but plays only a minor role in the Netherlands, where the market is an important purchaser and provider of childcare. The Dutch view on responsibility for childcare stresses the domination of economic logic above welfare state logic and leads to parents' dependence on family-friendly attitudes of employers. The voluntary sector provides most childcare in Germany, where churches and voluntary organizations run publicly financed and controlled kindergartens and pre-school and after school care.

The Swedish welfare state substantially contributes to parental leaves as well; mothers, and to a lesser extent fathers, are supported in taking care of their very young children without losing much of their financial resources. In Germany the state also facilitates parental care by providing a long parental leave; however payments are limited. In the Netherlands the state only supports its own civil servants with paid parental leaves, while other employees only have the legal right to unpaid parental leave and have to negotiate the payments in collective agreements. In this country the state behaves more as an employer than as a representative of the common interest with respect to care for young children.

The family, in particular the mother, is the main source of childcare in all countries and she is also the one who is ultimately responsible for packaging care if she is employed. Many German and Dutch mothers do not package care when their children are still very young; they just stay home to care for them themselves. Especially poorly educated mothers in both countries are full-time carers, resulting in an increasing income gap between well and poorly educated mothers, although to a lesser extent in Germany where mothers do at least receive some money during parental leave. Dutch mothers who want to stay in the labour market work part-time. The same applies to German mothers after the sometimes extended parental leave. In both countries, employed mothers claim and receive support from their partners or other kin. Fathers also provide care in all the countries, but grandparents are less involved in Sweden and former East Germany than in Holland or former West Germany (van Wel and Knijn, 2000; Knijn et al., 2003).

Most Swedish and German mothers take advantage of their right to paid leave, then use public childcare, and sometimes claim additional informal care to bridge changes in care or work. Swedish and German mothers package care by jig-sawing informal care and flexible working hours, but stable public childcare for pre-school and primary school children remains the cornerstone, offering continuity, security and quality. Dutch and German mothers do not however use either of the two if they stay home themselves, or take advantage of all kinds of resources in their care package. There is a sharp division between women who stay at home to care (often poorly educated) and those who stay in the labour market, usually part-time (often well-educated). If care is packaged during the child's first years, it is usually family members (fathers and grandmothers) who step in. Reducing and adjusting working hours and the support of grandparents and fathers are thus substantial elements of the care package in the Netherlands and Germany (Knijn et al., 2003).

Balbo was the first to apply the packaging thesis to care, adding an element we have not yet discussed. In her famous article 'Crazy Quilts' (1987) she clearly analyses how women's work mainly consists of packaging services. Via quilt-making or patchworking, women pool and package resources in a way that not only serves their families and neighbourhoods, but society at large as well.

> In today's society resources are channelled to individuals, or rather families, from a variety of external social institutions. They must choose from existing alternatives; 'combine' available resources from various agencies and institutions, whether public or private; 'adjust' them to the specific requirements of each family member, and provide services that are not available enough through other institutions (ibid., p. 48).

Nowadays family women fill in the gaps left by the welfare state. This patchwork thesis may be viewed as an extension of the packaging thesis. It not only states that women still play a major role in packaging care, but also that its character and momentum are no longer determined by the mother herself, not even in the familial context, but are shaped outside the family by external institutions. Nowadays companies and corporations, children's schools, athletic clubs, hospitals and childcare centres are deciding when and how long children are to be cared for elsewhere and what the rhythm and pace of a specific care package for a specific family member will be. The argument that external institutions are decisive to the care packaging of families as well as the argument that social solidarity does not replace familial solidarity, but just adds one potential source of cash and care to sources provided by the family itself, can be read as critique on the substitution thesis.

Complementary Thesis

Another alternative to the substitution thesis is the *complementary thesis*, which states that higher levels of collective solidarity increase the recipients' chances to get additional and complementary support from members of their family. This thesis accentuates that social solidarity strengthens rather than diminishes familial solidarity; they are cumulative. Strengthening familial solidarity by public means can mean that relatives are supported by public resources but it can also mean that people who already receive ample support will receive even more, whereas others still will not receive any at all. This is called the 'Matthew effect' (Komter et al., 2000).[3] There is a great deal of empirical evidence to confirm the complementary thesis as regards cash and care alike. Attias-Donfut and Wolff (2000b) argue that familial support for young adults does not diminish with public help. On the contrary, 'private and public support complement each other irrespective of the level of the parent's income' (ibid., 2000b, p. 53). Parents are even slightly more likely to support children who also receive some form of state allowance. As to financial transfers between middle-aged people and their elderly parents, the Matthew effect is also substantial; the more money the recipients have, the more they receive. This is a way of transferring wealth rather than improving the recipient's standard of living (ibid., 2000a, p. 33).

In care, complementary sources are the rule, not the exception. Frail elderly people who live on their own seldom exclusively rely on public help. Home care only supports very specific tasks for a limited number of hours a day or week, and indications for home care have become increasingly strictly regulated in almost all Western countries. The elderly can barely live on their own without some kind of family support and there is ample evidence that their relatives are aware of that. Neither the rise in public provisions in the 1970s and 1980s nor their decline in the 1990s resulted in a reduction of informal care by relatives. In addition, studies by Dykstra and De Jong-Gierveld (1997) and Komter et al. (2000) confirm that public care enhances family support and the most frequent recipients of informal support are the people who also use formal support to the largest extent.

As regards sources of childcare in lone mother families, van Wel and Knijn (2000) observe the same effect. Lone mothers who are not on welfare combine formal public and informal unpaid childcare much more (30%) than lone mothers who are on welfare (19%). They also note that of all the mothers who are not on welfare, the best educated ones not only use public childcare more frequently, but they also get more frequent childcare support from their ex-partners, relatives and close friends.

Like the packaging thesis, the complementary thesis emphasizes a balance in receiving public and private resources. While the packaging thesis shows how individuals and families combine sources from all the institutional levels to make ends meet, the complementary thesis accentuates that getting public support is not only a condition for getting additional family support, it also results in people who already receive public support having a better chance of getting additional family support.

Transmission Thesis

Lastly, the transmission thesis focuses on the conditions for family support that are created by public solidarity. This thesis holds that financial transmissions between family members occur because of and not in spite of state guaranteed income support such as pensions. Under the protection of the public pension system, gifts, donations and loans are transmitted from the older to the younger generations, and this is not solely done, if at all, in exchange for care. These private transfers undeniably contribute to family coherence and solidarity. Kohli (1999) observes inter vivo family transfers in Germany, the US and France, although not to the same degree. In each of these countries, transfers mainly go downwards from grandparents to their adult children and from the middle generation to their adult children. To a lesser degree, grandchildren and other relatives are also the recipients of financial family transfers. Interestingly, findings in the US, France and Germany strongly contradict the expectations of the substitution thesis. Based on this thesis, we would expect financial family transfers to decline in countries with strong welfare states, which by implication have generous public pension systems. However, Kohli (1999) concludes that family transfer patterns are much more complicated (see also Kohli et al., 2000). By comparing his German study with studies by Szydlik (1998) and McGarry (1997) in the US and Attias-Donfut (1995) in France, he notes rather similar transfer patterns in the residual welfare state of the US and the corporatist welfare state of Germany, and rather dissimilar patterns in the equally corporatist welfare state of France. Far more French parents (64% in the past five years) make financial transfers to their adult children than American or German parents (25 to 29% in the last 12 months). By comparing family transfers in former East and West Germany Kohli notes that pensioners in the East more often transfer financial resources to adult children than pensioners in the West, even though all the age groups have lower incomes in the East than the West. Since they receive public pensions, the oldest age group in the East of Germany see themselves as relatively wealthy compared to the younger generations, which may explain why they are more generous than their peers in the West of the country. In addition, not only do the highest income quintiles convey part of their financial resources to descending generations, the lower quintiles where pension dependency is highest also transfer substantial amounts. Based on these findings Kohli concludes: 'On the aggregate level, it forms a clear and surprising pattern: part of the public transfers from the employed population to the elderly are handed back by them to their family descendants' (1999, p. 94).

The implication is that welfare state provisions do not replace or downgrade family solidarity, in fact they seem to strengthen it by giving the older generations the resources to invest financially in their relationships with their descendants. Like the packaging and the complementary thesis, the transmission thesis criticizes the substitution thesis by confirming that family solidarity is made possible by social solidarity. The welfare state is an enabling institute with respect to family solidarity. Thanks to collective provisions such as public pensions, older family members can maintain relationships with their adult children.

FAMILY SOLIDARITY ... THE BEST THERE IS?

So far this chapter has given an empirically-based overview of alternatives for the substitution thesis, which does not ultimately prove to be based on firm grounds. Empirical studies on all kinds of family support show that at least three alternative theses are more firmly supported by empirical evidence. In addition, the alternative theses show that family solidarity is not confined to members of the nuclear family; there are also exchange relations between former family members (divorced parents) that can benefit family members and ex-family members. Moreover, limiting the context to the nuclear family would overlook the solidarity among secondary family members who do not live in the same household such as grandparents, grandchildren, parents-in-law and other relatives (see Tobío in this volume).

On the basis of the empirical findings that confirm alternatives to the substitution thesis, one might say the continuous strength of family solidarity is partly a consequence of welfare state provisions. Collective solidarity is conditional on and complemented by personal solidarity based on involve-ment with the people we know best and whose concerns we share. Public solidarity does not replace family solidarity and the welfare state does not break down family relationships, in fact it supports them. This might be an argument for preserving or even expanding public solidarity, since it would promote family solidarity. In view of the institutional effects of public solidarity on family relationships and the specific effects of family transfers on individuals, it might be said that family transfers are beneficial for individuals, even if they are paid by public means. This is how Kohli (1999) evaluates the relation between public and family solidarity. He stresses that public support for family solidarity should be preserved because it improves the position of the elderly within families by enhancing their status and enabling them to contribute to the social and financial position of their descendants. In a modernized dynamic society that tends to devaluate the elderly, this might be an appropriate compensation for their loss of power. According to Kohli, families are also better equipped to guarantee the welfare of the young than the welfare state is. Being an intermediate between the state and the individual, families have more effective systems for passing resources on to whoever needs them. The underlying assumption is that because of the altruistic and reciprocal character of family relationships, family transfers improve the quality of the exchange, reinforce the link between members of different family generations and thus reinforce social cohesion.

This is thus an argument in favour of preserving public support for the family as an intermediate institute between the state and the individual. It absolutely contradicts Popenoe's substitution thesis by stating that with-drawal of public support would undermine rather than strengthen family relations. It is however only one side of the coin. Another relevant issue is whether in itself the family is indeed the altruistic institution Kohli assumes it to be. Is the family really better able than the welfare state to guarantee soli-darity and divide income and welfare? Since the 1970s ample sociological evidence has demonstrated that the family is not such an undisputed pillar of society worth defending at all costs. Kohli seems to be aware of this when he says, 'If the arguments up to this point are charged with painting a too rosy picture of family relationships among adult generations, I plead guilty, but would be ready to supplement them with accounts of intergenerational dy-namics and conflicts' (1999, p. 100). Indeed, families are never completely without potential conflicts and they are indicative of the very aspects that characterize family relations. In the context of this chapter, however, I focus on the institutional characteristics of the family and its related values and norms, the principles of reciprocity and redistribution that dominate family relationships and the basis family members support each other on. Four as-pects of the family as an institution are crucial: 1) the family as a parochial community, 2) the family as a redistribution agency, 3) the family as a gen-erational system and 4) the family as a gender system.

The family is a parochial community, based upon inclusion as well as exclusion. As Cheal (2000) notes, drawing family boundaries is still an im-portant process in which criteria for belonging are articulated and redefined. These criteria are neither given nor evident and acquire meaning in relation-ships with relatives as well as outsiders. Family relations are thus arbitrary and vulnerable; even small conflicts that occurred long ago may result in avoidance or dismissal. Not only is family membership arbitrary, the same holds true of family support. Unlike the state, families are not supposed to equally support all their members or to fulfil all the needs of all their mem-bers to the same degree. In fact only some strictly defined family members can derive rights from family membership (spouses or children vis-à-vis their parents for instance). So being overly dependent on one's family is a risky affair. Janet Finch (1989) clearly concludes that family solidarity is not at all unconditional, especially as regards relatives outside the nuclear household. Many people feel the welfare state should take primary responsibility for their family members who do not belong to their household or nuclear family. They do not feel every claim for help is appropriate and are not willing to provide help regardless of the circumstance or condition. Family parochialism may also undermine social cohesion. Although many sociologists assume that a strong link between relatives automatically enforces social cohesion, the opposite trend should also be taken seriously. One need only think of the strong family cohesion in Sicily to understand this argument; excessive patriarchal family bonding is a potential threat to social cohesion.

This overview of the relation between family and social solidarity also highlights that the Matthew effect that can characterize the redistribution of income by tax systems is reinforced by familial solidarity. Complementing social by family support seems to increase rather than decrease social inequality. As the complementary and the transmission thesis demonstrate, some family members who already receive a great deal of public support also receive a great deal of family support and those who do not receive any public support at all hardly receive any family support either. Although families also support relatives who are in serious need, the general conclusion is that family redistribution increases social inequality because of the selectivity of family solidarity (Komter et al., 2000). The specific nature of the family as an institution can explain this. Since the family is an institution based upon kinship and tradition, it mainly protects and supports its members who are defined as being most qualified to receive support. Family support thus has to be claimed and which members are or are not defined as qualified to make claims depends on the unwritten rules of the family itself. Not surprisingly, many families mainly support the members who have been most committed to the family, are defined as proper representatives of the family or can be expected to contribute to the welfare of the family as a whole. In other words, family solidarity is anything but a reliable compensation for unequal redistribution or for injustice linked to social solidarity. On the contrary, family solidarity reinforces inequality and injustice. The more family solidarity is the main source of support, the more social inequality there is apt to be.

As a generational system, the family is assumed to guarantee equal flows of cash and care along generational lines. The well-being of the elderly partly depends on social solidarity by way of a guaranteed income, giving them a certain financial status and control vis-à-vis their younger relatives. But frail elderly people also need care, and if the family is the main care provider, the well-being of both the elderly and their adult children, especially their daughters, might be at stake. In Britain, studies on family care for the elderly, e.g. by way of payments for care (Qureshi and Walker, 1989; Ungerson, 2000) show that neither frail elderly people nor their caring relatives are very satisfied with the arrangements. One reason for their dissatisfaction is again related to the characteristics of the family as an institution. Much of the care given within this institution is not entirely a matter of free will, but is founded on duty and obligation as well. If no alternative care is available, family members provide care based on what Land and Rose (1985) call compulsory altruism. There is overwhelming empirical evidence of this kind of obligatory care (Qureshi, 1996; Komter and Vollebergh, 2002). Obligatory care may entail disregarding the needs of the older relative, even if the carer and the care recipient both started the care relationship on a voluntary basis. Excessive daily contact between family members may also result in the exclusion of the elderly person's friends and other social contacts and thus cause social isolation. The European Observatory shows that in countries where the elderly largely depend on family care and thus have the most intensive contact with their relatives, the elderly have the greatest sense of loneliness. Elderly people in Greece, Portugal and Italy have more daily contact with their family members and more feelings of loneliness than the elderly in Denmark, Germany, the UK and the Netherlands (Walker and Maltby, 1997). Affection and altruism are assumed to be core characteristics of family relationships but these feelings cannot be enforced. If care becomes obligatory it might well lose these qualities. It is often suggested that the individualization and fragmentation of family relationships weaken family ties and reduce compassion with the older generation. However, in the past excessive dependence on relatives may have resulted in disregard for individual needs. The family, in the end, is a private institution based upon kinship and thus does not guarantee the satisfaction of the needs of its older members.

The family is ultimately based on normative assumptions about gender. In the context of family relationships, some categories of family members, in particular women, are still supposed to sacrifice their own interests to the common good. Women invest much more than men in family life by caring for relatives and kin keeping. This attitude is taken for granted by women and men alike to the extent that family solidarity is often at the expense of women's individual well-being and role in society. Family solidarity may not only reinforce social inequality in general, it may also enhance inequality between male and female family members. Since the family is a private institute, laws and regulations can only protect family members from abuse and excessive financial discomfort, but how resources are divided within the family is determined by the normative structure of the family itself. Some categories of family members are neither willing nor able to liberate themselves from the obvious injustice this institute is founded on.

Concerns about substitution like the ones expressed by Popenoe actually boil down to a defence of parochial claims for inequality among families and family members. Their fears are not based on the kind of empirical evidence that is discussed in this chapter. Social solidarity does not replace family solidarity; it supports and reinforces it. Family solidarity is still very strong and crucial and beneficial for families as institutions, for family members and for society. However, exclusively relying on family solidarity or arguing that the family is a necessary intermediate between the state and the individual is not without risks. Sometimes family solidarity turns out to be a Sicilian offer that can hardly be refused.

NOTES

1. One of my sisters discovered that the current habit of only calling aunts and uncles by their names might confuse children. One day her six-year-old son came home from school desperately crying because his teacher asked the children to name all their aunts and uncles and he was the only one who didn't have any. Then my sister told him he had thirteen aunts and uncles, probably more than any of his classmates. He just had not realised that the people he knew as Hans and Myriam, Karien and Wilfried and many of his parents' other 'friends' were actually his aunts and uncles. A happy boy went to school the next day.

2. A recent headline in a Dutch newspaper was 'Mother leaves eleven-year-old boy home alone'. In fact both British parents had sent their son home when they discovered at the airport that he did not have a valid passport to join the family on a holiday in Portugal. Scandalous as this is, it was not the father who was held responsible.

3. The concept of Matthew effect was introduced by Merton (1968). It refers to a passage in St. Matthew's gospel stating that those who have will receive and from those who own nothing, what little they have will be taken away.

REFERENCES

Arber, S. and C. Attias-Donfut (eds) (2000), *The Myth of Generational Conflict. The Family and State in Ageing Societies*, London and New York: Routledge.

Attias-Donfut, C. (ed.) (1995), *Les solidarités entre générations: Vieillesse, familles, état,* Paris: Nathan.

Attias-Donfut, C. and F.-C. Wolff (2000a), 'The redistributive effects of generational transfers', in S. Arber and C. Attias-Donfut (eds), *The Myth of Generational Conflict. The Family and State in Ageing Societies,* London and New York: Routledge, pp. 22 - 46.

Attias-Donfut, C. and F-C. Wolff (2000b), 'Complementarity between public and private transfers', in S. Arber and C. Attias-Donfut (eds), *The Myth of Generational Conflict. The Family and State in Ageing Societies,* London and New York: Routledge, pp. 47 - 68.

Balbo, L. (1987), 'Crazy Quilts": Rethinking the welfare state debate from a woman's point of view', in A. Showstack Sassoon (ed.), *Women and the State. Shifting Boundaries of Public and Private,* London: Hutchinson, pp. 45 - 71.

Cheal, D. (2002*), Sociology of Family Life,* Hampshire/ New York: Palgrave.

Dykstra, P. and J. De Jong-Gierveld (1997), 'Huwelijksgeschiedenis en informele en formele hulp aan ouderen', *Bevolking en Gezin,* **3**, 35 - 61.

Finch, J. (1989), *Family Obligations and Social Change,* Cambridge: Polity Press.

Hartmann, H. and Hsiao-ye Yi (2001), 'The rhetoric and reality of welfare reform', in N.J. Hirschmann and U. Liebert (eds), *Women & Welfare. Theory and Practice in the United States and Europe,* New Brunswick: Rutgers University Press, pp. 160 - 76.

Hooghiemstra, E. and T. Knijn (1997), 'Onder moeders paraplu: alleenstaande ouders op de armoedegrens', in G. Engbersen, J.C. Vrooman and E. Snel (eds), *Arm Nederland. De Kwetsbaren. Tweede Jaarrapport Armoede en Sociale Uitsluiting,* Amsterdam: Amsterdam University Press, pp. 103 - 22.

Knijn, T., I. Jonsson and U. Klammer (2003), 'Betreuungspakete schnüren. Zur Alltagsorganisation berufstätiger Mütter', in U. Gerhard, T. Knijn and A. Weckwert (eds), *Erwerbstätige Mütter. Ein europäischer Vergleich,* München: Beck Verlag, 162 - 92.

Kohli, M. (1999), 'Private and public transfers between generations. Linking the family and the state', *European Societies,* **1** (1), 81 - 104.

Kohli, M., H. Kunemund, A. Motel and M. Szydlik (2000), 'Families apart? Intergenerational transfers in East and West Germany', in S. Arber and C. Attias-Donfut (eds), *The Myth of Generational Conflict. The Family and State in Ageing Societies,* London and New York: Routledge, pp. 88 - 99.

Komter, A., J. Burgers and G. Engbersen (2000), *Het cement van de samenleving,* Amsterdam: Amsterdam University Press.

Komter, A. and W. Vollebergh (2002), 'Solidarity in Dutch families. Family ties under strain?', *Journal of Family Issues,* **23** (2), 171 - 88.

Land, H. and H. Rose (1985), 'Compulsory altruism for some or an altruistic society for all?' in P. Bean, J. Ferris and D. Wynes (eds), *In Defence of Welfare,* London: Tavistock, pp. 74 - 98.

Lewis, J. (ed.) (1997), *Lone Mothers in European Welfare Regimes. Shifting Policy Logics,* London: Jessica Kingsley Publishers.

McGarry, K. (1997), 'Inter vivos transfers and intended bequests', Working Paper 6345, Cambridge: National Bureau of Economic Research.

Merton, R.K. (1968), *Social Theory and Social Structure,* New York: Free Press

Millar, J. and A. Warman (1996*), Family Obligations in Europe,* London: Family Policy Centre.

Parsons, T. and R.F. Bales (1956), *Family, Socialization and the Interaction Process,* London: Routledge and Kegan Paul.

Popenoe, D. (1996*), Life without Father,* Cambridge: Harvard University Press.

Qureshi, H. (1996), 'Obligations and support within families', in A.Walker (ed.), *The New Intergenerational Contract. Intergenerational Relations, Old Age and Welfare*, London: UCL Press, pp. 100 - 19.

Qureshi, H. and A. Walker (1989*)*, *The Caring Relationships: Elderly People and their Families*, Basingstoke: MacMillan / New York: Temple University Press.

Rainwater, L., M. Rein and J. Schwarz (1986*)*, *Income Packaging in the Welfare State: A Comparative Study of Family Income*, Oxford: Oxford University Press.

Spalter-Roth, R.M. and H. Hartmann (1994), 'AFDC Recipients as care-givers and workers: a feminist approach to income security policy for American women', *Social Politics*, **1** (2), 190 - 210.

Stacey, J. (1991*)*, *Brave New Families*, New York: Basic Books.

Szydlik, M. (1998), *Lebenslange Solidaritat: Beziehungen zwischen erwachsen Kindern und Eltern*, Berlin: Freie Universität.

Ungerson, C. (2000), 'Cash in care', in M. Harrington Meyer (ed.), *Care Work. Gender, Labor and the Welfare State*, New York: Routledge, pp. 68 - 88.

Walker, A. (ed.) (1996), *The New Intergenerational Contract. Intergenerational relations, Old Age and Welfare*, London: UCL Press.

Walker, A. and T. Maltby (eds) (1997*)*, *Ageing Europe*, Buckingham/Philadelphia: Open University Press.

Wel, F. van, and T. Knijn (2000), *Alleenstaande ouders over zorgen en werken*, The Hague: Elseviers Bedrijfsinformatie.

3. Shifting Patterns of Solidarity and Responsibility: in Search of a Micro Perspective[1]

Ruth Lister

The issue of the location of the boundaries of responsibility between the public and the private – or between state, family and market – lies at the centre of social and family policy and is critical to the construction of social citizenship. Its importance was underlined by Janet Finch in her influential text, *Family Obligations and Social Change*, where she pointed to the ways in which these boundaries shift over time and in different circumstances; to the politically contentious and gendered nature of this process; and to the 'deep ambivalence about the family and its relationship to the state' (1989, p. 11) it reveals. Since her book, the drawing of the line between public and private responsibilities has become an even more critical issue across welfare regimes.

There is a growing literature on the shifting geometry of public-private responsibility from a macro institutional perspective (discussed elsewhere in this volume). What this chapter attempts to address is the impact of this shifting geometry on individual families and on family relationships and the extent to which it does or does not accord with citizens' own expectations of and beliefs about the location of the boundaries of responsibility. Or, in other words, what are the implications of changing patterns of macro-solidarity for patterns of micro-solidarity? The first section underlines the complexities of the issues. These complexities stem from the fact that the shifts taking place do not follow a single model, reflecting both elements of path dependencies and variations between different institutional spheres within nation states. Likewise, how individuals respond to the shifting boundaries of responsibility will be shaped to some extent by the institutional conditions that prevail within their societies. These institutional conditions can be understood in terms both of welfare regimes and familial regimes, the latter categorized according to state definitions of family obligations.

Transformations in the relationship between public and private can be understood as processes of familialization, de-familialization or indeed, re-familialization. Cultural expectations and beliefs about the respective responsibilities of government and family will be reflected in the way citizens respond to these processes. These beliefs and expectations, in turn, are likely to be moulded by the familial regimes within which they live. A further complexity which is explored, arises from the ways in which such beliefs are likely to be mediated by social divisions such as gender, age, ethnicity and social class and also by socio-geographical location.

The chapter will then review some of the evidence on the nature and impact of shifts in the boundaries of responsibility between the public and the private. The final section will use a number of examples to illustrate how disjunctions can arise between, on the one hand, government policies, and on the other, the beliefs of family members. This could mean a tension between macro- and micro-solidarities.

COMPLEXITIES

In addition to a paucity of comparable cross-national evidence, there are a number of factors that make it difficult to generalize across countries (and indeed within countries) when trying to make sense of the ramifications at the level of individual families of shifting patterns of responsibility and solidarity.

Inter-national Variations: No Single Model

The first of these concerns the fact that these shifting patterns do not conform to a single model. Responses to economic and social change are to a greater or lesser degree 'institutionally path dependent'. In the words of Paul Pierson, 'key programmatic arrangements of mature welfare states reflect the operation of self-reinforcing processes over extended periods of time' (2001, p. 12), although path dependency should be understood as an orientation rather than a straitjacket. Also, the transformations that have taken place in Central and Eastern Europe are of a different order to those in Western Europe. Moreover, even within individual nation states, the changes do not always add up to a single coherent pattern. In the UK, for example, we can witness, on the one hand, a continued shifting of the boundary of responsibility for the financial support of older people from the public to the private sector, as New Labour prioritizes private over public pensions. Ministers have made clear in a succession of speeches that the aim is for individuals and families to take greater responsibility for their own welfare more generally. Yet, on the other hand, for the first time the UK has a government that acknowledges that childcare is a public as well as private responsibility, with a national childcare strategy (based on public-private partnerships) and the first faltering steps towards the kind of maternity and parental leave provisions taken for granted in many other European countries. The providing state is being transformed not just into the enabling partnership state, in which responsibility for provision lies increasingly with non-state partners, but also into the social investment state, which prioritizes 'investment in human capital' (Giddens, 1998, p. 117; Commission on Social Justice, 1994; Esping-Andersen, 2002). Children, as citizen-workers of the future, are primary targets of the social investment state (Jenson, 2001; Jenson and Saint-Martin, 2001; Lister, 2002).[2]

How individuals and families respond to changing state forms and to shifting boundaries of responsibility will be shaped to some extent by the institutional conditions within their societies. According to Bo Rothstein, institutional conditions, which include social welfare programmes, are to be understood not just as systems of rules but as 'normative arrangements' (1998, p. 17). As such they will influence what people believe is the proper balance of responsibility for welfare between the state, family and market (although, as the mid-1990s British and European Social Attitudes Survey underlines, attitudes towards welfare do not necessarily conform to the expectations enshrined in particular institutional regimes (Jowell et al., 1998).

Typically, these institutional conditions are discussed using variations of Gøsta Esping-Andersen's (1990) welfare regime analysis. But also important in this context is what we might call 'familial regimes', where the main focus is on state definitions of familial obligations. Millar and Warman (1996), drawing on Castles (1993), use the notion of 'families of nations' in their study of family obligations in Western Europe. They identify three broad groupings: those where obligations are minimal and the individual is the main locus of provision (the Scandinavian countries); those where obligations are placed on the nuclear family (mainly Northern Continental Europe plus the UK and Ireland – and according to Appleton and Hantrais (2000), the 'applicant' Central/Eastern European states) and those where obligations are placed on members of the extended family (Southern European countries).

Whereas welfare regime analysis has used the concept of '(de)-commodification' to capture the relationship between the individual on the one hand and the state and market on the other, familial regime analysis makes more explicit the parallel process of '(de)-familialization'. The concept of de-familialization was first used by feminist analysts to provide a gendered balance to Esping-Andersen's preoccupation with de-commodification, thereby providing a more rounded measure of economic independence. It refers to the characterization of welfare states 'according to the degree to which individual adults can uphold a socially acceptable standard of living, independently of family relationships, either through paid work or through social security provisions' (Lister, 1994, p. 37, 2003; McLaughlin and Glendinning, 1994). Esping-Andersen himself has subsequently appropriated the term 'to capture policies that lessen individuals' reliance on the family; that maximize individuals' command of economic resources independently of familial or conjugal reciprocities' (1999, p. 45).

How citizens respond to these processes will reflect their expectations and beliefs regarding the respective responsibilities of government and family for the care and support of younger and older generations. These, in turn, while not determined by the nature of the familial regime in which they live are likely to be moulded by it. Some evidence for this can be found in a 1998 Eurobarometer survey which asked for responses to the statement that 'in future working adults may have to look after their parents more than they do nowadays'. While just over half overall thought it 'quite a good thing', the proportions in southern European countries, together with Ireland, were higher, with as many as 90 per cent agreeing in Greece. In contrast, support for this view was as low as 30 per cent in Sweden and just under 40 per cent in the Netherlands, Belgium and Finland (Eurostat, 2000, pp. 87 - 8).

Intra-national Variations: Social and Spatial Divisions

To further complicate matters, expectations and responses will also vary within individual countries, reflecting social divisions such as class, gender, age and ethnicity. Indeed, the British and European Social Attitudes Survey found that 'there is more within-nation variation in attitudes to different service areas and policies than there is between-nation variation in overall public values' (Taylor-Gooby, 1998b, pp. 64 - 5). At the same time, the nature and extent of these variations may differ between countries. So, for example, the same survey found that support for the view that the government should definitely be responsible for providing a decent standard of living in old age declined with income, but that the differences between high and middle to low income groups were much less in Sweden than in Britain and Germany. The European Science Foundation's cross-national *Beliefs in Government* programme found that class identification was one of the most important factors in attitudes towards the role of the state in welfare (Borre and Scarbrough, 1995).

With respect to gender, one finding of the British and European Social Attitudes Survey was that women are consistently more supportive of the government's responsibility for welfare than are men (Taylor-Gooby, 1998b).

However, women's (and no doubt men's) attitudes also vary with age. Thus a report on Women's Social Attitudes in Britain found that women aged 18 to 34 were less likely than those aged 35 plus to say that government should definitely be responsible for providing a decent standard of living in old age (Jarvis et al., 2000). To what extent this is an age or a generational effect is not clear.

Another important dimension, which is not picked up in standard welfare attitudes surveys, is that of ethnicity. Two studies in the North of England throw some light on the question. The first, a study in Leeds of minority ethnic groups' experience of the benefits system, found 'compelling evidence that cultural and religious influences inhibit' the claiming of benefits within minority ethnic communities (Law et al., 1996, p. 141). The second, which involved three focus groups from the Bradford Muslim community, is suggestive of the significance of Islamic beliefs for understandings of responsibilities within the context of Western welfare states. It found that British Muslims place considerable emphasis on both personal responsibility and on 'the need for the state to continue to provide welfare as a right' (Dwyer, 2000b, p. 47; see also Dean and Khan, 1997). Such findings point to the potentially strong influence of cultural and religious beliefs on views about the boundaries of responsibility between state, family and market. But we do not know enough about how these influences operate in specific minority ethnic communities and among different groups within them.

In addition to group variations in attitudes, there may well also be socio-geographical differences within nation states, although such differences are more likely to be marked in some countries than others. Simon Duncan writes that 'people will hold different values, and act in different ways, in different places. The same values, and the same relationships, will mean different things in different places' (1998, p. 126). More recently, he has identified, within nation states, localized 'geographies of family forms', linked to gender relations, that are likely to impact on how individual family members perceive their responsibilities (Duncan and Smith, 2002, p. 21). There are also likely to be differences according to the area of welfare provision. Thus beliefs and expectations about the role of government in provision for older people may not correlate with those about provision for the young or for people of working age (see for instance Hills and Lelkes, 1999).

THE NATURE AND IMPACT OF THE SHIFTING PATTERNS

The nature and impact of the transformations is read here through British lenses, which reflect the experience of the neo-liberal experiment of the late twentieth century. The limitations (referred to previously) of any generalization that follows need to be borne in mind, not least since the impact of similar trends is likely to differ between more institutionalized and more residualized welfare states.

Broadly, as Mary Daly has noted, 'many of the changes [in cash benefits] under way in European welfare states have the effect of pushing the onus of support back on the family' (1997, p. 144). This applies with regard to both the young and the elderly. The processes involve greater 'targeting' of welfare, so that in some countries public welfare becomes increasingly confined to the less well off, with the better off expected to look to the market and entitlement is based more on the family than the individual (see also Saraceno, this volume). They also involve greater conditionality, with the result that more groups are expected to look to the labour market rather than the state as their primary source of income. At the same time, the state plays a stronger regulatory role both in terms of enforcing private maintenance obligations for children and of policing the increasingly stringent conditions applied to benefits.

More complex have been the shifting patterns of cash and care. On the one hand, as Daly and Lewis point out, we can see the growing 'marketization' of care; on the other hand, state payments for caring have become increasingly common, heralding they suggest, 'a new type of welfare state citizenship' (1998, pp. 3 - 4). The effects of such payments are highly gendered and differ according to context. Moreover, as Daly and Lewis also observe, the patterns of public-private responsibility for the care of older people and for children can shift in opposite directions in the same country. A further complexity derives from the fact that such shifts are not always the product of legislation. Millar and Warman highlight as a key policy trend the extent of changing practice, in terms of policy implementation, rather than changing policy, 'with potentially very significant effects on the family-state boundary'. Such 'silent' shifts in responsibilities can also result, for example, from the differential interpretation of policy at local level or from shifts in the pattern of receipt of different kinds of benefits. They are, Millar and Warman point out, 'difficult to track, and the changes they introduce are difficult to assess' (1996, p. 49).

Perhaps some of the most dramatic shifts have been in Central and Eastern Europe. Pascall and Manning (2000) argue that, given the nature of the social state under the former Communist regimes, the shift of responsibility to the family is having that much greater an impact, especially on women. The extent of the shift is generally less in Central than Eastern Europe. At the most extreme, Zsuzsa Ferge (2001) writes of the near collapse of the state in some of the former members of the Soviet Union, so that families and especially women have to take on the whole burden of care and support. Jacqueline Heinen (1997) has pointed to the impact on women's family responsibilities and citizenship of severe cuts in social programmes and social rights more generally in Eastern Europe (see also Kotowska in this volume).

The impact on overall inequalities of the transformations in the relationship between public and private will in part depend on how they interact with underlying economic, social and demographic trends which are, for the most part, fuelling greater socio-economic inequality. According to Eurostat, with reference to 1995, the latest date for which figures were available, 'following a downward trend, inequality has been rising in most Member States since 1980' (2000, p. 67). The increase was greatest in Denmark, Sweden, the Netherlands and the UK while it was negligible in Ireland and Finland, and Italy experienced a slight decrease. Subsequent national studies in the UK, Sweden and Finland 'indicate an increase in income inequality in the second half of the 1990s' (Eurostat, 2001, p. 47).

In the UK, earlier analysis by John Hills (1998) suggests that income inequality rose faster than elsewhere. More recent official figures indicate some levelling off at the start of the new century following a slight decline in the first half of the 1990s and a further rise in the second half (Lakin, 2002). In the UK considerable attention has been paid to the growing inequality between 'work rich' and 'work poor' families, i.e. between two-earner and one or no earner-families; the statistics also show growing inequality within the pensioner population. Esping-Andersen suggests that 'resource inequalities between household types are undoubtedly growing and we face the menacing spectre that access to social and cultural capital is polarizing between "winner" and "loser" families' (1999, p. 146; 2002).

There is a lack of information about the impact on individual families of the reconfiguration of public and private responsibilities. Some qualitative research in the UK about a decade ago found that changes in social security benefits, which placed greater responsibility on individual families, had caused anxiety and stress and had damaged relationships within families. The main burden was borne by women in both one and two parent families. The researchers, Craig and Glendinning, concluded that

> paradoxically, rather than increasing family responsibilities it seems that parents' abilities to fulfil what they perceived to be their normal obligations of parenthood were actually undermined. The overall effect of reducing dependency on the state may well have been to inflict some profound and lasting damage on the quality of life for these families (1990, p. 46).

A similar conclusion was reached by Dean and Taylor-Gooby (1992) in their study of the supposed 'dependency culture'.

A DISJUNCTION BETWEEN POLICY AND THE EXPECTATIONS AND BELIEFS OF FAMILIES?

Family Responsibilities

Dean and Taylor-Gooby's (1992) research also provides some indication of how families on benefit may react to the state's expectation that they should rely more heavily on private sources of welfare. Two-thirds of their sample either implicitly or explicitly rejected the idea that they should seek help from family or friends and only four participants expressed any approval. Analysis indicated either total disapproval of enforced family dependency or a sense of clear limits to how much was acceptable. In two-thirds of cases, the objection was principled, while the remaining third responded pragmatically on the grounds that their families were not in a position to help them.

This suggests a disjunction between the then Government's view of the proper balance of responsibility between state and family and the beliefs and expectations of families themselves. This appears to bear out the point made by Janet Finch that 'the lesson of our past is that governments are quite capable of promoting a view of family obligations which is out of step with what most people regard as proper or reasonable, and with the commitments people have arrived at themselves, through delicate processes of negotiation' (1989, p. 243).

Finch's research with Jennifer Mason in the UK highlighted how the responsibilities that family members feel towards each other do not follow automatically from family relationships but reflect the particular history of those relationships. What also came across strongly was that 'people do not want to have to rely on their relatives for extensive help (..). Policies which are designed to make people *more* dependent on their relatives breach a principle which many people hold dear' (1993, p. 179, emphasis in original). The conclusion they reached was that 'policies which rest on the assumption that people have a right to expect assistance from their relatives (even from their parents or their children) will not align with the realities of family life' (1993, p. 180).

If the same research were done in other countries, particularly those where wider family obligations are more embedded in law than they are in the UK, the results might look rather different. Also we do not know whether, over time, the re-drawing of the state-family boundary will mean the gap between individuals' expectations and the assumptions underlying policy will widen or whether individuals' expectations will come to reflect more closely those assumptions in line with the reality of attenuated state provision for some groups. The latter is a particularly plausible scenario in societies, such as the UK, where today's young people have been growing up in a political culture that emphasizes individual responsibilities.[3]

For now, there are other examples of the gap between policy assumptions and individual beliefs and expectations concerning the proper boundaries between public and private responsibility. For example, a study by van Drenth et al. (1999) of lone mothers in the Netherlands and the UK found that, whereas policy in both countries is increasingly predicated on the assumption that reliance on benefits equals dependence, the lone mothers themselves felt financially independent when on benefit. However where maintenance constituted a significant proportion of total income, the lone mothers tended to feel dependent. Both this and other British research (see for instance, Bradshaw and Millar, 1991) found little support for the principle that non-custodian fathers should pay maintenance for the mother (as opposed to the child), as was the case initially in the British Child Support scheme.

The same Anglo-Dutch study found that in both countries policies, which increasingly treat lone mothers as workers rather than mothers, run 'counter to the primary importance that lone mothers themselves afford to care' (van Drenth et al.1999; pp. 638 - 39). Indeed, the full-time work obligation imposed on lone parents in the Netherlands in the 1990s failed in its objectives, partly because of the combined opposition of lone mothers and caseworkers for whom the law contravened what they believed to be the proper responsibilities of lone mothers (Knijn and van Wel, 2001a,b). This contrasts with the situation in the US where, in the context of a culture where it is assumed mothers with young children will do paid work, there was much greater acceptance of the imposition of tougher work obligations (Orloff, 2002). Similarly in Norway, the intensification of the work requirements applied to lone parents has been relatively uncontroversial in the context of a strong gender-neutral work-ethic culture (Skevik, 2001).

The different responses in different societies to the expectation that lone mothers should look primarily to the market for support rather than to the state underline the importance of socio-cultural context, which is, in turn, 'linked to prevailing conceptions of [gendered] citizenship' (Rowlingson and Millar, 2001, p. 261). Such beliefs constitute what Birgit Pfau-Effinger calls the 'gender cultural system' (2002, p. 239). Moreover, the work of Duncan and Edwards (1999) suggests that this system and the more specific 'gendered moral rationalities' that lone mothers apply to these questions can be shaped by local as well as national norms and expectations.

Attitudes Towards the Role of the State in Welfare

More general surveys on attitudes towards welfare also provide some support for the thesis that the expectations of citizens and the assumptions underlying policy with regard to the proper boundaries between public and private responsibility for welfare do not always coincide (although these tend to focus on support for older people rather than children).

The International Social Attitudes Survey (based on 1990 data) suggested, according to Peter Taylor-Gooby, that public attitudes 'were (and are) out of sympathy with the prevailing international mood of politicians and governments in favour of market-led provision' (1993, p. 100). The more comprehensive survey of Western European attitudes towards the role of the state undertaken in the early 1990s, as part of the Beliefs in Government project, concluded that the great majority still believed that government should be responsible for health, education, housing, old age and unemployment (Borre and Scarbrough, 1995). Similarly, comparison of attitudes in West Germany and Britain in the mid-1990s as part of the British and European Social Attitudes Survey found 'as near universal agreement as there is ever likely to be in a sample survey that health care and basic old age pensions should be the responsibility of the state' (Kaase and Newton, 1998, p. 44). Kaase and Newton suggest that public opinion is resistant to the 'ebbs and flows of ideological debates (..) and political fashions' (ibid., p. 48), insofar as they promote radical shifts in the boundary of responsibility between the state and the individual/family. However, Taylor-Gooby (1998b) detects a slight tendency over time towards a belief in reduced government responsibility. If true, this might reflect the more fundamental shift that appears to have taken place, in some countries, in the ideological construction of the state's responsibility.

In the UK the consistent finding from a number of surveys, including one carried out for the then Department of Social Security, is that, while people are 'pessimistic about the future of state pension provision', there is 'a strong expectation and desire that the state should be responsible for providing a basic level of retirement pension, and that this should be higher than the current level of the basic state pension' (Williams et al., 1999). Likewise, in the 2001 British Social Attitudes Survey, four-fifths of respondents considered it definitely the responsibility of government to 'provide a decent standard of living for the old' and almost everyone else considered that it probably was (Hills, 2001). Both these surveys suggested greater acceptance of the idea that, above the basic pension, people should be encouraged to make provision for themselves. In the latter, for instance, nearly three-quarters agreed with the proposition that 'the government should encourage people to provide something for their own retirement instead of relying only on the state pension' and only one in seven disagreed (ibid.). However, another poll found that nearly two-thirds of workers surveyed believed that the government should provide an adequate state pension rather than expect people to top it up with a private pension or means-tested state support, as under current government policy (The *Guardian*, 7 April, 2000).

A qualitative study in the North of England, based on group discussions, found 'overwhelming endorsement' of the view that 'the state should continue to have a centrally important role in meeting future welfare needs' (Dwyer, 2000a, p. 192; see also Dean with Melrose, 1999). There was considerable hostility to the idea that individuals should be expected to take out private insurance and pensions and virtually no discussion of the role of the family in welfare provision.

Risk

Another area of research, which is relevant to an understanding of how individuals and families respond to transformations in the relationship between public and private responsibility is that relating to how people manage risk, in an increasingly individualized world (Beck, 1992; Beck and Beck-Gernsheim, 2002). A UK Economic and Social Research Council research programme provides one of the few empirical sources of evidence. Studies within the programme, which looked at long-term care of older people and private unemployment insurance, again revealed some disjunction between policy expectations and the capacity and willingness of individuals to respond to them (Taylor-Gooby, 1998a, 2000). However, the study of managing unemployment risks found 'a common feeling that "welfare" was changing and that more self provision was inevitable' (Abbott and Quilgars, 2001, p. 120).

Nevertheless, Peter Taylor-Gooby, the Programme Director, concludes that 'the cultural framework presumed by current directions in policy is not predominant among ordinary citizens. Many people still expect government rather than private citizens to take core responsibility for the improvement of the major welfare services through the enhancement of tax-financed public provision' (1998a, p. 220). The other main conclusion he reaches from the programme is the importance of social and cultural context to understanding how people respond to risk, choice and opportunity. This echoes my earlier point about the significance of 'institutional arrangements' and is also reflected in the work of feminist ethicists such as Selma Sevenhuijsen (1998) who emphasise the importance of context to the decisions people take with regard to welfare (see also, DiQuinzio and Young, 1997).

The findings suggest that reactions to transformations in the relationship between public and private responsibility do not necessarily reflect the rational calculations of 'economic man and woman', but are 'influenced by cultural expectations and preconceptions, by the norms prevalent in society, by the moral considerations that govern duty and obligation and by experience and learning from the experience of others' (Taylor-Gooby 2000, p. xi). This, he suggests, stands in contrast to assumptions about individual self-interest, which underlie the marketization of welfare and which are therefore potentially 'damaging to human interests in tackling the uncertainties that citizens face' (ibid., p. 11).

CONCLUSION

Cross-national analysis of welfare policies and regimes tends, not surprisingly, to concentrate on the macro institutional level. This chapter has attempted to shift the focus to the micro level and to answer the question: what are the implications for and responses of family members to shifts in the boundaries of responsibility for welfare between state and families/individuals? It has highlighted issues of solidarity between the generations rather than the sexes, although, generational relations are themselves gendered. A combination of the complex factors involved and limitations of data has made it difficult to answer the question. Nevertheless, the chapter has highlighted the importance of the interface between macro and micro levels of solidarity and has presented some evidence of possible tensions between the two.

This tension was first illuminated by Finch and Mason's study, carried out in the UK during the second half of the 1980s. There has, since then, been considerable further change in patterns of welfare, as well as in assumptions about gender and generational relationships. This suggests a research agenda, which would update and modify the kind of research Finch and Mason carried out, but on a cross-national basis. It would be helpful to know not just how individual citizens construct their own responsibilities for their welfare and that of other family members but also how they perceive and respond to the particular transformations in the relationship between the public and private in their respective national contexts. Without an understanding of what is happening at the micro level, we cannot have a clear picture of the transformations of solidarity between the sexes and the generations in Europe.

NOTES

1. I would like to thank the editors for their helpful comments on the first draft of this chapter.
2. The idea of the social investment state has been used to characterize the transformation of some liberal regimes, most notably Canada and the UK, into a rather different animal from that described in Esping-Andersen's original analysis (Dobrowolsky and Saint-Martin, 2002; Jenson and Saint-Martin, 2002). Esping-Andersen himself has identified a bifurcation between 'youth oriented' liberal regimes and a group that is 'ever more age-biased and service-lean' (1999, p. 166). He includes the UK in the latter (with the US) but this was before the emergence of New Labour's social investment state.
3. Research as part of the UK Economic and Social Research Council *Youth, Citizenship and Social Change Programme* (Award no. L134251039) found that young people were generally able to articulate their perceived responsibilities as citizens. Among these, they tended to include the responsibility to look after oneself and one's family and to be in waged employment and pay tax (Lister et al., 2002).

REFERENCES

Abbott, D. and D. Quilgars (2001), 'Managing the risk of unemployment: is welfare restructuring undermining support for social security?', in R. Edwards and J. Glover (eds), *Risk and Citizenship. Key Issues in Welfare*, London and New York: Routledge, pp.111 - 25.

Appleton, L. and L. Hantrais (2000), *Conceptualizing and Measuring Families and Family Policies in Europe*, Loughborough: Cross-National Research Group.

Beck, U. (1992), *Risk Society. Towards a New Modernity*, London, Thousand Oaks, New Delhi: Sage.

Beck, U. and E. Beck-Gernsheim (2002), *Individualization*, London, Thousand Oaks, New Delhi: Sage.

Borre, O. and E. Scarbrough (1995), *Beliefs in Government, Vol. 3: The Scope of Government*, Oxford: Oxford University Press.

Bradshaw, J. and J. Millar (1991), *Lone Parent Families in the UK*, DSS Research Report No. 6, London: HMSO.

Castles, F.G. (1993), *Families of Nations: Patterns of Public Policy in Western Democracies*, Aldershot: Dartmouth.

Commission on Social Justice (1994), *Social Justice: Strategies for National Renewal*, London: Vintage.

Craig, G. and C. Glendinning (1990), *Missing the Target*, Ilford: Barnardos.

Daly, M. (1997), 'Welfare states under pressure: cash benefits in European welfare states over the last ten years', *Journal of European Social Policy*, 7 (2), 129 - 46.

Daly, M. and J. Lewis (1998), 'Introduction: Conceptualising social care in the context of welfare state restructuring', in J. Lewis (ed.), *Gender, Social Care and Welfare State Restructuring in Europe*, Aldershot/Brookfield USA: Ashgate, pp. 1 - 24.

Dean, H. and P. Taylor-Gooby (1992), *Dependency Culture. The Explosion of a Myth*, New York, London: Harvester Wheatsheaf.

Dean, H. and Z. Khan (1997), 'Muslim perspectives on welfare', *Journal of Social Policy*, **26** (2), 193 - 209.

Dean, H. with Melrose, M. (1999), *Poverty, Riches and Social Citizenship*, Basingstoke: Macmillan.

DiQuinzio, P. and I.M. Young (eds) (1997), *Feminist Ethics and Social Policy*, Bloomington and Indianapolis, Indiana University Press.

Dobrowolsky A. and D. Saint-Martin (2002), 'Agency, actors and change in a child-focused future: problematizing path dependency's past and statist parameters', American Political Science Association Annual Meeting, Boston, 29 August – 1 September.

Drenth, A. van, T. Knijn and J. Lewis (1999), 'Sources of income for lone mother families: policy changes in Britain and the Netherlands and the experiences of divorced women', *Journal of Social Policy*, **28** (4), 619 - 41.

Duncan, S. (1998), 'Editorial: The spatiality of gender', *Innovation*, **11** (2), 119 - 28.

Duncan, S. and R. Edwards (1999), *Lone Mothers, Paid Work and Gendered Moral Rationalities*, Basingstoke: Macmillan, New York: St Martin's Press.

Duncan, S. and D. Smith (2002), 'Family geographies and gender cultures', *Social Policy and Society*, **1** (1), 21 - 34.

Dwyer, P. (2000a), *Welfare Rights and Responsibilities. Contesting Social Citizenship*, Bristol: Policy Press.

Dwyer, P. (2000b), 'British Muslims, welfare citizenship and conditionality', in M. bin Hamzah, M.- binBin, M. Harris and P. Dwyer, *Islamic Values, Human Agency and Social Policies, RAPP Research Working Paper*, Leeds: Department of Sociology and Social Policy, University of Leeds, pp. 31 - 56.

Esping-Andersen, E. (1990), *The Three Worlds of Welfare Capitalism*, Cambridge: Polity Press.

Esping-Andersen, G. (1999), *Social Foundations of Postindustrial Economies*, Oxford, New York: Oxford University Press.

Esping-Andersen, E. (2002), 'A child-centred social investment strategy', in E. Esping-Andersen with D. Gallie, A. Hemerijck, J. Myles, *Why We Need a New Welfare State*, Oxford and New York: Oxford University Press, pp. 26 - 67.

Eurostat (2000), *The Social Situation in the European Union 2000*, Luxembourg: Office for Official Publications of the European Communities.

Eurostat (2001), *The Social Situation in the European Union 2001*, Luxembourg: Office for Official Publications of the European Communities.

Ferge, Z. (2001), 'Welfare and "ill-fare" systems in Central-Eastern Europe', in R. Sykes, B. Palier and P.M. Prior (eds), *Globalization and European Welfare States*, Basingstoke and New York: Palgrave, pp. 127-152.

Finch, J. (1989), *Family Obligations and Social Change*, Cambridge: Polity Press.

Finch, J. and J. Mason (1993), *Negotiating Family Responsibilities*, London and New York: Routledge.

Giddens (1998), *The Third Way. The Renewal of Social Democracy*, Cambridge: Polity Press.

Heinen, J. (1997), 'Public/private: Gender – social and political citizenship in Eastern Europe', *Theory and Society*, **26**: 577 - 97.

Hills, J. (1998), *Income and Wealth. The Latest Evidence*, York: Joseph Rowntree Foundation.

Hills, J. (2001), 'Poverty and social security: What rights? Whose responsibilities?', in A. Park, J. Curtice, K. Thomson, L. Jarvis and C. Bromley (eds), *British Social Attitudes. The 18th Report*, London, Thousand Oaks, New Delhi: Sage, pp. 1 - 28.

Hills, J. and O. Lelkes (1999), 'Social security, selective universalism and patchwork redistribution', in R. Jowell, J. Curtice, A. Park and K. Thomson (eds), *British Social Attitudes. The 16th Report*, Aldershot/Brookfield USA: Ashgate, pp. 1 - 22.

Jarvis, L., K. Hinds, C. Bryson and A. Park (2000), *Women's Social Attitudes: 1983 to 1998*, Cabinet Office: London.

Jenson, J. (2001), 'Rethinking equality and equity: Canadian children and the social union', in E. Broadbent (ed.), *Democratic Equality: What Went Wrong?*, Toronto, Buffalo, London: University of Toronto Press, pp. 111 - 29.

Jenson, J. and D. Saint-Martin (2001), 'Changing citizenship regimes: social policy strategies in the investment state', Workshop on Fostering Social Cohesion. A comparison of new political strategies, Université de Montreal, 21 - 22 June.

Jenson, J. and D. Saint-Martin (2002), 'Building blocks for a new welfare architecture: from Ford to LEGO?', American Political Science Association Annual Meeting, Boston, 29 August – 1 September.

Jowell, R., J. Curtice, A. Park, L. Brook, K. Thomson and C. Bryson (eds) (1998), *British and European Social Attitudes. How Britain Differs. The 15th Report*, Aldershot/Brookfield USA: Ashgate.

Kaase M. and K. Newton (1998), 'What people expect from the state: plus ça change…', in R. Jowell et al., op. cit, pp. 39 - 56.

Knijn, T. and F. van Wel (2001a), 'Does it work? Employment policies for lone parents in the Netherlands', in J. Millar and K. Rowlingson (eds), *Lone Parents, Employment and Social Policy*, Bristol: Policy Press, pp. 107 - 27

Knijn, T. and F. van Wel (2001b), 'Careful or lenient: welfare reform for lone mothers in the Netherlands', *Journal of European Social Policy*, **11** (3), 235 - 51.

Lakin, C. (2002), 'The effects of taxes and benefits on household income, 2000 - 01', *Economic Trends*, **582** (May), 33 - 80.

Law, I., A. Deacon, C. Hylton and A. Karmani (1996), 'Black families and social security: evidence from fieldwork in Leeds', in H. Jones and J. Millar (eds), *The Politics of the Family*, Aldershot/Brookfield USA: Avebury, pp. 129 - 44.

Lister, R. (1994), '"She has other duties" – women, citizenship and social security', in S. Baldwin and J. Falkingham (eds), *Social Security and Social Change,* Hemel Hempstead: Harvester Wheatsheaf, pp. 31 - 44.

Lister, R. (2002), 'Investing in the citizen-workers of the future: New Labour's "third way" in welfare reform', American Political Science Association Annual Meeting, Boston, 29 August – 1 September.

Lister, R. (2003), *Citizenship: Feminist Perspectives*, 2nd edn, Basingstoke: Palgrave/New York: New York University Press.

Lister, R., N. Smith, S. Middleton and L. Cox (2002), *Negotiating Transitions to Citizenship. Report of Findings,* Loughborough: Centre for Research in Social Policy.

McLaughlin, E. and C. Glendinning (1994), 'Paying for care in Europe: is there a feminist approach', in L. Hantrais and S. Mangen (eds), *Family Policy and the Welfare of Women*, Loughborough: Cross-National Research Group, pp. 52 - 69.

Millar, J. and A. Warman (1996), *Family Obligations in Europe*, London: Family Policy Study Centre.

Orloff, A.S. (2002), 'Explaining US welfare reform', *Critical Social Policy* 22 (1): 96 – 118.

Pascall, G. and N. Manning (2000), 'Gender and social policy in Central and Eastern Europe and the former Soviet Union', *Journal of European Social Policy*, **10** (3), 240 - 66.

Pfau-Effinger, B. (2002), 'Changing welfare states and labour markets in the context of European gender arrangements', in J.G. Andersen and P.H. Jensen (eds), *Changing Labour Markets, Welfare Policies and Citizenship*, Bristol: Policy Press, pp. 235 - 56.

Pierson, P. (2001), 'Introduction. Investigating the welfare state at century's end', in P. Pierson (ed.), *The New Politics of the Welfare State*, Oxford, New York: Oxford University Press, pp. 1 - 14.

Rothstein, B. (1998), *Just Institutions Matter*, Cambridge, New York, Melbourne: Cambridge University Press.

Rowlingson, K. and J. Millar (2001), 'Supporting employment: emerging policy and practice', in J. Millar and K. Rowlingson (eds), *Lone Parents, Employment and Social Policy*, Bristol: Policy Press, pp. 255 - 63.

Sevenhuijsen, S. (1998), *Citizenship and the Ethics of Care,* London and New York: Routledge.

Skevik, A. (2001), 'Lone parents and employment in Norway', in J. Millar and K. Rowlingson (eds), *Lone Parents, Employment and Social Policy*, Bristol: Policy Press, pp. 87 - 105.

Taylor-Gooby, P. (1993), 'What citizens want from the state', in R. Jowell, L. Brook and L. Dowds (eds), *International Social Attitudes. The 10th BSA Report,* Aldershot/Brookfield USA: Dartmouth, pp. 81 - 101.

Taylor-Gooby, P. (ed.) (1998a), *Choice and Public Policy. The Limits to Welfare Markets*, Basingstoke: Macmillan and New York: St. Martin's Press.

Taylor-Gooby, P. (1998b), 'Commitment to the welfare state', in R. Jowell et al., op. cit, pp. 57 - 73.

Taylor-Gooby, P. (ed.) (2000), *Risk, Trust and Welfare*, Basingstoke: Macmillan and New York: St. Martin's Press.

Williams, T., M. Hill and R. Davies (1999), *Attitudes towards the Welfare State and the Response to Reform*, DSS Research Report No. 88, London: Department of Social Security.

4. Individualization and the Need for New Forms of Family Solidarity

Jane Lewis

Enormous behavioural change in the second half of the twentieth century has resulted in more family breakdown, more fluidity in intimate relationships, and a large increase in single person households. In addition, increasing numbers of women have entered the labour market. Indeed, this has become one point of convergence between EU member states. There has, in short, been more 'individualization' in the sense of the family becoming an 'elective relationship' rather than 'a community of need' (Beck-Gernsheim, 1999), and in the sense more commonly understood by policy makers of adult family members becoming more economically independent. However, the responsibility for caring for young and old dependants in the family has showed relatively little change. Time-use surveys show that men's behaviour has been less susceptible to change and that women still do the bulk of unpaid care work (Gershuny, 2000; Laurie and Gershuny, 2000).

It is increasingly expected that women will be in the labour market, although to what extent is not clear. Similarly, it is increasingly expected, although there is less consensus on this in some countries, that fathers will be 'involved' with their children in the sense of nurture and care, as well as breadwinning.[1] In respect of the first expectation, an 'adult worker model' holds out more promise for women than the dependence inherent in the traditional male breadwinner model family. Feminists have long argued for 'individualization' in the sense of economic independence for women. But individualization was conceptualized by many western governments in the 1990s more as an obligation to engage in the labour market, and increasingly as an expectation that adults will be capable of greater self-provisioning. Given the trend towards the 'individualization of the social' (Ferge, 1997; Guillemard, 1986) together with massive family change over the last quarter of a century resulting in a huge increase in lone mother families in many northern and western European countries, women need more access to wages. However, the acceptance of what might be called an 'adult worker model' (Lewis, 2001a) depends on the terms, not least because women continue to work fewer hours in lower paying jobs than men. 'Welfare-to-work' programmes and policies to 'make work pay' dominated the reform of social security in many Western European countries during the 1990s, as part of the strategy to enforce the obligation to work. But in countries outside Scandinavia and some continental European countries (particularly France and Belgium) there is relatively little attention to policies in respect of care work. Without these an adult worker model poses severe problems, not only for women but also for the wider society. In respect of the second expectation regarding the role of fathers as nurturers as well as providers, there is also relatively little sign of policies designed to promote care work by men.

The chapter suggests that there has been a shift towards individualization that is more evident at the level of prescription than behaviour. Adults are more economically autonomous and intimate relationships have become more elective. But care work, which is by definition relational, is inevitably characterized by interconnectedness, and is still marked by relations of dependence as well as inter-dependence. The changing nature of the contributions men and women make to families require an effort on the part of policymakers to promote new forms of social solidarity, both at the level of collective provision via policies to promote cash payments for care and care services (so-called de-famililialization), and within the family, by encouraging a more equal distribution of money and labour between men and women.

INDIVIDUALIZATION: BEHAVIOUR

The contributions of men and women to families have changed significantly, particularly in respect of women's increased financial contribution due to their greater labour market participation. But full individualization in the sense of economic autonomy is constrained principally by the need of dependants for care, although the decision to care (usually made by women) may of course be the expression of a preference.[2]

Labour force participation rates for the last twenty years show women's participation rising, and rising relatively steeply in most European countries, and men's participation rates falling. However, while the trend is similar in virtually all OECD countries, the baselines are very different. In 1980, Denmark had the highest female participation rate in the EC and in 2000 the second highest rate (behind Sweden). The Netherlands had one of the lowest rates of female participation in 2000, but one of the steepest rates of increase between 1980 and 2000. In addition, the nature of female labour market participation looks very different in these countries. In most European countries the percentage of women workers who are employed part-time has risen over the last twenty years, but in Denmark it has fallen; only Finland, Portugal, Spain and Sweden have lower proportions of part-time women workers. In The Netherlands and the UK virtually the whole post-war expansion of female employment has been part-time and a large percentage of women work short part-time hours. The majority of women workers are employed in the service sector, but in the UK a greater proportion are in private sector services than in The Netherlands or Denmark (Daly, 2000).

During the last quarter of the twentieth century, research revealed the extent to which the male breadwinner system no longer described behaviour for a significant proportion of families (Crompton, 1999; Lewis, 2001a). But nor have families become fully individualized, with both partners engaged in full-time work and economically independent of one another. The male breadwinner model has eroded but the social reality is still far from a family comprised of self-sufficient, autonomous individuals. While women's contribution to family income has risen and that of men has fallen, it cannot be assumed that women are or can be in any near future economically self- sufficient. While women's behaviour has changed substantially in respect of paid work, they still perform the bulk of unpaid care work, which was their obligation under the old work/welfare model.

Men have changed much less in respect of the amount of either the paid or unpaid work they do (e.g. Laurie and Gershuny, 2000). The pattern of paid work between men and women in households is now much more difficult to predict, but patterns of unpaid work have not changed so much, although the mix of provision in respect of unpaid work (from market, third sector and public sources) that accompanies unpaid informal provision varies between countries, and according to both the hours of paid work carried out by women and their partners' earnings (Lewis, 2000; Warren, 2000). In the UK, women who work full-time are most likely to use their own mothers as childcare providers with their spouses a close second, and women who work part-time are most likely to use their spouses and their mothers second. The dominant pattern of contributions to most Western European families follows some form of one-and-a-half earner model, with women working part-time, albeit that part-time work varies from the long and protected hours of the Scandinavian countries to the short and precarious hours of the UK. In other words, the problem of squaring the need to do care work has been reconciled mainly through the partial individualization of women, although the much more substantial part-time working of Scandinavian women rests in turn on the more substantial collective provision for care in terms of cash and services.

Men do contribute to childcare and, indeed to elder care. UK time-use data show a steady increase in fathers' care work for children, albeit from a low base (Gershuny, 2000), and the participation of men in care tasks has also advanced considerably in continental European countries. US data show similar trends, with men doing more relative to women in the household when women work full-time, although as Pleck (1997) pointed out, this was largely because women cut their unpaid contributions. However, for the USA, Furstenberg (1988) suggested that there may be polarity in the behaviour of fathers, with one group doing a lot more with their children, and a second group very little, a conclusion that probably also holds good for the UK.

Recent British surveys have stressed the long hours worked by fathers in two parent families: the longest in the European Union (at 48 hours a week) for fathers with children under 11 (Ferri and Smith, 1996; Lewis, C., 2000). When put together with the fact that fathers also still earn an average of two-thirds of the family income in the UK, the gender division of contributions to two-parent households still look quite traditional (Lewis, J., 2000). In respect of care for elderly people, the UK's General Household Survey shows spouses to be the most common informal carers; however men will usually provide less intimate and less intensive care than do women (Land and Lewis, 1998). Men are participating somewhat more in care work, and reducing their hours of paid work slightly. Women have increased their hours of paid work dramatically, but without a concomitant reduction in their hours of unpaid work. The resulting imbalance has given rise to considerable commentary, particularly in the USA, on the threat the resulting imbalance poses to family stability, to the pursuit of gender equality, and to those needing care (Hewlett, 1991; Hochschild, 1990).

Gerson's (1993) qualitative study of men in the US developed a typology of autonomous, breadwinning and involved male partners (married and cohabiting). The autonomous man was the individualist, who might encourage his female partner's economic independence, but who did not share either the work of the household or necessarily contribute to it economically. Such attitudes have been shown in other American studies to be more typical of men who cohabit (Lewis, 2001b). The sole breadwinner in Gerson's study was in a minority and often tended to a traditional view of male/female relationships, but nevertheless saw himself as a committed contributor to the welfare of the household. Men who were 'involved' (40% shared fully, the rest 'helped') had usually either started on a fast track at work and decided to quit, or had hit a dead-end at work. In other words, their contribution owed much to what had happened to them in the workplace. The fact that Gerson found it possible to identify these types shows the extent of change in the nature of the contributions that men and women are making to households.

INDIVIDUALIZATION: POLICY PRESCRIPTION

From the point of view of women, the key issue is the extent to which governments are moving towards assuming the existence of an adult rather than a male breadwinner model, and thus seek to treat men and women the same, whether by insisting on the obligation to work in return for state benefits, or by assuming that they will be able to make more provision for themselves, for example in respect of pensions. Evidence that this is happening is not hard to find, although that of the UK is among the most striking. The UK Labour Government has made the drive from welfare-to-work central to its social policy. Tony Blair's introduction to the document on welfare reform has been widely quoted – 'work for those who can; security for those who cannot' (Cm 3805, 1998, p. iii) – and contrasted with the Beveridgean promise of security for all. The introduction also made clear that this approach was to apply to women as well as men: 'the welfare state based around the male breadwinner is increasingly out of date' (p.13).

There are several strands of thought that have fed the profound shift that government has made in respect of assumptions about appropriate models of work for women (see also Lister, 2000). First, a major influence on Governments of the early and mid-1990s was the view that all those in receipt of state benefits have a concomitant obligation to engage in paid labour. Lawrence Mead (1986) presented this solution in terms of a model of equal citizenship, based on participation and responsibility, a perspective that has also been adopted by European social democrats in the 1990s (Vandenbroucke, 2002). Welfare-to-work, implemented first in the US, embodied these ideas and was applied to all able-bodied adults, lone mothers included, notwithstanding their particularly visible double burden of paid and unpaid work. However, in the context of the European social model, with its more elaborate provision for adults in terms of services and transfers, the new-found emphasis on the importance of an 'active welfare state' and labour market participation looks less punitive.

Second, social democrats have, like Mead but unlike more radical critics of 'welfare dependency' (such as Charles Murray), also stressed the overriding importance of employment as a means to social integration or inclusion. In this interpretation, the effort to get more lone mothers into the labour market has been justified as much by reference to improving the welfare of the mothers themselves as by condemnation of welfare dependency. This position is shared by many feminists, who, while they have long stressed the need to recognize the unpaid work of care (Finch and Groves, 1983) have also long campaigned for women's financial autonomy (McIntosh, 1981).

Third, the globalization thesis directs the attention of government to labour markets and competitiveness (Gough, 1996). Certainly, the European Commission has stressed the importance of adult labour market participation in order to increase competitiveness (CEC, 1993, 1995, 2000a, 2000b). Both the EC (CEC, 2000) and the OECD (2000) have emphasized the importance of policies to 'make work pay', and in the words of the EC, of strengthening 'the role of social policy as a productive factor' (CEC, 2000a, p. 2). In the economic strategy documents of the Commission, there is little reference to the family and family responsibilities, yet there is also obvious concern at the EU level with the work/family nexus, as expressed, for example, in the Directive on parental leave (EC96/34). The point is, that these two agendas remain parallel and separate and the former predominates. Thus, greater labour market participation is seen as the best way of securing competitive advantage, of keeping public expenditure down (especially in respect of the growing numbers of lone mother families), and of promoting social inclusion and reducing poverty.

A fully individualized adult worker model is not necessarily 'bad for women'. Everything depends on the conditions under which such a model is implemented. The problems of assuming the existence of a full adult worker model are fourfold:

- Unpaid care work is unequally shared between men and women, which has substantial implications for women's position in the labour market.
- Given the lack of good quality affordable care in the formal sector (public or private) in many countries, many women have little option but to continue to provide care.
- A significant number of female carers feel that it is 'right' to prioritize care over paid work.
- Women's low pay, especially in care-related jobs, means that full individualization is hard to achieve on the basis of long part-time or even full-time work.

Just as policy assumptions based on a male breadwinner model disadvantaged women in particular, so assumptions based on a full adult worker model are also likely to do so. First, individualization in the sense of an obligation to engage in paid work is likely to result in the 'double shift' (Hochschild, 1990) for women, and intolerable burdens if no attempt is made either to get men to share the care, or to de-familialize care. Second, any assumption that wages will enable more self-provision in the social arena, especially in respect of pensions, is fraught with danger for women. Pension reform has been carried out as if the implications are gender neutral. But privatizing pension provision means that women will do disproportionately badly because of their unequal position in the labour market, while lengthening the number of years of work required for a state pension disadvantages women who leave the labour market to care. Ginn et al. (2001) have argued powerfully and convincingly that pension reform in EU member states has systematically disadvantaged women who already suffer the greatest poverty in old age. The new welfare contract is moving from social contributions to individually defined contributions, premised on the idea that adults are in the workforce, but this is an unrealistic assumption in respect of women, whose labour market participation is limited by the assumption of care work responsibilities. Assumptions made by governments regarding the existence of a fully individualized adult worker model pose threats to women unless issues to do with the unequal gendered division of work and hence of life-time earnings are addressed.

Of course, the shift to an adult worker model is generally far from complete. Policy ambiguity and inconsistency are common, especially in the UK case (Rake, 2000; McLaughlin et al., 2001), but also in other continental European countries (Daly, 2000). Existing mechanisms for delivering cash benefits have not changed in line with new-found assumptions regarding an individualized adult worker model. The UK, with its heavy reliance on means-testing and hence joint assessment, faces particular problems in this regard. In the UK, the working families tax credit designed to 'make work pay' is administered on the basis of joint earnings and may thus actually reduce the incentive for partnered women to enter employment in low paid jobs. The New Deal for the Partners of the Unemployed (mainly women) treats them both as having an independent relationship to the labour market and as dependants. Their access to the programme is dependent on their being the partner of an unemployed man (see also Saraceno in this volume). Thus while ideas about individualization have been clearly expressed in the UK and The Netherlands, it is still assumed that married women can depend on their husbands as and when necessary. In the context of the new assumptions about an equal obligation to do paid work, it is significant that both the UK and The Netherlands have acted unequivocally to push lone mothers into the labour market, in the face of strongly shared values among women in both countries that prioritize care work (Duncan and Edwards, 1999; Knijn and van Wel, 2001).[3]

In respect of men's contribution to the family, there is considerable ambiguity in terms of the views that are held about the contribution men make to contemporary family life; in the UK and the USA this has resulted in considerable confusion and disagreement (Lewis, C., 2000). Stacey (1990) has commented that young working-class men in late twentieth-century California were not sure whether to regard one of their number who became a breadwinner as a hero or a chump. As the male breadwinner model family has eroded, it might be expected that prescriptions for fathers would move away from earning to more of a focus on caring, and the evidence suggests that this has indeed been more readily accepted in those European countries, particularly in Scandinavia where men have been given strong incentives to take parental leave.

However, the picture is not that simple. The processes of family change which have resulted in much larger numbers of lone-mother families have meant that governments, especially in the English-speaking countries, have tried to enforce financial support on the part of absent fathers. Orloff and Monson (2002, p. 88) have referred to the American government's effort to 'discipline fathers into breadwinnerhood' as part and parcel of the 1996 welfare reforms, and Smart and Neale (1999) have commented on the apparent desire of the British government to enforce traditional marital gender roles in relationships where marriage has ended or even where it has never taken place.

The responsibility of fathers to maintain their children is accepted in all Western European countries, and increasingly, in line with individualization, it is the parental and not the spousal obligation that is central in family law (Maclean and Eekelaar, 1997). In Sandinavian countries this was entrenched in family law since the early part of the twentieth century. However, nowhere does the contribution made by fathers to lone mother families constitute the major source of financial support (Millar and Warman, 1996). In Sweden, for example, almost two thirds of a lone mother's income comes from wages, and almost one third from state transfers; a very small percentage comes from fathers (Lewis and Hobson, 1998). As the 1974 UK Report on One-Parent Families (Cmd. 5269, para 4.49) recognized, the burden of support for lone mother families would inevitably fall on the state given that it was well-nigh impossible in a liberal democratic society to control marital and reproductive behaviour. It has since been noted in addition that despite the trend towards treating adults as able to fend for themselves in and outside of marriage, the financial support of children has also to encompass the provision of care for them, which is, in and out of marriage, largely provided by women (Lewis, 2001b).

Male irresponsibility in relation to the family has been defined largely in terms of the 'failure to maintain'. In the UK, child support legislation was implemented in 1991, following similar attempts in the US and Australia, in an attempt to give all biological fathers, unmarried and divorced, a persistent obligation to maintain. The legislation was billed as a means of securing greater provision for women and children, but research showed they made few gains. Any money raised from fathers was deducted pound for pound from the mothers' benefits. In other words, the legislation was intended above all to enforce private, parental responsibility and to reduce 'welfare dependency'. Faced with the doubling of expenditure on lone parents' bene-fits and the fact that by 1989 the children of lone parents accounted for three-fifths of all children of income support claimants (compared with under half in 1986), the UK government turned first to men as an alternative source of support, introducing the Child Support Act. However, when this measure proved a conspicuous failure, the Department of Social Security announced in 1996 a new incentive to assist lone mothers into paid employment, provid-ing individual help with job search and assistance with training for work. In other words, a more explicit effort was made to encourage individualization in the sense of self-support, something that also happened in the US and Dutch cases.

This legislative response to family change shows that the role of fathers as breadwinners has far from disappeared from the minds of politicians. As we have seen in the case of mothers, notwithstanding the generalization of the adult worker model to women, Western European governments still tend to assume that in two-parent families women can fall back on their partners for support. There is also evidence that men themselves also identify primar-ily as earners; in the UK, Warin et al. (1999) showed the extent to which men still define themselves primarily as economic providers. On the other hand, men are increasingly expected to care. As Williams (1998) has remarked, anxieties and concerns about 'fathering' have increasingly focused on father distance, as well as on father absence. Father involvement has been linked to higher achievement levels in children (Pleck, 1997), and to the wider proc-esses of social capital formation in neighbourhoods and communities (Furstenberg, 1988), although many communitarians are more concerned to encourage women not to neglect their care responsibilities (Fukuyama, 1999; Popenoe, 1993).

In the English-speaking countries, however, there has been little signifi-cant shift in prescription regarding the roles of fathers in terms of government policy. In the UK the first steps have been taken to promote parental leave, in line with the European Commission Directive on the issue (EC 96/34), but the very short 13-week leave has been confined to the parents of children born after December 1999 and remains unpaid. This compares to 18 months for Swedes, a year for Austrians and 10 months for Italians. In addition, the opt-outs from the European Commission's Directive on working time (EC 93/104) allow the very British male 'long hours culture' to persist. Men have only recently gained an entitlement to a two-week paternity leave. Tony Blair faced personal publicity on this issue when his fourth child was born.

Other European countries have shown considerable concern about the issue of care and its gendered dimension. Parental leave has been taken disproportionately by women, even in those countries paying generous sums to those taking it, and many Northern European countries have experimented with periods of leave available only to men – 'the Daddy month' – and with the right of men and women to work a shorter working day or a four-day week while they have young children. Again, individualization of leave is important if gender equality in the division of work, paid and unpaid is to be promoted. But even in the Scandinavian countries, there is a long way to go before there is equal acknowledgement between the sexes of the responsibility to care. It is significant, for example, that more men take parental leave if they are working in the public sector, where there is more support for it from both colleagues and managers. In The Netherlands, the government has promoted the sharing of paid and unpaid work by men and women in households via the 'Combination Scenario' set out in a 1997 White Paper, the policy goal being the promotion of economic independence by redistributing paid and unpaid work at the household level rather than by de-familializing care work (Knijn, 2001).

There is little doubt that the slowness of legislative action to promote a shift in men's behaviour in respect of care is matched by men's own attachment to the identity of breadwinner. But it is also fair to say that in many countries, particularly the English-speaking ones, legislation still emphasizes the importance of men's role as breadwinners and in so far as men are also being asked to take on more of the work and responsibility for care without much by way of support, the result is often confusion and frustration.

THE NEED TO PROMOTE NEW FORMS OF SOCIAL SOLIDARITY

If no action is taken to promote the sharing of care between men and women, to provide collectively for care, or to value care work more highly (whether it is carried out in the family or in the public sphere), then individualization in the sense of economic participation can only be achieved at the expense of care. Furthermore, even these approaches to policies for care may still be insufficient. They are most developed in the continental European countries and have been explicitly linked to women's increasing labour market participation. There is a long way to go in developing these policies, which are crucial for maintaining family solidarity, but it is additionally necessary to take a more care-centred perspective in order to build new structures of social solidarity in the family. Policies are needed on two levels: collective provision to secure a degree of de-familialization, but also to promote a redistribution of work and income at the household level between men and women.

Given the convergence towards an adult worker model it is necessary to think more closely about how a balance between paid and unpaid work is to be achieved. It is useful to look at the Scandinavian and American models in this regard as well. Both have a fully individualized, adult-worker model. However, in the US case, the obligation to enter the labour market is embedded in a residual welfare system that often borders on the punitive, whereas in Sweden and Denmark it is supported by an extensive range of care entitlements in respect of children and older people. The position of lone mothers – always a border case for the study of social policy – is particularly instructive in this respect because of the problem of combining unpaid care work and employment. The US has gone much more wholeheartedly than Britain down the road of treating these women as paid workers, imposing time-limited benefits. Employment rates of lone mothers are high in the US; the push factor is strong. But employment rates are higher still in Sweden and Denmark and lone mothers' poverty rates are much lower than in the UK or the US. Indeed, in Sweden all adult citizens have long been obliged to engage in paid work in order to qualify for a wide range of benefits, and are then permitted to leave the labour market for cause. However, Swedish lone mothers still get one third of their income from the state (Lewis and Hobson, 1998). The system is based on a commitment to universal citizenship entitlements, rather than, as in the US, grafting equal citizenship obligations on to a residual welfare model.

In general, attention has been paid to care policies only in association with the promotion of an adult worker model. Thus Korpi (2001) has sought to categorize policies according to the extent to which they enable the redistribution of care work with the policy goal of promoting women's labour market participation. Indeed, this has been the dominant approach of governments seeking to reconcile work and family life, whether at the individual level of the household, as in the Dutch Combination Scenario, or through the collective provision of care leaves and/or services. Such measures are extremely important, but more is needed to address the kinds of profound changes that have affected families.

A focus on unpaid care work directs attention above all to the importance of time, something that feminist analysis has stressed for three decades (see especially Balbo, 1975; Land, 1983). Some formal recognition of non-monetary data has been given in the revised system of national accounts, devized in 1993 and implemented in 2000. So-called 'satellite accounts' are intended to attach a value to unpaid work (Harrison, 2000; Short, 2000). As Nowotny (1994) has commented, time is no longer a private issue. Taking care seriously requires that due consideration be given to the 'time to care'. All too often women experience little genuine choice to care (Land and Rose, 1985). Indeed, the shift towards an individualized adult worker model entails modes of care provision that remain unarticulated. These are most striking in the case of lone mothers, who have no choice but to seek substitute carers for their children.

The literature that develops an ethic of care proposes an alternative model of relationship and connection and makes a strong case for enabling all human beings to care (Tronto, 1993; Sevenhuijsen, 1998). This means that policies must address the distribution of time. The French 35-hour week introduced at the beginning of 2000 for companies with more than 20 employees (with the possibility of working longer hours at peak times and fewer hours at others), comes closest to Schor's (1991) ideal of a 30 hour week for both sexes and has shown additionally that shorter working hours may raise productivity and competitiveness. But Creighton (1999) concluded from his analysis of working time, much like feminists in the 1970s, that policies to address the issue of sharing work, both paid and unpaid, are vital. The Dutch Government is alone in having explicitly encouraged the sharing of paid and unpaid work between men and women and The Netherlands has high rates of part-time work for men as well as women. However, in practice the majority of men working part-time are either young or over 55 years old, in other words they are unlikely to be sharing care work (Knijn, 2001). It may be that policy makers should begin to think more about the redistribution of paid work for men and women over the life course, with fewer paid working hours during periods of caring for young and old people.

But choice to care depends further on valuing care. This is enormously problematic. As Joshi and Davis (2000) have pointed out in respect of the new satellite accounts, the decision whether to use a fixed, flat rate of pay or an earnings related amount has very different distributory effects. In policy terms, any effort to take the time to care and the choice to care seriously must logically encompass discussion of some form of basic income. The idea of a participation income would encompass participation in the form of care work (and avoid the problem of the 'free lunch' that is perceived to accompany a universal basic income, especially at a time when governments are determined to promote active rather than passive welfare). However, deciding who is eligible for a 'participation' income would be difficult. Nevertheless some form of basic income is necessary for there to be the security to choose different forms of humanly and socially necessary activity, particularly care, which may be particularly important in respect of the problem of falling birth rates. In addition, policies must also encourage the valuing of care work inside households. For example, Barr (2001) has enclosed the idea that half the female partner's pension contributions should be put into her male partner's pension pot each year and vice versa in order to address the problem of the gendered division of paid and unpaid work.

In the face of rapid and dramatic family and labour market change, governments have tended increasingly to assume that they can treat men and women alike because they will all be in the labour market. This is to underplay the considerable differences that still exist in the nature of the contributions that men and women make to households in EU member states. Thus as governments have moved in the 1990s to insist on the responsibility to engage in paid work, and to make individuals, male and female, more responsible for providing for their own welfare, especially in respect of pension provision, women stand to be severely disadvantaged. This is why more by way of collective provision in the form of care services (for young and old) is necessary to enable women to reduce the double day and possibly to be employed for longer hours. However, care work is necessary and desirable, and is work. Thus collective provision is also needed in the form of cash payments to value it, and policies also need to promote a more equal valuing and sharing of care work between men and women at the level of the household. It cannot be assumed that this will come about automatically. 'Daddy leaves' and new forms of household sharing of pension entitlements are crucial elements here. If the shift to an individualized adult worker model is allowed to take place without any effort on the part of the state to ensure that care is compensated, then the outlook is bleak both for women and for those needing care.

NOTES

1. The concept of 'father involvement' has been developed by Lamb (1986).
2. However, Hakim's (2000) insistence that women's different combinations of paid and unpaid work in different countries reflects their preferences ignores the part played by government policies in addressing the constraints represented by the needs of dependants for care.
3. It is important to note that such preferences are not held in many other European countries, even in a country such as Norway where motherhood has relatively recently been prioritized over paid labour for women (Leira, 1992; Skevik, 2001).

REFERENCES

Balbo, L. (1975), 'The servicing work of women and the capitalistic state', *Politics Power and Social Theory*, **3**, 251 - 70.

Barr, N. (2001), *The Welfare State as Piggy Bank*, Oxford: Oxford University Press.

Beck-Gernsheim, E. (1999), 'On the way to a post-familial family. From a community of need to elective affinities', *Theory, Culture and Society*, **15** (3 - 4), 53 - 70.

CEC (1993), *Growth, Competitiveness and Employment – The Challenges and Ways Forward into the 21st , Century*, Luxembourg: CEC.

CEC (1995), *Equal Opportunities for Women and Men – Follow-up to the White Paper on Growth, Competitiveness and Employment*, Brussels: DGV.

CEC (2000a), *Report on Social Protection in Europe 1999*, Com (2000) 163 final, Brussels: CEC.

CEC (2000b), *Communication from the Commission to the Council, the European Parliament, the Economic and Social Committee and the Committee of the Regions: Social Policy Agenda*, Brussels: CEC.

Cmd. 5629 (1974), *Report of the Committee on One-Parent Families*, London: HMSO.

Cmd. 3805. (1998), *New Ambitions for Our Country: a New Contract for Welfare*, London: The Stationery Office.

Creighton, C. (1999), 'The rise and decline of the "male breadwinner family" in Britain', *Cambridge Journal of Economics* **23**, 519 - 41.

Crompton, R. (ed.) (1999), *Restructuring Gender Relationships and Employment. The Decline of the Male Breadwinner*, Oxford: Oxford University Press.

Daly, M. (2000), 'A fine balance: women's labour market participation in international comparison', in F.W. Scharpf and V.A. Schmidt (eds), *Welfare and Work in the Open Economy, Vol. II Diverse Responses to Common Challenges*, Oxford: Oxford University Press, pp. 467 - 510.

Duncan, S. and R. Edwards (1999), *Lone Mothers, Paid Work and Gendered Moral Rationalities*, London: Macmillan.

Ferge, Z. (1997), 'The changed welfare paradigm: the individualization of the social', *Social Policy and Administration,* **31** (1), 20 - 44.

Ferri, E. and K. Smith (1996), *Parenting in the 1990s,* London: Family Policy Studies Centre.

Finch, J. and D. Groves. (eds) (1983), *Labour and Love: Women, Work and Caring,* London: Routledge and Kegan Paul.

Fukuyama, F. (1999), *The Great Disruption. Human Nature and the Reconstitution of Social Order,* London: Profile Books.

Furstenberg, F. (1988), 'Good dads – bad dads: two faces of fatherhood', in A. J. Cherlin (ed.), *The Changing American Family and Public Policy, Washington*: The Urban Institute Press, pp. 193 - 218.

Gershuny, J. (2000), *Changing Times. Work and Leisure in Post-Industrial Society,* Oxford: Oxford University Press.

Gerson, K. (1993), *No Man's Land: Men's Changing Commitments to Family and Work,* New York: Basic Books.

Ginn, J., D. Street and S. Arber (eds) (2001), *Women, Work and Pensions,* Buckingham: Open University Press.

Gough, I. (1996), 'Social welfare and competitiveness', *New Political Economy,* **1** (2), 209 - 32.

Guillemard, A.M. (1986), *Le déclin du social: Formation et crise des politiques de la vieillesse,* Paris: Presses Universitaires de France.

Hakim, C. (2000), *Work-Lifestyle Choices in the Twenty-first Century: Preference Theory,* Oxford: Oxford University Press.

Harrison, A. (2000), 'National accounts for policy analysis', in N. Fraser and J. Hills (eds), *Public Policy for the 21st Century. Social and Economic Essays in Memory of Henry Neuberger,* Bristol: Policy Press, pp. 33 - 48.

Hewlett, S. (1991), *When the Bough Breaks: The Cost of Neglecting our Children,* New York: Basic Books.

Hobson, B. (ed.) (2002), *Making Men into Fathers,* Cambridge: Cambridge University Press.

Hochschild, A. (1990), *The Second Shift,* London: Piatkus.

Joshi, H. and H. Davies (2000), 'The price of parenthood and the value of children', in N. Fraser and J. Hills (eds), *Public Policy for the 21st Century. Social and Economic Essays in Memory of Henry Neuberger.* Bristol: Policy Press, pp. 63 - 76.

Knijn, T. (2001), 'Care work: innovations in the Netherlands', in M. Daly (ed.), *Care Work Security,* Geneva: ILO, pp. 159 - 74.

Knijn, T. and F. van Wel (2001), 'Does it work? Employment policies for lone parents in the Netherlands', in J. Millar and K. Rowlingson (eds), *Lone Parents, Employment and Social Policy,* Bristol: The Polity Press, pp. 107 - 27.

Korpi, W. (2000), 'Faces of inequality: gender, class and patterns of inequalities in different types of welfare states', *Social Politics,* **7** (3), 127 - 91.

Lamb, M. (ed.) (1986), *The Father's Role. Applied Perspectives,* New York: John Wiley.

Land, H. (1983), 'Who still cares for the family?', in J. Lewis (ed.), *Women's Welfare/Women's Rights,* London: Croom Helm, pp. 64 - 85.

Land, H. and H. Rose (1985), 'Compulsory altruism for some or an altruistic society for all?', in P. Bean, J. Ferris and D. Whynes (eds), *In Defence of Welfare,* London: Tavistock, pp. 74 - 96.

Land, H. and J. Lewis (1998), 'Gender, care and the changing role of the state in the UK', in J. Lewis (ed.), *Gender, Social Care and Welfare State Restructuring in Europe,* Aldershot: Ashgate, pp. 51 - 84.

Laurie, H. and J. Gershuny (2000), 'Couples, work and money', in R. Berthoud and J. Gershuny (eds), *Seven Years in the Lives of British Families,* Bristol: The Policy Press, pp. 45 - 72.

Leira, A. (1992), *Models of Motherhood,* Cambridge: Cambridge University Press.

Lewis, C. (2000), *A Man's Place in the Home: Fathers and Families in the UK,* York: Joseph Rowntree Foundation.

Lewis, J. (2000), 'Work and care', *Social Policy Review,* **12,** 48 - 67.

Lewis, J. (2001a), 'The decline of the male breadwinner model: the implications for work and care', *Social Politics,* **8** (2), 152 - 70.

Lewis, J. (2001b), *The End of Marriage? Individualism and Intimate Relationships,* Aldershot: Edward Elgar.

Lewis, J. and Hobson, B. (1998), 'Introduction', in J. Lewis (ed.), *Lone Mothers in European Welfare Regimes. Shifting Policy Logics,* London: Jessica Kingsley, pp. 1 - 20.

Lister, R. (2000), 'Dilemmas of pendulum politics. Balancing paid work, care and citizenship', Conference on Re-inventing Feminism: theory, politics and practice for the new century, Goldsmiths College, May.

McIntosh, M. (1981), 'Feminism and social policy', *Critical Social Policy,* **1** (1), 32 - 42.

McLaughlin, E., J. Trewsdale and N. McCay (2001), 'The rise and fall of the UK's first tax credit: the working families tax credit 1998 - 2000', *Social Policy and Administration,* **35** (2), 163 - 80.

Maclean, M. and J. Eekelaar (1997), *The Parental Obligation: A Study of Parenthood across Households,* Oxford: Hart.

Mead, L. (1986), *Beyond Entitlement. The Social Obligations of Citizenship,* New York: The Free Press.

Millar, J. and A. Warman (1996), *Family Obligations in Europe,* London: Family Policy Studies Centre.

Nowotny, H. (1994), *Time: The Modern and Post-modern Experience*, Cambridge: Polity Press.

Orloff, A. S. and R. Monson (2002), 'Citizens, workers or fathers? Men in the history of US social policy', in B. Hobson (ed.), *Making Men into Fathers. Men, Masculinities and the Social Politics of Fatherhood*, Cambridge: Cambridge University Press, pp. 61 - 91.

Pleck, J. H. (1997), 'Paternal involvement: levels, sources, and consequences', in Lamb (ed.), *The Role of the Father in Child Development*, 3rd ed., New York: John Wiley, pp. 66 - 103.

Popenoe, D. (1993), 'American family decline, 1960 - 1990: a review and appraisal', *Journal of Marriage and the Family,* **55** (August), 527 - 55.

Rake, K. (2000), 'Gender and new labour's social policies', *Journal of Social Policy* **30** (2), 209 - 32.

Schor, J. (1991), *The Overworked American*, New York: Basic Books.

Sevenhuijsen, S. (1998), *Citizenship and the Ethics of Care*, London, Routledge.

Short, C. (2000), Time-use Data in the Household Satellite Accounts, London: ONS.

Skevik, A. (2001), *Family Ideology and Social Policy. Policies towards Lone Parents in Norway and the UK*, Oslo: Norwegian Social Research NOVA Rapport 7/2001.

Smart, C. and B. Neale (1999), *Family Fragments*, Cambridge: Polity Press.

Stacey, J. (1990), *Brave New Families. Stories of Domestic Upheaval in Late Twentieth Century America,* New York: Basic Books.

Tronto, J. C. (1993), *Moral Boundaries. A Political Argument for an Ethic of Care*, London: Routledge.

Vandenbroucke, F. (2002), 'Foreword', in G. Esping-Andersen with D. Gallie, A. Hemerijck and J. Myles, *Why we Need a Welfare State*, Oxford: Oxford University Press, pp. viii - xxiv.

Warren, T. (2000), 'Diverse breadwinner models: a couple-based analysis of gendered working time in Britain and Denmark', *Journal of European Social Policy,* **10** (4), 349 - 71.

Warin, J., Y. Solomon , C. Lewis and W. Langford (1999*), Fathers, Work and Family Life,* York: Joseph Rowntree Foundation.

White, S. (2000), 'Social rights and the social contract – political theory and the new welfare politics', *British Journal of Political Science,* **30**, 507-32.

Williams, F. (1998), 'Troubled masculinities in social policy discourses', in J. Popay, J. Hearn and J. Edwards (eds), *Men, Gender, Divisions and Welfare*, London: Routledge, pp. 63 - 100.

5. De-Familialization or Re-Familialization? Trends in Income-Tested Family Benefits

Chiara Saraceno

All welfare states implicitly or explicitly support and define some degree of family solidarity. And the familialization of social rights and subsidiarity with regard to expected family solidarity are at the origin of all welfare states in so far as they are premised on and strengthen relations of dependence and interdependence between the genders and the generations. The concept of the male breadwinner model makes this clear with regard to married women: the male breadwinner, in fact, not only provides an income for his wife, he also provides access to social protection even after his death through the institute of the survivor pension. The same however holds true for children, since regulations on child labour and compulsory schooling have rendered them increasingly dependent, and for a longer period, on their father's income. Non-active individuals were thus first incorporated into the welfare state by being members of the family of a breadwinner with access to social protection (Crouch, 1999). As many feminist analyses have indicated, this not only implies the familialization of social rights for dependent family members, it also implies the familialization of care: if male breadwinners redistributed income and social security entitlements, adult women redistributed care within the household and the kinship network.

The degree to which welfare state regimes and provisions are familialized has increasingly differentiated since the post-war period. Women's labour market participation de-familializes women as regards access to income and social security; but it also requires some de-familialization of caring work and caring needs, either via the market or via the public provision of services. The degree to which intergenerational obligations and solidarity within the household and the kin network are expected and even legislated also varies among European countries.

These differences not only reflect different conceptions of gender and inergenerational relations. They also reflect different conceptions of the responsibilities of the state (including the local authorities), community, household and kin: in European Union jargon, we might say they reflect different conceptions of the principle of subsidiarity.[1] Subsidiarity might mean the state does not intervene except in the extreme cases where families are not able to solve their problems on their own, i.e. if they are for some reason inadequate or unfit. Subsidiarity might also mean the state has some obligation to support families and thus enable them to fulfil their 'normal' obligations. Viewed in this light, subsidiarity can motivate different policies. It might be applied to enable women to stay home with their children or to combine family and work responsibilities, or to enable parents to share childcare responsibilities.

Means testing is a crucial mechanism in implementing subsidiarity.[2] Referring to the household income as a criterion for accessing benefits has been the critical core of the male breadwinner concept and, at least partly, of comparative analyses of lone motherhood status. Yet, means testing not only involves gender relationships but intergenerational ones as well. It also represents one of the ways patterns of subsidiarity with regard to family obligations are not only defined on the basis of gender and intergenerational expectations, but also of class, or at least income.

DE-FAMILIALIZATION OR RE-FAMILIALIZATION? NON-UNIVOCAL TRENDS

Recent country specific and comparative research demonstrates that contemporary welfare state reforms seem to indicate the re-familialization of entitlements and de-familialization alike. Measures have been enacted strengthening individual rather than family entitlements, as in many pension reforms that have reduced the coverage of survivors' pensions or in the emerging expectation that mothers participate into the labour market (Lewis, 1997; van Drenth et al., 1999; Millar and Rowlingson, 2002). However, the increasing role of income-tested benefits in many countries, and the blurring of boundaries between social security and social assistance, strengthen the family base of entitlements, in so far as income testing occurs on the basis of household and not individual income. This in turn more strongly affects the entitlements of women who are married or living together than those of their partners. In Southern Europe it also affects the entitlement of the young in so far as they are defined as dependent on their parents' income for longer than in most other parts of Europe.

Here I am interested in comparatively analysing the kind of assumptions concerning gender and intergenerational interdependencies that are incorporated in family benefits in different European countries, with a particular focus on income-tested benefits. Specifically, I discuss
  a) variations and trends in income-tested benefits for and to spouses,
  b) variations and trends in the degree to which a spouse's income affects the access to or the amount of an individual benefit and
  c) variations and trends in the degree to which parents' income affects the access to or the amount of a child benefit.

The focus of this chapter is on three different policy dimensions: patterns of subsidiarity with regard to expected household and family solidarity, universality versus selectivity (thus also horizontal versus vertical redistribution) and individualization versus familialization of entitlements. In analysing these dimensions, assumptions should also emerge on what the family is and what intergenerational and inter-gender obligations are considered to be. If they are income-tested, in fact, family benefits render more explicit assumptions on intra-family solidarity and obligations, family boundaries and gender patterns, which emerge in all the measures addressing the family. In fact, they imply a definition of the family at no less than three levels: a) as a specific relationship which is accorded social relevance and is therefore considered an entitlement for receiving a benefit (marriage, generation, kin and so forth), b) as a solidaristic community within which resources are shared and obligations are allocated (who is responsible for whom) and c) as the relevant unit for testing income (whose income should be taken into account, what degree of sharing between whom should be assumed).

.At all three levels, the structure and rules of a given benefit define what a family is, i.e. which relationships make up a family, for policy and redistributive purposes. They also define patterns of citizenship along the familialization/de-familialization continuum. As a consequence, they define patterns of subsidiarity. Expectations concerning intergenerational and marital solidarity, in fact, are a crucial dimension in the division of responsibility between public and private solidarity.

INCOME TESTING FOR SPOUSES' BENEFITS AND INCOME TESTING SPOUSES FOR BENEFITS

Benefits for spouses, or more accurately for wives, rather than benefits for children accruing to fathers, have been cited as the epitome of the male breadwinner model: a man - a regular male worker - should be able to support his wife during as well as after his working life and even after his death. According to most feminist welfare state analysts (Lewis, 1992; Orloff, 1993; Ostner and Lewis, 1995), this model informed the early European welfare states and was still evident throughout the 1970s, when it started to break down due to changing family patterns and women's changing attitudes to paid work. Recent comparative research, however, indicates that this general model had a different intensity in various countries, depending not only on the degree to which attachment to a male/husband/ father was the sole means of access to social rights, but also on the degree to which the boundaries of the nuclear family solidarity were extended to include kin (e.g. Naldini, 2003).

My focus here is more limited. It concerns a) the complex interplay between the dimensions of familialization/individualization and universalism/ selectivity which takes place when income testing is involved, and b) the distinction between instances where income testing is used to assess a spouse's entitlement to a benefit as a spouse and instances where the combined spouses' income is used to define the individual's or household's entitlement to a given benefit. The benefits I analyse are old-age pensions, widows' pensions, spouse's allowances within social security provisions and tax allowances for spouses.

Old-age Pensions

In theory, old-age pensions are based on an individual entitlement, be it simply age, as in universal basic (citizenship) old-age pensions, or age plus a contributory record as in insurance-based pension systems. So they should not be considered family benefits. Yet there are instances where either the amount of the pension is defined in reference to the couple as a unit, or the entitlement to and the amount of an individual's pension is income-tested with reference to the married couple's income. These are two different instances of the familialization of entitlements, with the Dutch until the 1980s exemplifying the former and the Southern European countries, France and the UK, the latter.

In the Netherlands in the 1960s a minimum universal old-age pension (AOW) was introduced and the standard was set with reference to the minimum wage for couples, stipulating lower rates for lone parents and the unwed. This reference to the couple, and more generally to the household, was also extended to social security. As a consequence, married women were only entitled to an old-age pension as a member of a married couple, which received a higher benefit as such. Only in the mid-1980s was this system individualized and nowadays both members of a married couple, thus married women as well, can earn their individual contributory pension: each spouse receives half the amount set for the couple. So now the individualization of entitlement is granted on equal terms between spouses, although being part of a couple reduces the individual amount: each spouse receives less than the amount set for a single person. At the same time, reference to the couple in the minimum pension has a positive effect for low-income couples where only one spouse is above 65: while on principle only people above 65 are entitled to the minimum state pension, in cases where the spouse is younger but has no income of her/his own the couple receives an additional flat rate income to bring it to the level of a couple's minimum pension. Thus, the continuing reference to a couple's reciprocal obligations, linked with an individual test of income, serves to widen rather than restrict individual entitlement.

In contrast, reference to the couple's income restricts entitlement in countries where there is no basic citizenship pension. This is the case in Italy, Spain, Portugal, France and the UK. In these countries there is a basic social assistance pension for individuals above the age of 65,[3] without a minimum contributory record and with an income below a given threshold. Although the beneficiary is the individual and not the couple or the household, given its social assistance framework, this pension is income-tested on the basis of the couple's and not the individual's income in order to restrict access to the neediest. There are thus two different thresholds for assessing the individual's entitlement: one for individuals living alone (or at least not part of a married couple) and one for married couples. Since it is more often the wife who is not entitled to a contributory pension, it is her entitlement which is more explicitly linked to her husband's income.

In contrast to the Dutch case, reference to the couple and to the subsidiarity principle is thus used to restrict the number of beneficiaries rather than support the value of living as a married couple as such. At the same time, belonging to a couple reduces the individual entitlement. Thus, in this case, the familialization of entitlement weakens both individual rights and family welfare through income testing.

The same may also occur in contributory pensions, which are generally more firmly based on individual entitlements than social assistance ones. Thus, in Italy people whose contributory record is long enough to entitle them to a pension, but not high enough to grant them the minimum contributory pension, may have it supplemented up to the minimum if they fall below a given income threshold (higher than the one that makes people eligible to receive a social assistance pension). Until the pension reforms of 1992 and

1995, this income test was based on individual income. Following the reforms, the supplement was defined as having a social assistance dimension, and required that the test of income be made on the basis of the couple's and not the individual's income. This new regulation was only enforced on people who were of retirement age from that point on. Thus a number of people, again mostly women, suddenly lost their entitlement to the supplement they had been encouraged to expect, strongly reducing their individual as well as their couple's income. The rationale for the reforms stressed individual responsibility and acknowledgement of individual contributory records and income careers, and on the whole, the reforms encouraged a greater equity between workers and generations. From the point of view of at least a few cohorts, however, these reforms led to a greater familialization of entitlement and to a (male) breadwinner model, in so far as it strengthened the economically weaker spouse's dependence on the main income earner (see also Trifiletti, 1999). On the whole, this stricter targeting severely limited older women's financial autonomy and the financial welfare of couples with medium to low incomes.

Survivors' Pensions for Spouses

Survivors' pensions are the most important measure in the male breadwinner model: acknowledging both a man's long-lasting responsibility to support his family and the implicit marriage contract, where care and servicing were exchanged for financial support. The history of survivor pensions varies in different countries with regard to income testing. Over time, however, and by the end of the 1970s, income testing was eliminated with regard to survivors' social security pensions all over.[4] It was the status of the widow as such that entitled her to a pension.

Things started to change again in the late 1980s and early 1990s under the dual impact of changes in women's labour force participation (more women could earn their own contributory pension) and social security budget constraints. From two different standpoints, these two phenomena called into question the principle of the survivor's pension was based on, i.e. that it should grant the surviving spouse and children the standard of living provided by the deceased spouse and parent. Particularly in so far as women could earn their own pensions, their dependence could no longer be assumed and attention was refocused on 'needy survivors' versus 'non-needy' ones. Thus, income testing has re-emerged. In Italy, where survivors' pensions have the widest range of possible beneficiaries (either spouse, dependent children, kin whom there is a maintenance obligation towards, such as parents, parents-in-law, siblings, grandchildren, nieces and nephews), the 1995 pension reform stipulated that survivors' pensions were subjected to income testing and progressively decreased as the personal income and wealth of the beneficiary increased. The same changes were put into effect in Germany under the 1985 pension reform.

The redefinition of the spouse's survivor pension in social assistance terms is also evident in Italy even in the development concerning separated and divorced women's entitlement to a quota of their former husband's survivor pension. Entitlement to this quota is generally not only linked to the duration of the marriage but also to women's having been prior alimony beneficiaries, which in turn largely depends on their not having an income of their own. It also depends on the women's not having remarried. Thus, a progressive residualization of the survivor pension does not really refute the male breadwinner model. It only restricts it to the needy cases: expecting each spouse to 'normally' take care of their own pension contribution.

To a lesser degree, this is also apparent in the Swedish and Dutch cases, where there is a minimum citizenship pension. In Sweden, contribution-based survivor's pensions are being phased out if there are no children under the age of 12. Childless widows or widows with older children only receive the survivor pension for a year as a transitional or 'adjustment' resource. In the Netherlands, as in Germany and Italy, entitlement to a contributory survivor's pension is now income-tested and restricted to individuals with no pension of their own or only a very low one.

The history of survivors' and spouses' pensions thus seems to be directly related to women's labour force participation. Income testing has been eliminated and the breadwinner pattern reinforced during the expansion of the full-fledged one-earner family (leaving income testing only to social assistance pensions). Later, the individualization of rights emerged based on individual contributions and the progressive residualization of survivor's pensions for spouses.[5] In social assistance and consequently income-tested terms, individualization has in turn paved the way for a partial redefinition of the survivors' pension. As a consequence, unless there is a universal, citizenship-based minimum pension, the de-familialization of entitlement to an old-age pension for married women with no contributory record of their own has weakened their entitlement to this type of pension. Not only do these women need to have been married to a pension-earner, they also need to demonstrate their financial need. Individualization thus combines with familialization in restricting entitlement.

Assumptions on Dependent Spouses in Tax Policies

At the level of tax policies, since the 1980s there has been a common trend from joint to some degree of individual income taxation. Provisions for dependent wives, however, seem to last longer and to sidestep negative income testing. They also benefit higher incomes and the breadwinner model to a greater degree, somewhat contradicting the vertically redistributive and individualization trends I have noted with regard to old-age pensions. In her overview of the income tax system in fourteen countries in the mid-1990s with regard to the generosity of marital tax relief and their provisions for either joint or individual taxation, Sainsbury (1999) notes that although most countries tax labour market income on an individual basis, they differ on three counts: a) the presence or absence of a housewife tax bonus and the possibility of transferring tax relief, b) whether the tax-payer receives a tax allowance or credit for a dependent spouse, and c) whether tax allowances or credits can be transferred between spouses. Only France maintains pure and mandatory joint taxation and several other countries, e.g. Germany, Belgium and Norway, give taxpayers a choice between separate and joint taxation. Most countries, among which the UK, the Netherlands, Italy and Austria, have separate taxation but maintain a housewife tax bonus. In the UK, until recently there was even a marital allowance for husbands irrespective of their wife's working status. In the Netherlands, tax allowances and credits may be transferred between spouses. Only Sweden and Finland have a fully individualized tax system.

Although on the basis of Sainsbury's scheme Italy and Sweden would seem quite similar in having highly individualized taxation systems, from a wider perspective they represent two almost opposite trends. In Sweden, the individualization of taxation has proceeded to the point of eliminating all tax deductions for family dependents including children. In Italy as well, the principle of individual taxation has been in place since 1977. There, however, tax deductions for dependent family members have been strengthened in the last decade in response to critics who pointed out the unfriendliness of the Italian tax system to one-earner families and families with children. Until recently, tax deductions for dependent spouses have in fact been more generous than those for children (Saraceno, 2003). Since 1997, following the gradual increase of the latter, the dependent spouse's deduction became amount-tested on the basis of the taxpayer's income: the basic amount may be raised if the taxpayer's income falls below a given ceiling. In this case, the dual reference to income and maintenance obligations within the (married) couple works towards improving benefits for beneficiaries. [6]

Women's growing labour force participation has stimulated an increasing individualization of the taxation system. Yet it cannot be overly stimulated, since taxation has to take into account family dependencies and the intra-family distribution of income, including between spouses.

INCOME TESTING CHILD BENEFITS: DIFFERENT PATTERNS AND A NON HOMOGENEOUS DEVELOPMENT

Direct Child Benefits

In their historical development, child benefits (any kind of direct financial benefits for children) more clearly than spouses' benefits represent the friction between the aims of vertical and horizontal redistribution, i.e. between concern about poverty and concern about inter-household equity, as well as between concerns about population issues and concerns about individual entitlement, and between public and private responsibilities with regard to family matters and choices. This friction might well account for the diversity of child benefits in the various countries and the varying degrees of their perceived legitimacy (see also Gauthier, 1996).

Although the most generous, longest tradition of child benefits is found in Catholic countries, it is by no means the case that all Catholic countries, or all countries with a long history of a Catholic majority in government, have generous or non-income-tested child benefits. Actually the reverse is true: the European countries with less generous and more residual and income-tested child benefits include all the Southern European countries including Orthodox Greece. Residual and income-tested child benefits may, in this perspective, be taken as one indicator, although by no means the only one, of the 'Mediterranean' welfare regime (Naldini, 2000; Gonzalez et al., 2000).

In all the countries where they were introduced either by the state or by employers, child benefits were first income-tested in the sense that they only addressed core blue-collar workers. They were thus dually income-tested, firstly on the basis of income origin and secondly on the basis of income level. This not only excluded higher income families; it also excluded those whose income derived from agricultural work, self-employment and so forth. This dual feature, which in some cases, such as Italy, is still evident in existing income-tested schemes, indicates that it is not poverty in general that is the concern behind income-tested child benefits, but the poverty of the working poor, i.e. the 'deserving poor' and their children. In France and later in

Belgium, Germany and Italy, child benefits were aimed first and foremost at offsetting, but without affecting wages, the downward cycle in the life course of blue-collar working families when children are too young to work and mothers often have to give up their jobs. Even in countries like France where the pro-natalist aim was most explicit,[7] offsetting poverty in working-class families with numerous children was the main goal or was at least perceived as a necessary instrument to carry out a pro-natalist policy.

At present, general child benefits are only income-tested in Southern European countries, with the recent exception of Greece. In the other countries, income testing is reserved for the other additional child benefits such as the ones for lone mothers (see also Dumont, 1998). Within this general trend towards the universalization of child benefits, however, the friction between horizontal and vertical redistribution, and thus between universal and income-tested child cash benefits, has apparently never been solved once and for all, but is liable to return to the fore in times of budget constraints. So in all the countries where child benefits have eventually become universal - the UK, France, Belgium, The Netherlands, Sweden, Denmark, Germany and Ireland - there have been times when they either reverted to income testing, as in Denmark from 1977 to 1987, in Germany (only for the amount) in 1983, in France for higher income families in 1997- 98, or there has been a debate about the option of using income testing to cut social expenditures or increase the amount available for the lower income households.

Although differentiation in the financing and amount on the basis of occupational category is now only evident in conventionally corporatist welfare states, not all the countries usually included in this group have a categorically differentiated system of child benefits. Although France and Germany partly finance child benefits through contributions, they pay flat rate universal benefits similar to the ones in Denmark, Sweden and the UK. The Netherlands also pays the same benefit to everyone irrespective of income and category, although it differentiates on an age basis. These countries thus differ in generosity, but not in access rules (see also Bradshaw, 2000).

There are now solely means-tested child benefits from the point of view of either entitlement or amount or both in Italy, Spain and Portugal and until very recently in Greece (Montigny and Saunier, 1998; MISSOC, 2000). Italy and Spain possibly represent the two most different cases of income-tested child benefits, and Portugal and Greece fall somewhere in between. In fact since 1991 child benefits in Spain, previously linked to working status as in Italy, have become universal social assistance benefits. In other words, all the children whose household income is below a given, equalized, income threshold are entitled to them, irrespective of their parents' labour market position. Since 1985 they have become more strictly income-tested in Italy on the basis of household income as well as labour market position. Only people who receive at least 70% of their household income from dependent/wage work can receive them. Child benefits are also income-tested for the amount, which differs according to the equalized household income bracket. In 1999 a non-categorical income-tested benefit with regard to entitlement as well as the amount was introduced for low income households with at least three underage children, which can be added to the standard one for the low-income households of wage workers.

Following the democratic revolution, in Portugal child benefits, which were formerly income-tested and work status-tested as in Italy and Spain, became universal. In 1997 Portugal reverted to income testing, but only for the amount. Greece, which has a child benefit system somewhat similar to the Belgian one with different schemes for the public and private sector, supplements child benefits with income-tested social assistance benefits for orphans, large families, or the mothers of large families. These additional benefits were not income-tested in the past, but have become so in recent years.

European countries can thus be divided in two categories: the majority of them that support the costs of children as such, and the minority that only support them in low-income households. Subsidiarity in the former case means the state helps parents as such raise their children. In the latter case it means the state only intervenes if parents are unable to provide. The individualization of the rights of children thus appears to be greater in the former than the latter case.

The Interplay between Child Benefits and Tax Allowances for Children

The cost of children may be taken into account in taxation in various ways, depending on the overall system (see also Wennemo, 1992). There is a continuum between the two poles of the French family quotient, where children count in defining the amount of taxable income, and the highly individualized Swedish system, where no deductions are allowed. The most usual situation is the one with tax relief either from income (tax allowance) or from tax (tax credit). These forms of tax relief are usually not income-tested. Actually, they might even cause a kind of reverse income testing, as in the case of tax allowances. To avoid this risk, tax allowances for children have recently been eliminated in Sweden. Flat rate child benefits and generous services constitute the public package provided to help households bear the cost of children.

In most countries, however, there is a combination of the two systems – cash benefits and tax reliefs usually in the form of tax credit (and child benefits are not taxed) (see also OECD, 1997). In the absence of negative income tax mechanisms, however, only households with incomes high enough to be taxed benefit from child-related tax reliefs (including allowances for expenses on behalf of children). While in most countries the value of non-income-tested cash benefits as well as their incidence compared to income-tested ones has gone down (Bradshaw, 2000), child-related tax reliefs in many countries have gone up, and more generally redistribution through taxation rather than direct cash benefits has been favoured.

Italy is a good example of this trend. The value of tax relief for children there had constantly decreased since the post-war years. Until the mid-1990s it was among the lowest in the most developed countries (OECD, 1997). Since 1997 the trend has reversed, with child-related tax credits substantially upgraded. Children may be of any age, and may not live in their parents' household, as long as they do not have an income of their own, since their parents are deemed financially responsible for them.[8] With the 2002 financial law, this general upward trend, which had a horizontal redistributive goal, also incorporated a vertical redistributive aim: the tax credit for dependent children may be almost doubled for middle to low income tax-payers.

Germany lies in between the various situations that, like Sweden and the Scandinavian countries in general, have moved towards a simplification of the system in an effort to neutralize its vertical reverse redistributive effects, and the ones that maintain the dual and sometimes contradictory system of child benefits and tax allowances. After many changes back and forth, since 1996 parents can either claim tax allowances or child benefits, whichever is more beneficial. And the value of the benefit and the tax allowance has been set at the social assistance minimum level by a Constitutional Court decision that went farther than simply stipulating an equal value to be calculated for each child. It declared, in fact, that the value of the benefit/deduction should be no lower than what is deemed necessary for subsistence as defined by the social assistance minimum (not merely a symbolic addition or allowance to the parents' income).

In 1996, tax relief for children was eliminated in the Netherlands just like in Sweden in favour of child benefits, but it was re-introduced in 2001. Even more than dependent spouses, the issue of children tests the implications of full individualization in the tax system. Individualization, in fact, overlooks intra-household and inter-generational redistribution and solidarity. Only a generous system of monetary and in kind transfers can offset this blindness to family obligations and dependencies. At the same time, acknowledging these obligations solely or mainly through the tax system may result in reverse redistribution with no impact on lower income households.

PATTERNS OF FAMILIALIZATION VERSUS INDIVIDUALIZATION IN PROVIDING BENEFITS

References to households in policy provisions may belie two distinct and op-posing aims: helping households meet their needs and dependencies and in-terdependencies versus using references to household and even kin redis-tributive solidaristic obligations to ration benefits and services. This is par-ticularly evident if benefits are calculated on the basis of some kind of household income test. The way countries take account of and define family dependencies in providing benefits and income testing them reveals in fact two somewhat symmetrical patterns in the familialization and the individu-alization of entitlements, which are in turn indicative of different patterns of subsidiarity with regard to public-private responsibilities (Table 5.1). Both familialization and individualization may in fact serve either as a means to ration benefits or as a means to include a wider range of individuals.

Table 5.1: Patterns of familialization and individualization through benefits

Inclusive familialization	Rationing familialization	Rationing individualization	Inclusive individualization
- non income-tested survivor pension - old-age couple pen-sion - splitting and family quotient in taxation - family supplements in social security benefits - additional income-tested child benefits - married man's tax allowances - tax allowances for dependent family-members - additional income-tested tax allowances for dependent family members	- income-tested social assistance pensions based on couple's in-come - solely income-tested child benefits - household income-tested maternity grants - care allowances in-come-tested on the basis of carer's household income - working family tax credit for dual-parent households	- income-tested survivor pensions - supplement up to the basic contributory pension based on couple's income	- basic universal old-age pension - universal child benefits - social assistance - minimum income for lone mothers of young children - working family tax credit for sin-gle parent house-holds

And subsidiarity may mean the state does not intervene to support family obligations and solidarity but in the case of low-income households, using either individualization or familialization to reduce the amount of benefits and/or the range of beneficiaries. Or it may mean the state intervenes to actively and positively support intra-household and intra-generational redistribution, acknowledging its costs either by providing generous benefits for dependent family members or by supporting an individualization of entitlements, thus reducing family dependencies.

Actually, rationing familialization and rationing individualization greatly overlap and can be viewed as inter-dependent. However, inclusive familialization is the opposite of inclusive individualization. No country presents a fully coherent package. Yet the overall country packages can be classified as belonging more to either the one or the other pattern.

The inclusive familialization pattern does not fully coincide with the male breadwinner pattern since it also includes underage children and, in the southern countries, adult children and some of the kin. Its full-fledged manifestation with regard to the nuclear family could be found in the Netherlands until the 1970s, and it was how the otherwise rudimentary Mediterranean welfare states managed to include most of their population (Naldini, 2003). It represented a specific pattern of subsidiarity in so far as the welfare state channelled resources and entitlements – to individuals who would otherwise be left out – through families (and breadwinners). At present, however, no country follows this pattern. Instead the countries defined as inclusive familialized prior to the 1970s moved either towards rationing familialization or towards either of the forms of individualization.

Only Sweden and Denmark, and to a lesser degree Norway, have systematically moved towards full inclusive individualization, even at the expense of reduced generosity. Universal flat rate benefits are the rule, and only under-age children are considered legitimately dependent.[9] The subsidiarity principle in these countries thus appears in its minimum form, at least with regard to expected family solidarity and redistribution.

The Netherlands, the most inclusive familialized country in the 1960s and 1970s, has progressively moved towards inclusive individualization both in benefits and taxation. This includes also an individualization of children, with flat rate benefits until they are 17, and grants for students over 18. From this perspective, the country viewed as the epitome of subsidiarity for so long seems to have moved quite far from it, at least with regard to the family as the main provider of income security for women and children. Substantial aspects of the inclusive familialized approach nonetheless remain: in the calculation of the basic old-age pension, in the possibility of transferring unused tax allowances between spouses and more generally between partners living together, in the tax deductions allowed for dependent family members, including unemployed children under 21 and older children who do not receive study grants or are too old for them.

Germany has also moved a long way towards the universalization of benefits in the case of dependent children, in so far as generous flat rate benefits have become the rule, notwithstanding the parents' income. Yet the individualization of children has not gone as far as in the Netherlands and in Sweden or Denmark, as there is no universal study grant and children with no income of their own are deemed dependent on their parents. Inclusive familialization, limited to the couple, persists in the taxation system which is premised on the couple, while rationing familialization is emerging in the pension system.

In France, where the male breadwinner model has never fully informed the social security system and the focus has been on supporting households with children, there seems to be a balance between inclusive familialization and individualization (a family-friendly taxation system, generous universal child benefits), with some space for rationing familialization in the case of old-age and disability pensions. Belgium also approaches this pattern, although its taxation system is neither as favourable to the couple as the German one nor as favourable to families with children as the French one.

The Mediterranean countries and the UK, though they have quite different welfare regimes according to prevalent typologies, show similar traits of rationing familialization sometimes coupled with rationing individualization. In the case of the UK, however, the family is mostly restricted to the couple and the underage children for benefit and tax purposes, and the rationing focus is balanced by a flat rate benefit system which, in the case of children benefits, is fully universal. In the Mediterranean countries, references to the 'family' for assessing means as well as dependencies may extend well beyond the household, and there are virtually no universal non-income-tested family benefits nor universal income-tested minimum benefits. Thus, it seems that where family solidarity is most expected and family dependencies most extended (and even enforced by civil law), families and individuals receive less support and are thus more vulnerable in times of stress.

What role does income testing play in these patterns? It is certainly a crucial means of rationing familialization and rationing individualization and thus a way the principle of subsidiarity with regard to family obligations and solidarity is more clearly used as a device for restricting entitlement and reducing provisions. Yet it cannot be left at that, since it may also be a way to equalize households that otherwise have widely different resources and to deter reverse redistribution. Overall, I think income testing with regard to family-related benefits has at best an ambiguous record. There is more than one reason why.

Firstly, one should consider the disincentive that income testing on a household basis represents to a second earner in the family, particularly a wife. Discouraging women/wives/mothers from working for decent pay represents the strongest blow to the ability of a family to protect itself. This was true in the past, in the golden age of the male breadwinner model, when a striking percentage of the poor were widows and orphans. It is even truer nowadays, when labour market security and marriage stability have both weakened in an era of flexible labour and rising divorce rates. Interestingly, the risk of this discouraging effect is increasingly considered in policies targeting lone mothers and less so in those targeting dual-parent households.

Secondly, there are contradictions in the benefit and tax benefit package that can strongly reduce the vertical redistributive impact of income testing.

Thirdly, and perhaps more significantly, the risks as well as the efficacy of income testing on an individual or even more so a household basis depend on the degree to which it affects all the relevant entitlements and enforces long-term dependencies. If income testing concerns only a small portion of the benefits while the relevant part of the resources – health services, education, basic pensions, child benefits – is received as an individual citizenship entitlement, and labour market participation is supported, income testing may offer further support to people who have additional needs or who temporarily cannot manage in the labour market.

At the same time, it is only fair to note that not even universal benefits are totally free from gender and income-specific discouraging effects. Looking at the French case, for instance, Strobel (2000) observes that its mixture of universalism and targeting has proved fairly efficacious in protecting households with children from poverty (see also Jeandidier, 1995; Bradshaw, 2000). Thus, one might argue that notwithstanding its effects of reverse redistribution, in the end universalism through horizontal redistribution proves efficacious even in terms of vertical redistribution. At least this is true in the case of families with children, particularly if universal benefits are integrated by targeted benefits as well as a universal offer of services to help women remain in the labour market.[10] Yet, Strobel himself points out that while this mixture has not totally shielded households with children from poverty, especially in times of rising unemployment, it has proven even less efficacious in reducing gender inequality. In addition, some of even the most recent and universal measures encourage particularly low-skilled women to exit the labour market when they have a second child, thus strengthening the gender division of labour in the household as well as class differences among women. Family benefits are not neutral, nor are implemented in a neutral world in terms of gender or class divisions. Income testing on the household basis means membership can either serve to reinforce inequality and crystallized patterns of household organization or to weaken them.

At a broader level, the same may be said for the two poles that policies with regard to households and families seem to oscillate between: strengthening family solidarity versus strengthening individualization. Inter-dependencies and dependencies are the fabric households are made of, kinship networks are sustained, individuals develop their feelings of belonging. In addition, individualization can only go so far, particularly in the case of children, and to some degree also the frail elderly and those responsible for their support and care. Yet exclusive attention devoted to family solidarity and all the expectations related to it may turn inter-dependencies into an iron cage for everyone involved, particularly for those who have neither a voice nor any exit options: young children first and foremost, but also a number of full-time mothers and wives.

NOTES

1. Subsidiarity is a well-known concept in Catholic social doctrine and is an entrenched feature of some very specific European welfare states, such as the Dutch, the Belgian and partly the Austrian and German ones, where the presence of deeply rooted religious and/or ethnic divisions has given rise to distinct social institutions which have become acknowledged partners, or parts, of the national welfare state. In European Union jargon, it assumes that no higher body should perform what is better performed by a lower body.

2. See for instance Daly (2000) and Sainsbury (1996). These authors, however, are almost exclusively concerned with women.

3. In the case of women, some countries such as the UK set the minimum age at 60.

4. In some countries such as Italy, gender inequality was in principle also redressed in so far as the surviving spouses (and children) of women pensioners could now also receive a survivor pension.

5. The impact of individualization is quite different on various cohorts, whose life course patterns and contributory record have been shaped by different circumstances, norms, expectations, behaviours, as Allmendiger et al. (1993) have demonstrated for Germany. See also Gin et al. 2001.

6. This might disincentive women's labour force participation in the lower income brackets. See also Sainsbury (1999). Dingeldey (2001) argues that it is not possible to detect any clear shaping effects of the taxation system on wives' employment, since one has to look at the whole policy package.

7. For a rich comparison of the story of demands and rationales for child benefits in UK and France in the years between World War I and World War II see Pedersen (1993).

8. On the basis of the same principle, analogous deductions may be claimed for dependent kin, although in this case taxpayers have to demonstrate that they actually support them.
9. In recent years, due to the tightening of the eligibility criteria, some form of rationing individualization or rationing familialization is appearing. This, however, is more apparent in social assistance where, for instance, adult children living with their parents used to be considered an independent household for income-testing purposes, but are now increasingly considered part of their parents' household.
10. In their study of the comparative redistributive performance of eleven welfare states, Wildeboer Schut, Vrooman and de Beer (2001) indicate that in the social democratic countries (Scandinavia), due to a lack of targeting, poor families with many children have no special status, contrary to what occurs in both the corporatist and the liberal welfare regimes.

REFERENCES

Allmendinger, J. H. Brückner, E. Brückner (1993), 'The production of gender disparities over the life course and their effects in old age. Results from the West German Life History Study', in A.B. Atkinson and M. Rein (eds), *Age, Work and Social Security*, New York, U.S: St. Martin's Press, pp. 188 - 223.

Bradshaw, J. (2000), 'Jusqu'où les minima sociaux contribuent-ils à lutter contre la pauvreté des enfants?', in C. Daniel and B. Palier (eds), *La protection sociale en Europe*, Paris: La Documentation Française, pp. 177 – 194.

Crouch, C. (1999), *Social Change in Western Europe*, Oxford: Oxford University Press.

Daly, M. (2000), *The Gender division of welfare*, Cambridge: Cambridge University Press.

Dingeldey, I. (2001), 'European tax-system and their impact on family employment patterns', *Journal of Social Policy*, 30, 653 - 672.

Drenth, A. van, T. Knijn and J. Lewis (1999), 'Sources of income for lone mother families: policy changes in Britain and The Netherlands and the experiences of divorced women', *Journal of Social Policy*, 28, 619 - 41.

Dumont, J.P. (1998), *Les systèmes de protection sociale en Europe*, Paris: Economica.

Gauthier, A.H. (1996), *The State and the Family*, Oxford: Clarendon.

Gin, J., D. Street and S. Arber (eds) (2001), *Women, Work and Pensions*, Buckingham, UK: Open University Press.

Gonzalez, M.J., T. Jurado and M. Naldini (eds) (2000), *Gender Inequalities in Southern Europe. Women, Work and Welfare in the 1990s*, London: Frank Cass.

Jeandidier, B. (ed.) (1995*), Analyse et simulation des politiques de prestations familiales en Europe. Une comparison entre la France et l'Allemagne, La Belgique, l'Irlande et le Luxembourg*, rapport for CNAF. ADEPS-Université de Nancy2-CNRS.

Lewis, J. (1992), 'Gender and the development of welfare regimes', *Journal of European Social Policy*, **2** (3), 159 – 73.

Lewis, J. (ed.) (1997), *Lone Mothers in European Welfare Regimes. Shifting Policy Logics*, London: Jessica Kingsley Publishers.

Millar, J. and K. Rowlingson (2002), *Lone Parents, Employment and Social Policy*, Bristol: Policy Press.

MISSOC (2000), *Social Protection in the Member States of the European Union on 1ˢᵗ January 1999*, Luxembourg: European Commission.

Montigny, P. and J.-M. Saunier, (1998), *Les dépenses liées à la famille au sein de l'Union Européenne*, Solidarité Sauté – Etudes Statistique, **213**, 81 - 91.

Naldini, M. (2000), 'Family allowances in Italy and Spain. Long ways to reform', in Astrid Pfenning and Thomas Bahle (eds), *Families and Family Policies in Europe*, Frankfurt am Main: Peter Lang, pp. 70 – 89.

Naldini, M. (2003), *The Family in the Mediterranean Welfare States*, London: Frank Cass & Co.

OECD, (1997), *Tax/benefit Position of Production Workers*, OECD: Paris.

Orloff, A.S. (1993), 'Gender and the social rights of citizenship: the comparative analysis of gender relations and welfare states', *American Sociological Review*, **58**, 303 - 28.

Ostner, I and J. Lewis (1995), 'Gender and the evolution of European social policy', in S. Leibfried and P. Pierson (eds), *European Social Policy: Between Fragmentation and Integration*, Washington D.C.: Brookings Institution, pp. 159 - 93.

Pedersen, S. (1993), *Family, Dependence and the Origins of the Welfare State. Britain and France, 1914 - 1945*, Cambridge: Cambridge University Press.

Sainsbury, D., (1996), *Gender, Equality and Welfare States*, Cambridge: Cambridge University Press.

Sainsbury, D. (1999), 'Taxation, family responsibilities and employment', in D. Sainsbury (ed.), *Gender and Welfare State Regimes*, Oxford: Oxford University Press, pp. 185 - 209.

Saraceno, C. (2003), *Mutamenti della famiglia e politiche sociali in Italia*, Bologna: Il Mulino.

Strobel, P. (2000), 'La contribution des politiques familiales à la réduction et de la pauvreté et des inégalitées: les paradoxes du cas français', in C. Daniel and B. Palier (eds), *La protection sociale en Europe*, La Découverte: Paris, pp. 195 – 208.

Trifiletti, R. (1999), Southern European welfare regimes and the worsening position of women, *Journal of European Social Policy*, IX, 1, February, pp. 49 – 64.

Wennemo, I. (1992), 'The development of family policy: A comparison of family benefits and tax reductions for families in 18 OECD Countries', *Acta Sociologica*, **35** (3), 201 – 217.

Wildeboer Schut, J.M., J.C. Vrooman and P.T. de Beer (2001), *On Worlds of Welfare*, The Hague: Social and Cultural Planning Office.

PART TWO

Cross-National Comparisons of Demographic Trends

6. Changes in Family Patterns and People's Lives: Western European Trends

Pearl A. Dykstra

In the past decades, western European countries have witnessed marked demographic changes (Coleman, 1996; Ditch, et al., 1996; Sardon, 2000).[1] There has been a common pattern characterized by increased longevity (particularly at advanced ages), postponement of marriage and declining marriage rates, a rise in divorce, postponement of childbearing and a drop in birth rates, a rise in births out-of-wedlock, and increased numbers of couples cohabiting. Basically, similar trends have been revealed, but the changes have not been equally profound across the continent, with differences in the timing and tempo of change. Moreover, the situation in the late 1960s, at the onset of the changes, was far from uniform.

Scholars differ in their views of these changes. Some (e.g. Jones, 1993; Roussel, 1992) view the demographic trends in Europe as a process of continuing convergence. Economic, technological, cultural and social forces will move all European countries towards the same situation. Supposedly, between-country variability is attributable to time lags. Certain countries are 'stragglers', whereas others are 'forerunners' on the unidirectional and uniform path of the second demographic transition (van de Kaa, 1987, 1994; Lesthaeghe and van de Kaa, 1986; Allan et al., 2001). The consistency in developments is supposedly inspired by the process of individualization, which entails that people are increasingly freed from the shackles of family, church and community - taking their lives into their own hands rather than following the prescriptions, demands and needs of the wider collective. Another way of looking at the demographic changes in Europe is to emphasize the persistence of cross-national and regional differences (e.g. Reher, 1998). According to this perspective, cultural and historical differences within Europe cannot be disregarded: the past is never the same for two countries. Religious traditions together with social policies create distinct differences within Europe. Kuijsten (1999) argues that both the 'uniformity in trends' view and the 'persistence of differences' view are supported by the data. What one finds, depends on one's focus, and neither view can be proven conclusively.

Though I harbour no illusions about solving the 'uniformity' versus 'diversity' debate, new insights can be gained from viewing the demographic changes in terms of changing patterns of solidarity in families. I am defining family solidarity as the dependency relationships that are evident in work-care arrangements within households and families – those between men and women in intimate relationships and those between family members of different generations. As Knijn and Komter argue in the introduction to this book, patterns of family solidarity are created and maintained by developments in the political economy. Countries, because they differ in the generosity of provisions made available to families, differ in the extent to which they encourage or discourage certain forms of family solidarity. Differences in economic dependencies are reflected in demographic behaviour: leaving home, union formation, childbearing, union disruption and co-residence. Women's position in families is crucial here: 'what matters is the degree to which social policy frees women from the burden of family obligations' (Esping-Andersen, 1999, p. 51). Is public policy built on the assumption that the care of frail older adults, handicapped family members and minors is provided free of charge by female family members? Alternatively, to what extent does public policy provide women with opportunities to be active in organizing their own lives, independently of men and independently of parents?

Drawing upon the previous considerations, I will be looking at cross-national differences in demographic behaviour in the light of the support countries provide to women to live independently (or in a non-married state) and to combine motherhood and a paid job. The focus in the first part of the chapter is on family patterns as evident in demographic statistics, and more specifically, trends in childlessness, births out of wedlock and one-person households. In the second part of the chapter, a closer look is taken at changing life courses. Of interest here is the interplay between family life and work.

FAMILY PATTERNS

To capture and describe differences in family patterns in Europe, researchers often construct clusters of countries. An example is Reher's (1998) north/south divide, with Scandinavia, the British Isles, the Low Countries, and much of Germany and Austria characterized by 'relatively weak family links', and the Mediterranean region by 'strong family ties'. In countries with 'strong' family ties, frail elderly are cared for by family members, grandparents take care of their children's offspring while they are at work, and young adults remain in the parental home until they get their first stable job. In countries with 'relatively weak' family ties, social and market services play a greater role in child- and elder-care, and adult family members are more strongly committed to residential autonomy.

Ireland's demographic profile tends to differ from that of other 'northern' countries, and for that reason, a Catholic/Protestant distinction is often used to describe 'traditional' and 'modern' patterns of family formation (Hobcraft and Kiernan, 1995). The traditional pattern, which is characteristic of Catholic southern Europe, implies that childbearing and child rearing are more likely to take place within formal marriage and with both parents present. The modern pattern with higher levels of extramarital births and lone parenthood is characteristic of the social democratic Scandinavian countries.

Mellens (1999) developed a clustering that also takes into account levels of women's labour force participation, policy arrangements and the cultural climate. He identified three clusters of countries in western Europe: the maternalistic, pragmatic and paternalistic. The maternalistic cluster includes the Nordic countries Denmark, Finland, Iceland, Norway and Sweden. 'Maternalistic' refers to the relatively high proportion of women with paid jobs, the high level of childcare arrangements, and the fact that typically feminine values such as cooperation tend to be espoused in these countries. The 'pragmatic' cluster includes the countries of Austria, Belgium, France, Germany, Ireland, Luxembourg, the Netherlands, Switzerland and the United Kingdom. In this region, economic wealth is of prime importance, and though women's emancipation and alternative lifestyles are accepted, policy measures aimed at achieving equality are limited. The 'paternalistic' cluster consists of the Mediterranean countries Italy, Greece and Spain, and also Portugal. In these countries, traditional family values and conservatism dominate, there is little gender equality and childcare arrangements are not well developed.

In this chapter I make use of Esping-Andersen's (1999) distinction between so-called familialistic and de-familialistic welfare regimes, implying that the work-care arrangements in families and households reflect and are shaped by the way welfare regimes organize the production of personal and social services. Countries such as Spain and Italy have 'familialistic' welfare regimes, which are built on the assumption that caring needs are serviced in households. Paradoxical as it may seem, the lack of policies to support young families or older adults is characteristic of familialistic regimes. Countries such as Denmark, Sweden, Norway, Finland, Belgium and France have 'de-familialistic' welfare regimes, where caring burdens are assigned to the state. In these countries, the availability of services enables women to participate on the labour market and enables family members to set up independent households. Esping-Andersen does not specify where Germany (FRG), the Netherlands, the United Kingdom and Switzerland fit on the 'familialistic'-'de-familialistic' continuum. Presumably, their welfare regimes fall somewhere in between the two extremes.

Living Alone

One indicator of family 'self-servicing', to use Esping-Andersen's terminology, is intergenerational co-residence (three-generation households, young adults living in the parental home). Living alone may be seen as the flip side of family self-servicing. In countries with familialistic welfare regimes, one can expect to find low proportions of one-person households, whereas high proportions of one-person households can be expected in countries with de-familialistic welfare regimes.

As Table 6.1 shows, there are clear country differences in the extent to which living alone is a viable household form. Whereas the proportion of one-person households has risen in each of the selected countries, the increase has been stronger in certain countries (e.g. Denmark, Germany, Luxembourg and the Netherlands) than in others (e.g. Austria, Belgium, France and Finland). In addition, the share of one-person households differs strongly between the countries. Overall, proportions are highest in the Scandinavian countries, and lowest in the Mediterranean countries. The high proportion of one-person households in the Scandinavian countries is consistent with their de-familialistic welfare regimes. Likewise, the low proportion of one-person households in the Mediterranean countries is consistent with their familialistic welfare regimes. However, France and Belgium, which are part of the de-familialistic cluster, are not among the countries with the highest proportion of one-person households, whereas Germany, the Netherlands and Switzerland are. The proportion of one-person households in the latter countries is higher than one would expect given their mixed welfare regimes.

Clearly then, the familialism of welfare regimes does not provide a full explanation for cross-national differences in the proportion of one-person households. Other factors should also be considered. Scarcities on the housing market are among them. As regards the low levels in Spain, for example, one should take into account that there are few single person dwellings in that country. Perhaps the most important development contributing to the rise in one-person households is the increase in prosperity (Kobrin, 1976; Pampel, 1983).

Table 6.1. Proportion of one-person households in all private households, selected European countries, 1950 - 1990.

	1950	1960	1970	1980	1990
Scandinavian countries					
Denmark	14	20	23	30	34
Finland	19	22	24	27	32
Norway	15	14	21	28	34
Sweden	21	20	25	33	36
Continental Europe					
Austria	18	20	26	28	27
Belgium	16	17	19	23	28
France	19	20	20	25	27
Germany (FRG)	12	17	25	31	34
Netherlands	9	12	17	23	30
United Kingdom	11	11	18	22	26
Switzerland		14	20	29	32
Mediterranean countries					
Greece	9	10	11	15	16
Italy	10	11	13	18	21
Portugal	8	11	10	13	14
Spain			7	10	13
Turkey	7	3	3	6	5

Source: Kuijsten, 1996.

More and more people have the financial means to live on their own. Among home-leavers, particularly in northern and western European countries, it has become more common to set up a household of one's own before entering a partnership. Rising divorce rates have also contributed to the growth in one-person households. Increasing numbers of women who have outlived their husbands – given the difference in life expectancy and the fact that women tend to marry men who are senior in age – are another determinant of the growing proportion of one-person households.

Non-Marital Births

The last decades have shown an increase in so-called alternative partnerships such as consensual unions, partners who are members of separate households, and commuter marriages. Evidence suggests that the dependencies between men and women differ by partnership type (Batalova and Cohen, 2002; Blumstein and Schwartz, 1983). Marriages are more likely to be character-ized by a gender-based division of tasks with a male breadwinner and a fe-male homemaker, whereas consensual unions are more likely to be character-ized by an egalitarian division of tasks with both partners engaging in house-hold work and employment. Here I examine differences across time and across countries in whether marriage is chosen as the arrangement for part-nerships and for raising children. The differential importance of formal mar-riage as the milieu for having children is evident in the statistics on non-marital births.

Rates of childbearing outside of marriage have increased in virtually every European country (see Table 6.2). Nevertheless, there is considerable cross-national diversity. The Scandinavian countries together with France and the United Kingdom are at the one end, where between 40 per cent and 55 per cent of all children currently born have mothers who are not formally married. Note, however, that these women are not necessarily single; the majority are in consensual unions (Kiernan, 1999). Greece, Italy, Spain and Switzerland are at the other end. In these countries less than 15 per cent of all births are non-marital. The Netherlands, Austria and Portugal occupy inter-mediate positions. The statistics show a rather clear divide between the coun-tries with de-familialistic welfare regimes on the one hand (high proportion of non-marital births) and countries with familialistic welfare regimes on the other hand (low proportions of non-marital births). But there are exceptions too: France, the UK, Switzerland, Portugal cannot be categorized according to the assumptions of the typology. Interestingly, France and the United Kingdom almost approach the Scandinavian trends, while Portugal does not fit the pattern observed in the other southern European countries and Switzer-land deviates from other continental European countries.

Childlessness

People's opportunities to combine paid employment and caring tasks differ between welfare states. De-familialistic welfare regimes best enable people to engage in both spheres of life, whereas the lack of institutional support for families in familialistic regimes means that people are more or less forced to choose between gainful employment and care giving.

Table 6.2. *Proportion of non-marital births (of 100 births), 1970 - 1999, in selected European countries*

	1970	1980	1990	'98/'99
Scandinavian countries				
Denmark	11	33	46	45
Finland	6	13	25	39
Norway	7	14	39	49
Sweden	19	40	47	55
Continental Europe				
Austria	13	18	24	31
Belgium	3	4	12	
France	7	11	30	41
Germany (FRG)	6	8	11	
Netherlands .	2	4	11	23
United Kingdom	8	12	28	39
Switzerland	4	5	6	10
Mediterranean countries				
Greece	1	2	2	4
Italy	2	4	7	9
Portugal	7	9	15	20
Spain	1	4	10	14

Source: Sardon, 2000.

The recent rise in childlessness has been attributed to the difficulties women face in combining career aspirations and motherhood (Hakim, 2000). Of course the wide and easy availability of contraceptives has better enabled women to remain childless. What cross-national differences in rates of childlessness do we see in western Europe?

The trend across time is remarkably similar for all the countries listed in Table 6.3. The proportions childless women in the oldest cohorts hover around 20 per cent. Subsequent cohorts show a steady decline in the proportions childless women to between 10 and 16 per cent for the 1930s and 1940s cohorts. In the youngest cohorts, the proportions childless women are on the rise, but they are not reaching the levels of the cohorts born at the beginning of the twentieth century. Portugal and Spain are exceptions; the pattern in these countries is that of a steady decline in the childlessness rate, with perhaps a levelling off in the youngest cohorts. Of course, the reasons for childlessness have changed over time. The oldest cohorts have high proportions of childless women because many remained unmarried. In the younger cohorts women are remaining childless while in stable partnerships.

Despite the similarity across countries in the general trend, countries differ in the level of childlessness. For the present chapter, childlessness in the youngest cohorts is most relevant. The highest rates are found in Germany, the Netherlands, England and Wales (which have 'mixed' welfare regimes), the lowest rates are found in the Mediterranean countries (which have famialialistc welfare regimes), while the childlessness rates in the Scandinavian countries (which have de-familialistic welfare regimes) are in between. It is illuminating to compare the childlessness rates with women's labour force participation rates. These are relatively low in the Mediterranean countries, relatively high in the Scandinavian countries and moderate in the Continental European countries (OECD 1996, 2000). Taken together, one can conclude that the Scandinavian policy context best provides the conditions under which women can be both mothers and employees. Such conditions are less well developed in the Mediterranean and in the Continental European countries. In the former, the response of several women seems to have been to forgo paid employment, whereas in the latter, the response of several seems to have been to forgo motherhood.

Individual Lives

So far, attention has been paid to national statistics only. The reason for looking at them is that they tell us something about social change. As Saporiti (1989) maintains, 'demographic facts can be considered as indicators, as

Table 6.3. *Percentages of all women childless by age 45, 1900 – 1959 birth cohorts*

Five year cohort:	1900/1904	1905/1909	1910/1914	1915/1919	1920/1924	1925/1929	1930/1934	1935/1939	1940/1944	1945/1949	1950/1954	1955/1959
Scandinavian countries												
Denmark										9	11	13
Finland	26	22	20	18	16	15	16	15	14	14	15	16
Norway		12		10		10		9	9	9	11	14
Sweden							14	13	13	13	15	13
Continental Europe												
Austria	16						16	14	15	15	17	
Belgium	16	14		13	12		16	14	13	13	14	20
England-Wales			21	19	17	17	14	13	12	10	14	17
France	25	23	20	18	16		13	11	11	11	12	13
Germany former F.R	26	22	19	18	17	14	10	10	12	14	18	20
Netherlands	23	22	20	16	15	14	12	12	12	11	15	17
Switzerland	22	20				16		16	16	18		
Mediterranean countries												
Italy	18	19	17	15	16	15	13	10	14	12	12	14
Portugal	21	21	20	19	17	17	14			11	10	10
Spain	14	14	14	13	14	12			12	11	10	10

Source: Prioux, 1993; Rowland, still in press; Sardon, 2000; Toulemon, 1996.
Where figures differed between sources, normally the more recent ones were used.

signs revealing inner tendencies that concern society as a whole' (p. 195). Social change is brought about by changes in individual behaviour (Riley, 1987).To understand developments at the macro level, it is informative to analyse changes at the level of individual behaviour. In what follows, I would like to make that visible by showing some of the ways in which people's lives have changed over the course of the past decades. To examine changes in individual lives, one cannot rely on registry data. Censuses are not an appropriate source either, because they tend to have little information on the timing and sequencing of life transitions and on the combination of public and private roles. Survey data are required, and preferably surveys in which retrospective life history data have been collected.

Family Life Forms Project

Unfortunately, cross-nationally comparative life history data are limited. That is what makes the *Family Life Forms* project so unique (Kaufmann et al., 1997). This is a coordinated effort of researchers from ten European countries to chart changes from the beginning of the 1980s to the end of the 1980s in the family forms of women in the 'early parental phase' and women in the 'post-parental phase'. Secondary analyses of existing data sets were carried out – both large-scale (e.g. Labour Force Surveys) and small-scale surveys were used. 'Family life form' pertains not only to marital status and household arrangement, but also to the economic activity of adult household members. The inclusion of information on labour force participation makes it a richer concept than the ones traditionally used in household classifications. Given the limited international harmonization of definitions and classifications – in household research and in the field of labour force statistics – 'comparable research is no easy task' (Kuijsten, 1996, p. 128), and it should not come as a surprise that not every researcher succeeded in delivering data in the desired formats. Comparable data for two dates in time are available for four out of the ten countries: Italy, Germany (FRG), the Netherlands and Great Britain. The data are from repeated cross-sectional surveys. Note that, for Germany in particular, the sample sizes are quite small. The number of 'family life forms' differed between the country tables: the most elaborate categorization was given for the situation in Italy, whereas the least elaborate categorization was given for Germany.

Table 6.4 shows partnership, parenthood and employment combinations of young women (women in the so-called 'early parental phase', defined as the 25 - 29 age range) at two points in time: the early and the late 1980s. Among the married, the numbers were large enough to distinguish those with jobs from those without jobs. Distinctions by employment status were not made for women living alone and for women in consensual unions. Italy stands out from the other countries with its relatively high proportion of young women living in the parental home, and its low proportions of young women living alone or in consensual unions. Note that those living with their parents are not necessarily dependants. Virtually half of those living at home had incomes of their own (Menniti et al., 1997).

In each of the four countries, fulltime homemaking mothers occupy a majority position (numerically). Their numbers in the 25 - 29 age category are decreasing however, as is evident in the dropping proportions between the early and late 1980s. The Netherlands and Great Britain have a relatively high proportion of married childless women with paid jobs. This pattern is probably attributable to the high age at which women become mothers in the respective countries (Beets, 1997; ONS, 1999). The Netherlands has a particularly low proportion of married working mothers in the 25 - 29 age range. An increase in the proportion of young women living alone is observed in each of the four countries. Note though, that in Italy the number of young women living alone is quite small. The proportion of single women is higher in Germany than in the Netherlands. On the basis of these data, one cannot say why this might be the case. One possibility is that Dutch women enter partnerships at an earlier age than do the German. In Germany and the Netherlands, the proportions of young women in consensual unions increase over time, a pattern that is not observed in Italy (data on consensual unions in Great Britain are not given). Over time, an increase is observed in the proportions of young women living in the parental home. The reasons differ between the two countries for which data are available. In Great Britain, the increase is linked to postponement of the age of leaving home. In Italy, the increase is linked to the rising age at marriage. Great Britain shows an increase over time in the proportion of lone mothers. This group consists of both never and formerly married women. The findings in Table 6.4 cover a relatively limited time period. Nevertheless, considerable shifts in the life course patterns of young women are observed, attesting to the rapidity of social change.

Table 6.5 shows partnership, parenthood and employment combinations of middle-aged women (women in the so-called 'post-parental phase', defined as the 45 - 49 age range) in the early and the late 1980s. In three of the four countries, married women who are not employed and have children at home form the largest category in the 45 - 49 age range. Great Britain is the exception. Married women who do have jobs and have children at home form the second largest category, followed at a distance by married women who have no children living at home and are either employed or not employed. The proportion of women in this age range who are in consensual unions, is negligible. In each country, a slight increase over time in the proportion of working mothers is observed. Whereas Italy shows an increase over time in the proportion of jobless married women with children at home, the Netherlands, Germany and the UK show a decrease for this category.

Table 6.4 Partnership, parenthood and employment combinations of women, aged 25 - 29[a] in four European countries in the early and late 1980s (percentages)

	Germany (FRG)		Italy		Great Britain		The Netherlands	
	'80/'82	'88/'90	'83	'88	'81	'91	'81/'82	'89/'90
Living alone	18	22	1	3	6	9	10	16
Married, no children, employed	11	9	8	9	14	15	19	19
Married, no children, not employed			6	7				
Married, children, employed	14	11	17	14	16	14	5	4
Married, children, not employed	35	27	33	28	34	19	40	22
Consensual union	1	9	1	1			6	15
Living with parent(s)			29	36	6	9	5	7
Single parent			1	1	9	15		

Note: Open cells mean that no information for the specific category was provided by the original authors.

[a] In Italy the women were slightly younger: aged 24 - 28.

Sources: Clarke and Henwood, 1997; Federkeil, 1997; Kuijsten, 1996; Kuijsten and Schulze, 1997; Menniti et al., 1997.

A comparison of the two tables reveals that the 1980s have brought greater changes in the lives of young women than in those of middle-aged women. Kuijsten (1996) attributes the greater changes in the lives of the young as compared to the old to the cohort-drivenness of social change: the arrival of new cohorts with innovative behaviour is viewed as the source of social change (cf. Ryder, 1965). In my view, this is only part of the story. Characteristics of the specific life phases should also be considered. In young adulthood, many life options are still open: decisions about employment, entering a partnership and having children have yet to be made. By middle-age, most have committed themselves to jobs and families. Given that their courses for action are more restricted, it is not remarkable that the life course patterns of middle-aged women show less change than do those of the young.

Table 6.5 Partnership, parenthood and employment combinations of women, aged 45 - 49[a] in four European countries in the early and late 1980s (percentages).

	Germany (FRG)		Italy		Great Britain		The Netherlands	
	'80/'82	'88/'90	'83	'88	'81	'91	'81/'82	'89/'90
Living alone			3	4	6	12	7	8
Married, no children, employed	11	11	5	4	25	32		16
Married, no children, not employed	6	15	9	8	9	9		
Married, children, employed	16	18	18	20	28	20	21	26
Married, children, not employed	33	28	47	51	15	5	49	35
Consensual union			1	1			5	10
Single parent			8	8	6	5	4	9

Note: Open cells mean that no information for the specific category was provided by the original authors.

[a] In Italy the women were older: ages 49 - 53.

Sources: Clarke and Henwood, 1997; Federkeil, 1997; Kuijsten, 1996; Kuijsten and Schulze, 1997; Menniti et al., 1997.

Changing Lives Project

Recently, a study (Liefbroer and Dykstra, 2000) on changes in the trajectories that people's lives follow was carried out at the Netherlands Interdisciplinary Demographic Institute (NIDI) in preparation for a Netherlands Scientific Council for Government Policy report on solidarity between generations (WRR 2001[1999]). The project encompasses all of the life course rather than one particular stage in life. It maps changes in both family life and work, and studies the interplay between those domains. It focuses on a wide range of birth cohorts, including those born at the very beginning of the twentieth century. Finally, given that life-history information on more than 25,000 people is available, life course changes can be examined in a much more thorough and reliable way than was the case in earlier studies. One drawback is, of course, that the project focuses on the Netherlands only.

The project draws upon several large-scale Dutch surveys with life-history information, which have never been used in combination before. Piecing together data from the 1900 - 1970 birth cohorts, the study looks at shifts in the timing and sequencing of family - and employment - related transitions. Not only are single transitions considered (e.g. the age at leaving home, the birth of the first child, the death of one's parents) but also combinations of roles and the time spent in them (e.g. the number of years spent as a member of a couple, in gainful employment and with dependent children living at home). In what follows I will focus on family-work combinations and women's economic independence. Of interest is to what extent people's lives followed the 'standard' pattern, with its fixed sequence of life phases and gender-specific division of activities (male breadwinner and female homemaker).

The study reveals that people are living longer, but the course of their lives has become less predictable. Though many lives still follow the 'standard' pattern, increasing numbers are deviating from it. Women's lives have changed more dramatically than men's. This is illustrated in Figure 6.1 and Figure 6.2, which present changes in men's and women's family and work roles at age 40. The figures are limited to the 1900 - 1950 birth cohorts; data for the life circumstances at age 40 were not available for the younger cohorts. The roles are those of (a) partnership, defined as living with a partner either in marriage or in consensual union, (b) parenthood, defined as co-residence with children, and (c) employment, which might be full-time or part-time. Inspection of Figure 6.1 reveals few cohort differences in men's roles at age 40. The pattern is virtually identical in each of the birth cohorts. More than 75% of men combined the three roles of partnership, parenthood and paid employment. Their lives followed that of the 'standard pattern', of being providers. Across successive cohorts, there is a decrease in the proportion of men who at age 40 had a job and no other roles. This finding reflects the growing propensity to enter stable heterosexual relationships, and thus to combine work and partnership roles. In the oldest cohorts, higher proportions of men remained single, but they were never more than 10%. An increase is visible across successive cohorts in the percentages of men who at age 40 had a partner and children but were not employed. In the youngest cohort – those born between 1941 and 1950 – it is 6%. The men in this category were not househusbands; most were unemployed, as the result of the economic recession at the beginning of the 1980s.

Whereas Figure 6.1 (men's lives at age 40) shows a relatively stable picture across successive cohorts, Figure 6.2 (women's lives at age 40) shows considerable variation. For example, there is a steady increase in the proportion of women who at age 40 were combining work and family life. Concomitantly, there is a decrease in the proportion of women who had a partner and children at age 40, but were not employed. Nevertheless, this specific combination, also known as the 'standard' life course, exemplified by early marriage and motherhood and an almost exclusive focus on household tasks, characterizes the lives of the majority of women at the age of 40 in each of the cohorts. As was the case for their male counterparts, the figure for women shows decreasing proportions of women who at age 40 had jobs, but did not have a partner or children. This pattern reflects the decreasing proportion of women who never married or never cohabited. In the 1900 - 1910 cohort, this group encompassed 12% of women at age 40; in the 1941 - 1950 cohort, it was under 2%. Across cohorts, there is a growth in the proportion of women who had children at home but had neither a job nor a partner. The numbers of women whose lives fit this pattern remain relatively small, however. Even in the youngest cohort, they encompass no more than 5% of women— lone mothers, caring for their children full-time after divorce.

Another remarkable finding is that the changes in the lives of people born between 1900 and 1970 have taken place quite gradually. The life course patterns have evolved slowly, with few abrupt changes. The absence of clear discontinuities fits notions of modernization, which assume that transformations in society are part of a long-term ongoing process. It is, however, contrary to what generation theorists (Becker, 2000) suggest, namely that specific birth cohorts are distinguishable from others, due to the specificity of the historical circumstances of their formative years. Though the changes in life course patterns across successive cohorts were shown to follow a steady and slow rhythm, evidence of a clear break in history was also found. In the study, this turning point is described as the 'watershed of the 1970s'. The effects of the 1970s vary, depending upon the life course stage in which the cohorts find themselves. The existence of a turning point is most clearly evident in the changes in family formation. The oldest cohorts showed a continuous decline in the age at marriage and the age at which the first child is born. This continuous decline was reversed in cohorts born in and after 1945: people started marrying later and postponed having children.

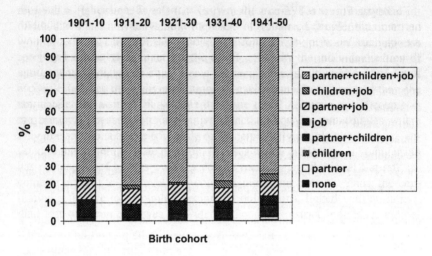

Figure 6.1. Family and work roles of 40 year old men, by birth cohort
Source: Liefbroer and Dykstra, 2000.

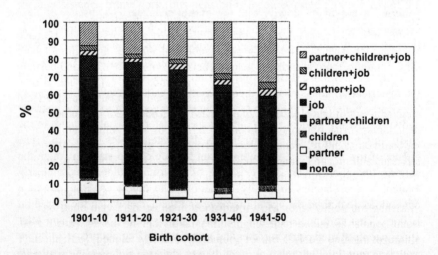

Figure 6.2. Family and work roles of 40 year old women, by birth cohort
Source: Liefbroer and Dykstra, 2000.

Starting with the 1945 cohort, there was a decline in family size, an increase in childlessness, and cohabitation outside of marriage gained popularity. The cohorts bringing about the change in life course patterns had their formative years (roughly between the ages of 15 and 25) in the late 1960s and early 1970s. Interestingly, changes are also visible in the lives of the older cohorts, but in different ways. For example (see Figure 6.3), the likelihood that middle-aged women had a paid job already showed an increase in the cohorts born between 1930 and 1940. More than 40 per cent of women in these cohorts were gainfully employed either full-time or part-time at the age of 40, whereas this figure was five to ten per cent lower for older cohorts.

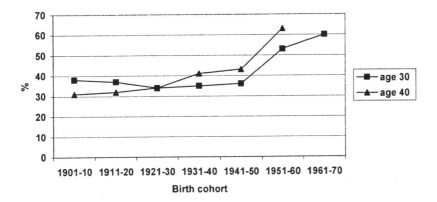

Figure 6.3. Women in full-time or part-time employment by birth cohort
Source: Liefbroer and Dykstra, 2000.

CONCLUSION

Post-war welfare regimes were built around a family prototype according to which people left the parental home to get married, subsequently had children, and stayed together until one of the partners died. A gender-based division of tasks, with men financially supporting the family and women providing unpaid care, was also part of the prototype. Cross-national comparative data presented in this chapter show that this prototype is becoming less and less representative of European families today. Though I do not think we have the empirical basis to substantiate Boh's (1989) provocative claim that European family patterns are converging to diversity, we do have repeated indications of the declining role of formal marriage as the arrangement for partnerships and child rearing, the decreasing prevalence of co-residence of parents and adult children, and increasing economic independence of women.

National registry data and censuses were used to chart these changing family patterns. A drawback is that they have only limited life history information. Unfortunately, cross-nationally comparative life history data are limited. Insofar the data are available, they cover only a short period of time, as in the *Family Life Forms project*, a unique and ambitious undertaking of European demographers that has comparable data for women at two dates in time (early and late 1980s) for Germany (FRG), the Netherlands, Italy and Great Britain. Findings show that full-time homemaking mothers occupy a majority position (numerically) in each of the four countries, but their numbers are declining whereas the proportion of working mothers is increasing.

The Dutch *Changing Lives* project covers a wider range of historical time. Data from this project provide a wealth of information on the developments that have taken place in the life courses of men and women born between 1900 and 1970. Results indicate that the prototypical life course has not been that prototypical at all. It best describes the life courses of men and women born between 1931 and 1945. Many in these cohorts entered marriage and they did so at a relatively early age. Many had children and also at a relatively early age. Furthermore, their lives in marriage were characterized by a gendered division of tasks with breadwinning husbands and home-making wives. The lives of the cohorts born before 1930 and of those born after 1945 showed greater diversity. Similar findings have been reported for the United States. Analyses of family change reveal that the marriage and childbearing patterns of the American cohorts born in the 1930s and early 1940s are characterized by the greatest uniformity ever (Cherlin, 1980; Uhlenberg, 1993). It seems then, that the one-earner-plus-housewife family, that served as the model for post-war welfare state reformers (and is still the linchpin of policy in many countries) is an historical anomaly rather than an institution.

Though some parallelism in demographic developments across western Europe can be observed, unmistakable country differences continue to exist. 'Non-prototypical' family patterns are most notable in the Scandinavian countries, least common in the Mediterranean countries, with the Continental European countries occupying intermediate positions. To a certain extent these differences mirror the familialism of the welfare regimes of the respective countries. The countries that, through policies and services, best enable women, young adults and older adults to be economically independent, show the highest rates of non-marital births, one-person households and working mothers. Nevertheless, I do not think differences in welfare regimes make up the whole story. Economic circumstances and the normative climate also shape people's behaviour in families. Of course, the way in which countries organize their welfare regimes is not independent of their prosperity and cultural and religious traditions. For that reason, future research efforts should be aimed at unravelling the interlinkages between welfare regimes, labour markets, changes in the economy and changes in cultural systems. In doing so, we should initiate and support efforts to create cross-nationally comparative databases.

NOTE

1. In this chapter, the term 'western' Europe is used rather broadly, and refers to the countries of the European Union as well as Switzerland and Norway.

REFERENCES

Allan, G., S. Hawker, S. and G. Crow (2001), 'Family diversity and change in Britain and Western Europe', *Journal of Family Issues*, **22**, 819 - 37.

Batalova, J.A., and P.N. Cohen (2002), 'Premarital cohabitation and housework: Couples in cross-national perspective', *Journal of Marriage and Family*, **64**, 743 - 55.

Becker, H.A. (2000), 'Discontinous change and generational contracts', in S. Arber and C. Attias-Donfut (eds), *The Myth of Generational Conflict: The Family and State in Ageing Societies*, London: Routledge, pp. 114 - 132.

Beets, G. (1997), 'Kinderen worden later geboren: Een demografische analyse' [Children are born later: A demographic analysis], in G. Beets, A. Bouwens and J. Schippers (eds), *Uitgesteld ouderschap*, Amsterdam: Thesis Publishers, pp. 13 - 42.

Blumstein, P. and P. Schwartz (1983), *American Couples: Money, work and sex*, New York: Morrow.

Boh, K. (1989), 'European family life patterns – A reappraisal', in K. Boh, M. Bak, C. Clason, M. Pankratova, J. Qvortrup, G.B. Sgritta and K. Waerness (eds), *Changing Patterns of European Family Life: A Comparative Analysis of 14 European Countries*, London: Routledge, pp. 265 - 98.

Cherlin, A. (1980), 'Changing family and household: Contemporary lessons from historical research', *Annual Review of Sociology*, **9**, 51 - 66.

Clarke, L. and M. Henwood (1997), 'Great Britain: The lone parent as the new norm?', in F.-X. Kaufmann, A. Kuijsten, H.-J. Schulze and K.P. Strohmeier (eds), *Family Life and Family Policies in Europe, Volume 1: Structures and Trends in the 1980s*, Oxford: Clarendon Press, pp. 155 - 94.

Coleman, D. (1996), *Europe's Population in the 1990s*, Oxford: Oxford University Press.

Ditch, J., H. Barnes, J. Bradshaw, J. Commaille and T. Eardley (1996), *A Synthesis of National Family Policies 1994*, Commission of the European Communities: Social Policy Research Unit, University of York.

Esping-Andersen, G. (1999), *Social Foundations of Postindustrial Economies*, Oxford: Oxford University Press.

Federkeil, G. (1997), 'The Federal Republic of Germany: Polarization of family structure', in F.-X. Kaufman, A. Kuijsten, H.-J. Schulze and K.P. Strohmeier (eds), *Family Life and Family Policies in Europe, Volume 1: Structures and Trends in the 1980s*, Oxford: Clarendon Press, pp. 77 - 113.

Hakim, C. (2000), *Work-Lifestyle Choices in the 21st century: Preference Theory*, Oxford: Oxford University Press.

Hobcraft, J. and K. Kiernan (1995), *Becoming a Parent in Europe*, London: London School of Economics, Welfare State Program, WSP/116.

Jones, G.W. (1993), 'Is demographic uniformity inevitable?', *Journal of the Australian Population Association*, **10**, 1 - 16.

Kaa, D.J. van de (1987), 'Europe's second demographic transition', *Population Bulletin*, **42**, Washington, DC: Population Reference Bureau.

Kaa, D.J. van de (1994), 'The second demographic transition revisited: Theories and expectations', in G.C.N. Beets, J.C. van den Brekel, R.L. Cliquet, G. Dooghe and J. de Jong Gierveld (eds), *Population and Family in the Low Countries 1993: Late Fertility and Other Current Issues*, Lisse: Swets and Zeitlinger, pp. 81 - 126.

Kaufmann, F.-X., A. Kuijsten, H.-J. Schulze and K.P. Strohmeier (eds) (1997), *Family Life and Family Policies in Europe, Volume 1: Structures and Trends in the 1980s*, Oxford: Clarendon Press.

Kiernan, K. (1999), 'Childbearing outside marriage in Western Europe', *Population Trends*, **98**, 11 - 20.

Kobrin, F.E. (1976), 'The fall in household size and the rise of the primary individual in the United States', *Demography*, **13**, 127 - 38.

Kuijsten, A.C. (1996), 'Changing family patterns in Europe: A case of divergence?' *European Journal of Population*, **12**, 115 - 43.

Kuijsten, A. (1999), 'Households, families and kin networks', in L.J.G. van Wissen and P.A. Dykstra (eds), *Population Issues: An Interdisciplinary Focus*, New York: Kluwer Academic / Plenum Publishers, pp. 87 - 122.

Kuijsten, A. and H.-J. Schulze (1997), 'The Netherlands: The latent family', in F.-X. Kaufman, A. Kuijsten, H.-J. Schulze and K.P. Strohmeier (eds), *Family Life and Family Policies in Europe, Volume 1: Structures and Trends in the 1980s,* Oxford: Clarendon Press, pp. 253 - 301.

Lesthaeghe, R. and D.J. van de Kaa (1986), 'Twee demografische transities [Two demographic transitions]?', in D.J. van de Kaa and R. Lesthaeghe (eds), *Bevolking: Groei en Krimp,* Deventer: Van Loghum Slaterus [Special issue *Mens en Maatschappij*), pp. 9 - 24.

Liefbroer, A.C. and P.A. Dykstra (2000), *Levenslopen in Verandering: Een Studie naar Ontwikkelingen in de Levenslopen van Nederlanders geboren tussen 1900 en 1970* [Changing Lives: A Study on Changes in the Life Courses of the Dutch 1900 - 1970 Birth Cohorts], WRR Voorstudies en achtergronden V 107, Den Haag: Sdu Uitgevers.

Mellens, M. (1999), 'Uniformity and diversity defined', in J. de Beer and L. van Wissen (eds), *Europe: One Continent, Different Worlds. Population Scenarios for the 21st century*, Dordrecht: Kluwer Academic, pp. 33 - 44.

Menniti, A., R. Palomba and L.L. Sabbadini (1997), 'Italy: Changing the family from within', in F.-X. Kaufman, A. Kuijsten, H.-J. Schulze and K.P. Strohmeier (eds), *Family Life and Family Policies in Europe, Volume 1: Structures and Trends in the 1980s*, Oxford: Clarendon Press, pp. 223 - 52.

OECD (1996), *Employment Outlook*, Paris.

OECD (2000), *Employment Outlook*, Paris.

ONS (1999), 'Key demographic and health indicators', *Population Trends,* **98**, 68.

Pampel, F.C. (1983), 'Changes in the propensity to live alone: Evidence from consecutive cross-sectional surveys, 1960 - 1976', *Demography,* **20**, 433 - 48.

Prioux, F. (1993), 'L'Infécondité en Europe', in A. Blum and J.L. Rallu (eds), *European Population 2. Demographic Dynamics,* Paris: John Libbey Eurotext, pp. 231 - 54.

Reher, D. S. (1998), 'Family ties in Western Europe', *Population and Development Review,* **24**, 203 - 34.

Riley, M.W. (1987), 'On the significance of age in sociology', *American Sociological Review,* **52**, 1 - 14.

Roussel, L. (1992), 'La famille en Europe occidentale: Divergences et convergences' [The western European family: Patterns of divergence and convergence], *Population,* **47**, 133 - 52.

Rowland, D.T. (still in press), 'Historical trends in childlessness', in P. Dykstra and G.O. Hagestad (eds), *Ageing without Children. A Cross-national Handbook on Childlessness in late Life,* Newport, CT: Greenwood Press.

Ryder, N. (1965), 'The cohort as a concept in the study of social change', *American Sociological Review,* **30**, 843 - 61.

Saporiti, A. (1989), 'Historical changes in the family's reproductive patterns', in K. Boh, M. Bak, C. Clason, M. Pankratova, J. Qvortrup, G.B. Sgritta and K. Waerness (eds), *Changing Patterns of European Family Life: A Comparative Analysis of 14 European Countries*, London: Routledge, pp. 191 - 215.

Sardon, J.-P. (2000), 'Évolutions récentes de la démographie des pays développés' [Recent demographic trends in developed countries], *Population*, 55, 729 – 64.

Uhlenberg, P. (1993), 'Demographic change and kin relationships in later life', in G.L. Maddox and M. Powell Lawton (eds), *Annual Review of Gerontology and Geriatics (Vol. 13): Focus on Kinship, Aging, and Social Change*, New York: Springer, pp. 219 - 238.

Toulemon, L. (1996), 'Very few couples remain voluntarily childless', *Population: An English Selection*, 8, 1 - 28.

WRR (2001 [1999]), *Generationally-aware Policy*. Reports to the government no. 58. Den Haag: Sdu-Uitgevers. [Extensive summary in English of the 1999 WRR-report 'Generatiebewust beleid'].

7. Fertility and Nuptiality in the CEE Countries in the Context of Weakening Families and a Weakening State

Irena E. Kotowska

The changes in fertility and nuptiality in the Central and Eastern European (CEE) countries undergoing transformation to a market economy, observed in the 1990s, are similar to the earlier ones in developed European economies. They constitute a core of the demographic change described as the second demographic transition (SDT) (van de Kaa and Lesthaeghe, 1986; van de Kaa, 1987, 1994, 1999; Lesthaeghe, 1991, 1995). The conceptual framework underpinning the analysis of the SDT focuses on fertility and marriage rates as they relate to changes in family formation and dissolution patterns, decisive in the emergence of a course of reproduction far removed from what was expected – under the demographic transition theory – for the last stage of demographic development.

This chapter starts with a brief description of reproduction developments in selected CEE countries in the 1990s. The selection includes the Czech Republic, Hungary, Poland, Slovakia, Slovenia and the former GDR (Central Europe), Bulgaria, Romania (Southeast Europe), Estonia, Latvia, Lithuania (Baltic republics), and the Russian Federation. The main components of the transformation processes are discussed, which can be considered a driving force behind the observed demographic change. The discussion refers to the explanatory framework formulated by van de Kaa (1994) to show similarities and differences in structural, cultural and technological processes underlying shifts in demographic attitudes and behaviour in the CEE countries in comparison to those observed in developed market economies.

The last part focuses on problems related to the transformation that seem to be decisive for the demographic changes in the CEE countries: a weakening state position, not accompanied by the construction of effective markets and a system of income transfers, a shift from more equality towards more inequality, the transition from a system where individuals have fewer opportunities and less responsibility for their situation to a system that offers more opportunities but also more challenges and responsibility. As a result, increased polarization and a decreased solidarity between losers and winners is observed. This imbalance between opportunities and challenges also pertains to the family level. Although state support for the family is substantially reduced and more responsibility has been shifted to the family, changes in the labour market and welfare arrangements make it more difficult to fulfil the standard functions of the family.

FERTILITY AND NUPTIALITY CHANGES IN SELECTED CEE COUNTRIES IN THE 1990s

A brief look at reproductive developments in countries in transition shows that, despite their diversity, they do have certain common features similar to those observed in developed countries under the SDT. The radical changes in fertility and marriage rates observed in developed countries since the 1960s exhibit two patterns: first, a decline in fertility to below replacement level accompanied by changes in the pattern of fertility such as the postponement of birth, a growing percentage of children born out of wedlock to cohabiting couples and single mothers, and a growing percentage of childless couples; and second, an increasingly widespread use of contraceptive practices by all social groups to limit family size according to preference. These trends are accompanied by an increasing social acceptance of childlessness and children born out of wedlock, a decline in the propensity to marry and the postponement of marriage, an increase in cohabitation and Living-Apart-Together (LAT) relations, rising divorce rates and a growing number of single parents.

To illustrate fertility and nuptiality changes in the CEE countries, basic demographic indicators are used: the total fertility rate (TFR), the mean age of women at the birth of their first child, the percentage of extramarital births, the total first marriage rate of females, the mean age of women at their first marriage, the crude divorce rate. The changes are situated among the trends observed in European developed countries grouped as follows by Kuijsten (1995) according to the type of arrangement for partnership and raising children:

Group A: Denmark, Sweden, Finland
  Fertility – relatively high, divorce – high, cohabitation – high, extra-marital fertility – moderate/high

Group B: France, Norway, The Netherlands, United Kingdom
  Fertility – low, divorce – high, cohabitation – low, extramarital fertility – moderate
Group C: Austria, Belgium, FRG, Luxembourg, Switzerland
  Fertility – very low, divorce – high, cohabitation – moderate, extramarital fertility – moderate/high
Group D: Italy, Greece, Portugal, Spain
  Fertility – very low, divorce – low, cohabitation – low, extramarital fertility – low
Group E: Ireland, Iceland, Poland, Hungary, Bulgaria, Romania
  Fertility – high, divorce – heterogeneous, cohabitation – low, extramarital fertility – heterogeneous.

Table 7.1 presents data around 1988 given by Kuijsten (1995) to illustrate the family types by groups. They are supplemented by relevant indicators based on data around 2000 to demonstrate the spectacular changes pertaining to the group E, which includes the CEE countries. Poland, Hungary, Bulgaria, Romania are relatively homogenous in terms of fertility (high), nuptiality (high), divorce (low) and cohabitation (low), remain homogenous in terms of fertility and nuptiality and become more heterogeneous in terms of extramarital fertility. However, the levels of the relevant indicators changed: fertility – very low, divorce – moderate, cohabitation – moderate, extramarital fertility – moderate. Ireland and Iceland, mainly included in that group because of their fertility levels, become out-layers.

At the beginning of the 1980s the countries under focus have relatively high fertility rates by developed countries' standards – the TFR is above 2.0 for almost all the countries (Table 7.2).

The drop in fertility is observed in the 1980s in almost all the countries, but at a relatively slow pace. In the Baltic countries and the Russian Federation, the TFRs fluctuate along an upward trend and reach peaks in 1986–8, depending on the country (Macura, 1995).[1] At the end of the 1980s, the countries in transition are still among those with a relatively high fertility. The rapid decline in fertility over the subsequent decade situates the CEE countries among those with the lowest fertility rates. They become more homogenous in terms of fertility levels, with the lowest TFR in the Czech Republic (1.14).

The decline in fertility is accompanied by shifts in the age distribution of mothers, a feature that can be synthesized by changes in the mean age of childbearing, especially by the mean age of the mother at the birth of the first child. The postponement of births is demonstrated by an increase in both of these indicators. However, these changes are more diversified across countries. The mean age of the mother at the first birth ranges from 23.5 (Bulgaria) to 27.6 (the former GDR, 1999) in 2000.

Table 7.1 Typology of European families

Countries	TFR 1988	TFR 2000	Total first marriage rate of females 1988	Total first marriage rate of females 2000	Divorce per 100 marriages 1988	Divorce per 100 marriages 2000	Percentage of births outside marriage 1988	Percentage of births outside marriage 2000
Group A								
Denmark	1.62	1.77	572	730	46	37	45	45
Sweden	2.02	1.54	601	530	41	54	50	55
Finland	1.78	1.73	592	620	38	53	25	39
Group B								
France	1.81	1.75	540	620	31	41	28	42
Norway	1.89	1.85	558	520	37	39	28	50
Netherlands	1.55	1.72	601	590	28	39	10	25
United Kingdom	1.81	1.65	665	530	42	53	25	39
Group C								
Austria	1.45	1.34	599	540	30	50	23	31
Belgium	1.58	1.66	718	520	31	60	8	15
FRG	1.39	1.38	598	640	32	44	10	18
Luxembourg	1.52	1.79	579	550	37	48	12	22
Switzerland	1.51	1.50	663	640	33	51	6	11
Group D								
Italy	1.29	1.23	695	620	8	12	6	10
Greece	1.50	1.29	870	520	12	21	2	4
Portugal	1.53	1.50	787	730	11	30	14	22
Spain	1.30	1.24	640	610	11	18	8	16
Group E								
Ireland	2.11	1.89	710	610	Forbidden		12	32
Iceland	2.21	2.08	470	700	36	31	52	66
Poland	2.15	1.34	840	630	17	20	6	12
Hungary	1.81	1.32	750	490	28	50	12	29
Bulgaria	1.96	1.26	852	520	18	30	11	38
Romania	2.31	1.31	870	640	21	23	4	25

Source: Kuijsten (1995), Table 3.1, p. 55; for 2000 data: Recent Demographic Developments in Europe 2001, Council of Europe.

Table 7.2. Main fertility indicators for selected Central and East European countries in 1980, 1990, 2000

Countries	Total fertility rate			Mean age of woman at first birth			Extra-marital births (per 100 births)		
	1980	1990	2000	1980	1990	2000	1980	1990	2000
Bulgaria	2.05	1.82	1.26	21.9	22.2	23.5	10.9	12.4	38.4
Czech Republic	2.10	1.90	1.14	22.4	22.5	24.9	5.6	8.6	21.8
Estonia	2.02	2.04	1.39	23.2	22.9	24.0	18.3	27.1	54.5
Former GDR	1.94	1.50	1.22	23.5	24.6	27.6[a]	22.8	35.0	49.9[a]
Hungary	1.91	1.87	1.32	22.4	23.1	25.1	7.1	13.1	29.0
Latvia	1.90	2.01	1.24	22.9	23.0	24.4	12.5	16.9	40.3
Lithuania	1.99	2.02	1.27	23.8	23.2	23.8	6.3	7.0	22.6
Poland	2.26	2.05	1.34	23.4	23.3	24.5	4.7	6.2	12.1
Romania	2.43	1.84	1.31	22.4	22.6	23.6	2.8	4.0	25.5
Russian Federation	1.86	1.90	1.21	23.0	22.6	22.7[b]	10.8	14.6	28.0
Slovak Republic	2.31	2.09	1.29	22.7	22.6	24.2	5.7	7.6	18.3
Slovenia	2.10	1.46	1.26	22.8	23.7	26.5	13.1	24.5	37.1

Notes:
a) data for 1999.
b) data for 1995.

Source: Recent Demographic Developments in Europe, Council of Europe, 2001.

At the same time, and parallel to the fertility decline, extramarital births increase visibly, although with a strongly differentiated intensity: in 2000 the lowest percentage of extramarital births is observed in Poland (12.1), the highest in Estonia (54.5) and in the former GDR (49.9, 1999).

The spread of out-of-wedlock births is related to changes in marital behaviour. Nuptiality changes mainly emerge in the declining propensity to marry and the postponement of marriage (Table 7.3). In 1980 the proper rates are relatively high by the standards of developed countries. The downward trend is already evident in the 1980s and largely results from the decline in the number of first marriages. This change seems to indicate growing homogeneity with respect to the propensity to marry although the timing of the onset of the rapid decrease in first marriages is strongly diversified across countries.[2]

Changes in the marriage age pattern can be illustrated by shifts in the mean age of women at their first marriage. In the 1980s the striking increase in this indicator occurs in the former GDR, the Slovak Republic and Slovenia, while the Czech Republic experiences a slight rise. In the other countries the mean age remains roughly stable. During the transition period, the postponement of marriage prevails in most of the countries and is even more intensive than the rise of the mean age of the mother at the birth of her first child. The mean age of females at their first marriage rises by at least by 1.2 years. The timing effects and the reduced percentage of women getting married contribute to the overall nuptiality decline.

Unfortunately, there are no official data on cohabitation and LAT relations to show the extent to which the increase in extramarital births in the 1990s might be attributed to cohabitation being on the rise and to the increasing number of single mothers. Sobotka (2001) demonstrates a large variety among countries with respect to single motherhood and cohabitation. Rabušic (2001) indicates that cohabitation is becoming a routine lifestyle in the Czech Republic. In Poland as well, premarital cohabitation and LAT relations are on the rise, especially among the younger generation.

In 1990 divorce rates are relatively low compared to those in the developed countries: the lowest divorce rate is in Slovenia (0.9) and the highest in Latvia (4 divorces per 1000 people). In 1990–1998 some countries either stabilize or exhibit a slight increase in their divorce rates (the Czech Republic, Slovakia, Bulgaria, Poland, Slovenia, Hungary), in other countries the relatively high divorce rates decline (Estonia, Latvia, Lithuania, the Russian Federation), and Romania experiences a visible increase. As a result the crude divorce rate ranges from 1.1 (Poland, Slovenia) to 4.3 (the Russian Federation) in 2000.

Linking changes in the CEE countries in the 1990s to developments in other European countries, the following conclusions can be drawn. In the beginning of the 1990s the CEE countries constitute a visibly separate group in terms of fertility and nuptiality levels as well as the mean age of mothers at the birth of their first child. In 2000 this group still differs greatly from other European countries (groups A, B, C and D), though its position has changed from the highest to the lowest fertility and nuptiality rates. The European countries become more homogenous in this respect, but the picture is diversified: there are increases in many countries but in others the decline continues. Changes in fertility patterns consistently result in an increase of the mean age of mothers at first birth and the mean age of childbearing but at different paces and the rising heterogeneity holds true for developed countries as well.

Table 7.3 Main nuptiality indicators for selected European countries in 1980, 1990, 2000

Countries	Total first marriage rates-females (below age 50)			Mean age at first marriage-females			Crude divorce rates (per 1000 of population)		
	1980	1990	2000	1980	1990	2000	1980	1990	2000
Bulgaria	0.97	0.90	0.52	21.3	21.4	24.1	1.5	1.3	1.3
Czech Republic	0.90	1.02	0.50	21.5	21.6	24.5	2.6	3.1	2.9
Estonia	0.94	0.79	0.39	22.6	22.5	24.8	4.1	3.7	3.1
Former GDR	0.81	0.64	0.47[a]	21.8	23.3	25.3[b]	2.7	2.0	1.9[a]
Hungary	0.89	0.77	0.49	21.2	21.9	24.6	2.6	2.4	2.4
Latvia	0.97	0.92	0.40	22.8	22.3	24.5	5.0	4.0	2.6
Lithuania	0.94	1.06	0.51	23.0	22.3	23.5	3.2	3.4	2.9
Poland	0.90	0.91	0.63	22.7	22.6	23.9	1.1	1.1	1.1
Romania	1.02	0.92	0.64	21.5	22.0	23.4	1.5	1.4	1.4
Russian Federation	0.96	1.00	0.75[b]	22.4	21.9	22.0[b]	4.2	3.8	4.3
Slovak Republic	0.87	0.96	0.52	21.9	21.9	24.0	1.3	1.7	1.7
Slovenia	0.79	0.51	0.45	22.5	23.7	26.7	1.2	0.9	1.1

Notes:
a) data for 1999.
b) data for 1995.

Source: Recent Demographic Developments in Europe, Council of Europe, 2001.

In the beginning of the 1990s the CEE countries are heterogeneous in terms of the percentage of extramarital births, be it at lower levels than in most of the other countries (similar to values found for group D). The diversified increase of this behavioural indicator leads to growing heterogeneity in all the countries.

So the observed convergence between the countries in terms of fertility and nuptiality levels and divergence in terms of their patterns seem to confirm opinions on the persistent diversity in family patterns, rooted in cultural and societal contexts (Coleman, 1996; Kuijsten, 1996).

MAIN PROCESSES UNDERLYING DEMOGRAPHIC CHANGES IN SELECTED CEE COUNTRIES IN THE 1990s

There is a growing consensus that fertility and nuptiality trends in countries in transition follow those in more developed countries but the changes are faster. However, a similarity of trends does not necessarily mean the change determinants are identical. There is little consensus about the interpretations and explanations of changes observed in the CEE countries. To authors who feel these changes represent a demographic crisis resulting from transformation processes, the economic determinants are crucial. Other authors (Kotowska, 1998; Lesthaeghe and Moors, 2000; Rabušic, 2001) who suggest applying the SDT concept to recent developments in the CEE countries also note that changing values might be relevant.

In the discussion presented here on possible explanations for nuptiality and fertility changes, I refer to the SDT conceptual framework. This approach distinguishes three groups of modernization processes underlying behavioural changes in developed economies (van de Kaa, 1994):

1. Structural processes (industralization, urbanization, development of services and other processes leading to the development of the post-industrial society and welfare state).
2. Culture (silent revolution, progress in democracy, the rise of universalistic values and norms, ideological pluralism, secularization, individualization, higher need orientation).
3. Technology (second contraceptive revolution and spread of television information, improvements in transport, communication, health care, medical technology, contraceptive technology).

Instead of opposing the two common explanations for social change and economic determinants, I would argue that although the two groups of determinants do shape the observed demographic changes, their impact seems to be diversified across countries and changes over time. The structural component plays a much more important role in terms of economic restrictions and incentives than in developed economies. Moreover, the crisis hypothesis implicitly assumes that the fertility decline might be viewed as an adjustment to all the shocks related to the transformation processes, and an improved economic situation would lead to a return to previous fertility patterns. However, reforms in countries in transition are related to deep institutional changes affecting people's perception of their life choices. And a return to old fertility and nuptiality patterns is unlikely.

The transition to a market economy is also at different stages. The Central European countries are more successful at implementing reforms whereas other countries, especially Bulgaria, Romania and the Russian Federation, are still experiencing an economic and social collapse. Together with the cultural context, this can lead to a differentiated interplay between economic and social change. The adjustment to economic constraints seems to play a crucial role at the beginning of the transition and remains highly important, especially in countries at a stage of economic deterioration. In the course of the transformation, demographic changes might be increasingly affected by shifts in attitudes and behaviour shaped by changing norms and values. However, economic determinants still continue to exert influence.

Two components of the transition process can be identified as exogenous factors or forcing development variables: The reassignment of economic functions between the state, the enterprise and the household and the changing conditions of labour market participation (Kotowska, 1994, 1998). In all the CEE countries, social solidarity declines; the state is no longer the main employer and provider of social services and support. Similarly, public and private sector employers no longer provide social services relevant to families (e.g. childcare services – nurseries, kindergartens, after-school programmes, children's summer or winter camps, sports, health, tourism). This shift leads to a growing responsibility on the part of household members for welfare. Individuals become more dependent on family solidarity. Personal resources such as personal income and the skills and abilities of household members become more important in the new circumstances. There are new consumption opportunities and more efforts are required to acquire income due to the new labour market conditions, and this all contributes to the importance of economic factors in individual choices. However, the reassignment of economic functions is not accompanied by the construction of effective markets or a system of income transfers covering protection from poverty. This is why an increase in economic and social inequality seems to be considered a non-transient effect of the reforms in the CEE countries.

Changing labour market participation results from institutional changes related to the labour market conditions, economic reforms (restructuring of the economy and employment, changes in the demand for labour) and changes in the labour supply. Economic reforms in all these countries impose a fundamental reconstruction of labour market control mechanisms aimed at more effective management of the workforce, greater labour productivity and a better quality of work. People are now, in general, confronted with more professional career and lifestyle opportunities and possibilities to influence their economic and social position as well as their life course. Under the previous system, professional careers were strongly affected by political affiliations. Currently, individuals' positions are more dependent on their personal skills and ability to act in new circumstances. However, gaining a desired status on the labour market is relatively difficult and uncertain due to the increased competition, changes in the employment status of workers (from employed to self-employed and employer, and from the state to the private sector) and the threat of unemployment. Visible unemployment is a new phenomenon in the CEE countries. Its high incidence strongly restricts possibilities to shape professional and family carriers.

These two forcing development variables result from the institutional changes underlying economic reforms, political structures and the reorganization of the state and society. They have considerable impact at the macro-level (e.g. income redistribution effects, the changing position of the state, labour market structures) as well as the micro- and meso-levels. For individuals there is more responsibility and competition, and for families and households, there are changes in household welfare, increasing links between household welfare and human resources. There are also striking changes in social stratification, with losers and winners as a result of the transition.

Change in Household Welfare

A lowering of the household welfare level is widely noted in all the countries. The household budget is hit from two directions by reforms: the average household income has decreased due to lower wages, unemployment, and a reduction in the financial support for the family, and household expenditure has increased due to inflation (especially early in the transition) and the rising costs of raising children, housing and health care. A severe cut in public spending on social services (education, childcare facilities, housing and health care) has led to a shift in the costs of education and health care from the state to the family, with numerous households having a difficult time obtaining enough income to live on.

Due to the decreases in output experienced by all the transition econo-mies, at any rate at the early stages of the transformation, the average income has declined. From 1989 to 1993 the real GDP per capita declined substan-tially in all the CEE countries. The same holds true for the real income per capita (except in Hungary) (Milanovic, 1997). Despite the economic recovery in a growing number of transition countries, economic and social inequality and a considerable incidence of poverty still characterize the population's absolute and relative deprivation. Income inequality has increased rapidly, mainly as a result of sharply rising wage differentiation (Milanovic, 1997;

Rutkowski, 1995, 1996). Income differences are becoming similar to those in developed economies, but the process goes from more equality to more inequality. This change has been accompanied by the universal increase in poverty, at least until 1995. Unemployed, less educated people, single parents, farmers, families with three or more children, young adults, more often women than men, and retired people (in some countries) are subject to a higher poverty risk (Milanovic, 1997). As a result of rising economic inequality, social diversification is on the rise as well.

Weakening Position of the Family

A substantial reduction in financial support for the family has also contributed to the economic decline in many households. In the centrally planned economy, social solidarity supported family life via widely accessed childcare services (nurseries, kindergartens, after-school programmes) provided and subsidized by the state or the company. Moreover, various family and child-related benefits, payments and allowances created a family supportive environment. Parental leaves, often paid, with a guarantee of re-employment facilitated a combination of paid work and family duties despite rigid work patterns (full-time jobs, fixed working hours) and the under- developed service sector. Furthermore, the provision of housing related to family status and the number of children, special loans for young couples and free or inexpensive education and social services (children's summer or winter camps, sports, health, tourism) kept the costs of raising children low.

This family-supportive environment has changed dramatically during the transition. Due to the declining role of the state in the economy and rapidly diminishing state resources, the state is no longer the single employer and provider of social services and benefits. Cuts in social programme first strike women as mothers, and whoever is mainly responsible for families. Income support to families have declined, as have institutional childcare facilities. The decreasing number of places at public nurseries and kindergartens has been accompanied by an increase in their costs. At the same time company-run nurseries and kindergartens have disappeared and state institutions now act on the basis of market principles.[3] Maternity entitlements, in contrast, have remained relatively stable and in some countries the duration of maternity leaves has increased. However, there are now fewer parents on leave and the effects of longer maternity leaves on women's labour market participation can be negative. Since maternity leaves are predominantly related to employment, the loss of jobs during the transformation also has a negative impact on women's access to maternity benefits (Women in Transition, 1999, pp. 49 - 57).

Summing up, during the transition families have come to rely less and less on state support. Moreover, legally guaranteed support is considerably mitigated by labour market conditions. There has been a parallel rise in the costs of raising children due to the higher costs of education and health care and the rising opportunity costs.

Poorer Labour Market Situation for Women

The conversion from a job-rights to a job-search economy has dramatically changed labour market conditions. New principles now apply to the economy (efficiency and cost criteria), restructuring employment under the persistent oversupply of labour. Economic growth, which does not generate a proportional increase in the demand for labour, and the increasing value of labour force mobility now differentiate men's and women's labour market positions; Puhani, 1995; Heinen, 1995; Kotowska, 1995; Kowalska, 1999; Ingham, Ingham and Dománski, 2001). They are now confronted with a new phenomenon – open unemployment, in most countries on a large and often unanticipated scale (only the Czech Republic is an exception). The risk of unemployment varies by gender, age, place of residence and educational level. Young people (under 35), unskilled workers (most of whom have no more than a basic vocational education), and women (except in Hungary and Estonia) are the groups most exposed to the threat of unemployment (Central European countries' employment and labour market review, 1999, 2000, 2001).

Under the socialist regime, women's labour market participation was high. Women's wide access to paid work mainly resulted from the labour-intensive economy, its low productivity and its wage policies. Low wages led to a need for two incomes to support a family. Women's employment was also ideologically supported by equating emancipation with employment and presenting it as one of the main advantages of the communist system. The high labour market participation of women coexisted with a traditional model of the family. Despite the social acceptance of the dual-earner family model, the female role was still mainly perceived as that of wife and mother, and the husband's main responsibility was to provide an income for his family. This model has been called the externally directed model of women's participation in paid work (Siemieńska, 1997). Conditions for labour participation (job-rights economy) and the provision of the childcare facilities made it possible for women to combine family duties and paid work, but it meant an increasingly heavy burden on their shoulders (Kotowska, 1995; Rabušic, 2001;

Titkow, 2001).

In developed market economies, however, women's labour market participation has gradually increased in different economic settings (services, flexible work patterns, part-time jobs) and is shaped by changing norms and values related to women's role in the society. This model is called the internally directed model (Siemieńska, 1997). The various conditions underlying women's economic activity in both types of economies have led to much higher female labour force participation in the CEE countries than in many Western countries at the beginning of the 1990s.

The economic and ideological reasoning underpinning women's participation in paid work has been rapidly replaced by purely economic arguments. The evident weakening of women's position on the labour market may be illustrated by a relatively high unemployment risk, far more hardship resulting from leaving the market, and worsening working conditions.

Social Change

The social dimensions of the transformation processes in the CEE countries pertain to the slow development of the middle class, growing stratification due to economic and social inequality, absolute and relative deprivation, a loss of security at the social and individual level, the slow and gradual development of civil society, the increasing role of political and religious groups, the need to be mobile and flexible to take advantage of whatever opportunities there are, the tendency to become economically independent at a later age, which are all different from the trends observed in developed economies. There are also certain similarities: the increase in the opportunity costs of marriage and childbearing, greater independence from partners, increasing difficulty combining the social roles of partners and parents and so forth. These macro- and micro-level effects define constraints for individual choices, e.g. for demographic decisions.

Despite new restrictions, mostly economic ones, the younger generations now bear more responsibility for their life course, and their individual ability to shape their life course is still increasing. In the course of the transition from a uniform ideology to a more liberal free market ideology, people are becoming more receptive to new ideas and influences. Moreover, processes related to technology, i.e. the revolution in information technology, have resulted in a rapid spread of information and tools and a striking reduction in their costs. In addition, improved transport and communication have stimulated the dissemination of new ideas, norms and values. Be it with varying intensity among the CEE countries, alternative lifestyles are generally more accepted and tolerated, and individualistic attitudes and a focus on self-fulfilment are more common, especially among younger generations. Widespread know-how on family planning, a growing availability of modern contraceptives, the growing acceptance of sex outside marriage and sexual initiation at an earlier age all combine to create a favourable environment for alternative lifestyles.

These changes can be attributed to modernization accompanied by an adoption of Western ideas, norms and behaviour patterns as well as the globalization of culture. However, people's attitudes and behaviour are affected by a permanent confrontation between two systems of norms and values – those related to the socialist regime versus those generated by the new capitalist economic and political regime (Sztompka, 2000). Individualization, self-realization, autonomy and responsibility for one's own position constitute values strongly preferred under the new circumstances and reinforce the pursuit of personal lifestyles and new attitudes to marriage, children and family.

Unfortunately, only very few studies have been conducted on value changes in the CEE countries that can directly document these interpretations. Studies by Siemieńska (1997) and Titkow (2001) illustrate the visible change in the perception of women's role, especially among the younger generation. The socially accepted family model is a mixture of features attributed to the traditional model as well as the partner model, but with the emphasis on the former. However, partner relations have gradually become more and more valued, especially among the well-educated (Siemieńska, 1997; Titkow, 2001). The statistical data on time use in households seem to confirm that household duties are still mainly women's responsibility. There are some indicators of changes in the division of household work between men and women, especially in the younger generation (Kotowska, 2001). The analysis by Rabušic (2001), based on the European Values Study, confirms that the younger generations in the Czech Republic no longer consider self-realization and life fulfilment as exclusively meaning having children and a family. Piscová (2001) uses the same set of data to demonstrate a similar change in values in the Slovak Republic.

The increasing value of human capital is one of the main social dimensions of the transformation in the CEE countries. Labour market analyses and changes in wage distribution indicate sharply increasing returns to education (Rutkowski, 1995, 1996; Kotowska, 1997; Liwiński, et al., 2000). University attendance has sharply increased despite the rising cost of education.[4] However, this process is accompanied by rising inequality in the access to education, mostly due to strong income disparities among different groups.[5]

CONCLUSIONS

The predominantly structure-based processes might be viewed as reflecting intended and non-intended changes in collective solidarity as well as ongoing and desired changes in family solidarity patterns. The CEE countries have simultaneously undergone processes directly related to the transition to a market economy and to large-scale structural and cultural transformation processes. A demographic response expressed by family-linked behaviour could thus be even more intense and differentiated than in developed economies and be accompanied by increasing social diversification in relatively less well-off societies that would require special attention for social solidarity.

Changes in fertility and nuptiality have taken much the same path in the CEE countries as in developed economies, but with a different intensity. However, although there are also certain similarities, the underlying processes differ greatly. The main differences relate to the role of the structural component: increasing income diversification, economic inequality and poverty result in sharp social differences that are reflected in a shift to greater inequality. In principle, people are confronted with more behavioural options and more freedom than under socialism, but with fewer possibilities to take advantage of them. Simultaneously, no efficient networks have been created to facilitate mobility between transition's losers and winners. As a result, economic factors seem to be more important as regards the demographic changes in the CEE countries than in developed economies.

The weakening position of the family is one of the crucial changes in the CEE countries. The same change has been noted in developed economies, but its context is different. In some countries the development of a market economy and a simultaneous welfare state has undermined the family's role as society's fundamental building block and primary welfare institution. The displacement of household functions has been facilitated since the 1960s and combined with the ideational change, this has led to a reformulation of the family model.

In countries in transition, two basic counter-processes define the position of the family and household: a) a reformulation of the responsibilities of the state, the company and the household, resulting in the household taking more responsibility for its welfare, and b) a striking reduction of the family support network, changes in labour market participation, and the marketization of social services, jointly making the household's welfare more insecure. All this has resulted in an increase in the structural incompatibility between the labour market and the family.

The weakening position of the family in the CEE countries has been accompanied by a weakening of the state. It is clear that under new economic and political regimes, the role of the state is subject to change. However, the weakening of the state in the CEE countries has not solely been the result of a redefinition of its position and rapidly diminishing state resources. The main reason has been the lack of ideas on how to respond to the new social challenges emerging during the transformation.

Despite the transition-specific context, like the changes in the fertility and marriage rates observed in developed economies, the changes in the CEE countries can be considered in terms of the reconciliation of work and family commitments (Pailhé, 2000). Reconsidering work and family commitments means examining gender roles, which was not done in public debates under socialism and would be necessary in order to reformulate the perception of women's labour market participation.

There are other transition-specific phenomena related to the increasing opportunity costs of marriage and fertility. First, fertility changes in the CEE countries are jointly affected by the basic factors usually cited as factors in a fertility decline: the rising costs of children, causing a fertility decline in developed economies before 1960 (i.e. the quantity - quality shift) and the rising marriage and parenthood opportunity costs relevant after 1960 (Becker, 1960, 1981). Easterlin (1961, 1968, 1987) shows that rising competition on the labour market and increasing consumption aspirations might affect professional career orientations and attitudes to starting a family among the younger generations. Altogether it diminishes the attractiveness of a traditional life path (early and almost universal marriage and early first childbearing) and makes becoming a family economically disadvantageous. In addition, new consumption opportunities and the promotion of a consumption and leisure culture cause shifts towards a materialistic, pragmatic approach to life.

Second, in all the countries in transition there is a need for simultaneous investments in the human capital of children and adults (including parents). This results from the rising competition on the labour market and the necessary adjustment of the labour force to the new demands for skills generated by the transformation processes and general trends in the labour markets. Parallel investments in the human capital of children and adults (parents) not only contribute to a rise in the relative costs of children, they also contribute to an incease in the opportunity costs of marriage and parenthood. Due to the labour market changes, this seems to be of special relevance in the CEE countries.

NOTES

1. His detailed study on time patterns of fertility and nuptiality changes in 1982–1993 gives two different patterns of fertility timing and magnitude, one for Central European countries and one for Baltic countries and the Russian Federation. The first pattern is relatively diversified among the countries, with the fertility decline at varying speeds and clearly accelerated in the early 1990s. The second one is more similar for the countries considered, with the upward tendency turning into a sharp decline in the 1990s.

2. In Poland, Hungary and the former GDR, the changes in nuptiality begin a year earlier than the changes in fertility whereas in the Slovak Republic and Estonia they begin at the same time as the changes in fertility. In the other countries the onset of the fertility decline is followed by the onset of the decrease in first marriages (Macura, 1995).

3. In 1996–1997 kindergarten enrolments stabilize or even improve in most countries. Changes in enrolment rates do not closely follow the changes in female labour force participation rates, which suggests that an interplay of household income, family structure, cultural patterns and policy choice is becoming more important (*Women in Transition*, 1999).

4. In Poland the number of students tripled in 1990–2000, as did the enrolment rates.

5. Survey data for Poland indicate inequality between urban and rural areas at the secondary school level, which only increases at the university level (Jóźwiak et al., 2000).

REFERENCES

Becker, G.S. (1960), 'An economic analysis of fertility', in *Demographic and Economic Change in Developed Countries, A Conference of the Universities – National Bureau for Economic Research*, Princeton University Press, Princeton.

Becker, G.S. (1981), *A Treatise on the Family*, Harvard University Press, Cambridge.

Central European Countries' Employment and Labour Market Review, *Studies and Research*, European Commision – Eurostat, no. 1/1999, 2/2000, 1/2001.

Coleman, D. (1996), 'New patterns and trends in European fertility: International and sub–national comparisons', in D. Coleman (ed.), *Europe's Population in the 1990s*, Oxford, pp. 1–61.

Easterlin, R.A. (1961), 'The American baby boom in historical perspective', *American Economic Review*, **51**, 869–911.

Easterlin, R.A. (1968), *Population, Labour Force, and Long Swings in Economic Growth*, New York: National Bureau for Economic Research.

Easterlin, R.A. (1987), *Birth and Fortune: The Impact of Numbers on Personal Welfare.*, 2nd ed., New York: Basic Books.

Heinen, J. (1995), 'Unemployment and women's attitudes in Poland', *Social Politics*, **2** (1), 91–110.

Ingham, M., H. Ingham, H. Donmánski (eds.) (2001), *Women on the Polish Labour Market,* Budapest: Central European University Press.

Jóźwiak, J., I.E. Kotowska and A. Kowalska (2000), 'Demographic processes, the labour market and education', in *Economic and Social Effects of Education* (in Polish), Warsaw: Institute for Problems of Contemporary Civilization, pp. 87–120.

Kaa, D.J. van de (1987), 'Europe's second demographic transition', *Population Bulletin,* **42** (1), Washington DC: Population Reference Bureau, Inc.

Kaa, D.J. van de (1994), 'The second demographic transition revisited: Theories and expectations', 1993, in G.C.N. Beets, R.L. Cliquet, G. Dooghe and J. de Jong Gierveld (eds), *Population and Family in the Low Countries 1993. Late Fertility and Other Current Issues,* Amsterdam, Lisse: NIDI–CBGS Publications, Swets & Zeitlinger B.V., pp. 81 – 126.

Kaa, D.J. van de (1999), 'Europe and its population: The long view', in D.J. van de Kaa, G. Gesano, H. Leridon and M. Okólski (eds), *European Populations: Unity in Diversity,* Dordrecht: Kluwer Academic, pp.1–49.

Kaa, D.J. van de and Lesthaeghe R. (1986), 'Twee demografische transities', in D.J. van de Kaa and R. Lesthaeghe (eds), *Bevolking: groei en krimp,* Deventer: Van Loghem Slaterus.

Kotowska, I.E. (1994), *Household Projections. Problems and Methods* (in Polish), Monografie i Opracowania, no. 396, Warsaw: Warsaw School of Economics – SGH.

Kotowska, I.E. (1995), 'Discrimination against women in the labour market in Poland during the transition to a market economy', *Social Politics,* **2** (1), 76–90.

Kotowska, I.E. (1997), 'Equality of women and men in the labour market', in R. Siemieńska (ed.), *Around Problems of Occupational Equality by Gender* (in Polish), Warsaw: Scholar Publisher Company, pp. 85–106.

Kotowska, I.E. (1998), 'The second demographic transition and demographic changes in Poland in the 1990' (in Polish), *Studia Demograficzne,* **4,** 134, 3–35.

Kotowska, I.E. (2001), 'Demographic and labour market developments in the 1990s', in M. Ingham, H. Ingham and H. Domański (eds), *Women on the Polish Labour Market,* Central European University Press, pp. 77–110.

Kowalska, A. (1996), *Females Economic Activity and their Position in the Labour Market,* Studies and Statistical Analyses, Central Statistical Office, Warsaw.

Kowalska, A. (1999), 'Women in the labour market' (in Polish), in I.E. Kotowska (ed.), *Demographic Changes in Poland in the 1990s from the Perspective of the Second Demographic Transition,* Monografie i Opracowania, no. 461, Warsaw: Warsaw School of Economics, pp. 35–81.

Kuijsten, A. (1995), 'Recent trends in household and family structures in Europe: An Overview', in E. van Imhoff, A. Kuijsten, P. Hooimeijer and L. van Wissen (eds), *Household Demography and Household Modeling*, New York and London: Plenum Press, pp. 53–84.

Kuijsten, A. (1996), 'Changing family patterns in Europe', *European Journal of Population*, **12** (2), 115–43.

Lesthaeghe, R. (1991), *The Second Demographic Transition in Western Countries: An Interpretation*, IPD Working Paper 1991–2, Brussels.

Lesthaeghe, R. (1995), 'The second demographic transition in western countries: an interpretation', in K.O.Manson and A. M. Jensen (eds), *Gender and Family Change in Industrialized Countries*, Oxford: Clarendon Press, pp. 17–62.

Lesthaeghe, R. and G. Moors (2000), *Recent trends in fertility and household formation in the industrialized world. Interface Demography*, IPD Working Paper 2000–200, Brussels: Department of Social Research, Vrije Universiteit.

Liwiński, J., M.W. Socha and U. Sztanderska (2000), 'Education and the labour market', in *Economic and Social Effects of Education* (in Polish), Warsaw: Institute for Problems of Contemporary Civilization, pp. 27–85.

Macura, M. (1995), 'Fertility and nuptiality changes in Central and Eastern Europe: 1982–1993', *Studia Demograficzne*, **4**, 122, 9–34.

Milanovic, B., (1997) *Income, Inequality and Poverty during the Transition from Planned to Market Economy*, Washington DC: World Bank.

Pailhé, A. (2000), *Family responsibilities and discrimination on the labour market*, paper presented at the Workshop on Gender Relations, Family and Work, Zahradky Castle, Czech Republic, September 2000.

Piscová, M. (2001), *The changes in family behaviour and family strategies in Slovakia*, paper presented at EAPS European Population Conference, Helsinki, June 2001.

Puhani, P. (1995), *Labour supply of married women in Poland. A microeconometric study based on the Polish labour force survey*, Discussion Paper no. 95–12, Zentrum für Europäische Wirtschaftsforschung GmbH, Labour Economics, Human Resources and Social Policy Series.

Rabušic, L. (2001), 'Value change and demographic behaviour in the Czech Republic', *Czech Sociological Review*, **1**, 99–122.

Recent Demographic Developments in Europe (2001), Council of Europe Publishing, Strasbourg 2001.

Rutkowski, J. (1995), *Changes in the wage structure during economic transition in Central and Eastern Europe*, World Bank, Data Report Series, Paper No.1, May 1995.

Rutkowski, J. (1996), 'High skills pay off: The changing wage structure during economic transition in Poland', *Economics of Transition*, **4** (1), 89–112.

Siemieńska, R. (1997), 'Values and attitudes conditioning the female presence in the labour market', in R.Siemieńska (ed.), *Around Problems of Occupational Equality by Gender* (in Polish), Scholar Publisher Company, Warsaw, pp. 61–83.

Sobotka, T. (2001), *Ten years of rapid fertility changes in European postcommunist countries: Evidence and interpretation*, paper presented at EAPS European Population Conference, Helsinki, June 2001.

Sztompka, P. (2000), *Trauma of Change. Social Costs of Transformation* (in Polish), Instytut Studiów Politycznych Polskiej Akademii Nauk, Warszawa.

Titkow, A. (2001), 'On the appreciated role of women', in M. Ingham, H. Ingham and H. Domański (eds), *Women on the Polish Labour Market*, Central European University Press, pp. 21–40.

Women in Transition. The MONEE Project CEE/CIS/Baltics, Regional Monitoring Report. UNICEF, International Child Development Centre, no. 6, 1999.

PART THREE

Shifting Patterns of Family Solidarity

8. Some Darker Sides of Family Solidarity

Aafke Komter

In most Western countries, children and intergenerational bonds are still important sources of support for the elderly, but concern for the continuity of this support is widespread. Over the past two centuries, drastic changes have affected the nature and extent of family solidarity. In the absence of social security and institutions of social welfare, kin served as the most essential resource for economic assistance and security, but there has been a gradual weakening of kin interdependence. In the past, commitment to the survival and economic well-being of the family took priority over individual needs. Anthropological studies suggest that 'kinship dues' were traditionally the main source of family support (Sahlins, 1972). The instrumental orientation toward the family has gradually been replaced by a more individualistic and affective one and a greater emphasis on individual needs and personal happiness (Hareven, 1995). This has given rise to concern about the vitality of family bonds and intergenerational solidarity. Demographic changes have significantly added to this concern (Bengtson, 2001). Never before have the elderly lived so long and never before has the younger generation been relatively so small. The greater variety in family structure is also thought to have caused weaker traditional family patterns and values. International studies on cultural and other values show that greater individualization is accompanied by less family loyalty and identification (Inglehart, 1977; Popenoe, 1988).

In addition to demographic trends, life course changes can impact family solidarity. Recent research in the Netherlands shows that the phase of childhood and adolescence has become longer in that societal responsibility is postponed and the period of dependence on societal transfers is prolonged (Liefbroer and Dykstra, 2000). In adulthood the period of participation in paid labour has become shorter. In the Netherlands, the percentage of working people in the 55 - 64 age group has decreased from 35% in 1975 to 28.7% in 1998 (SCP, 1999). The phase of old age has become longer because of increased longevity. More and more old people will need care and support, though fewer people, especially women, will be available to provide them. At the same time, more young elderly people will be available to provide financial as well as care support for the younger generation. Both these trends can affect family solidarity.

Family solidarity is also influenced by the wider social context of the welfare state and its social security and care arrangements. Since their introduction, western welfare regimes have incorporated an implicit social contract between the generations based on intergenerational as well as intragenerational transfers of resources by means of taxation and social expenditure (Walker, 1996; Bengtson and Achenbaum, 1993). Public pensions and health and social care are the core of this social contract. There is a similar but informal social contract specifying care obligations and relations in the family. In the welfare state social contract as well as the implied contract between the generations in the family, the idea of reciprocity is quintessential. The welfare state has institutionalized and encouraged an expectation of reciprocity in its system of inter- and intragenerational transfers. Similarly, Bengtson et al. argue that the contract between the generations in a family 'calls for the parents to invest a major portion of their resources throughout their adult years in the rearing of children; in old age, the care-giving is expected to be reversed' (1990, p. 255). Walker (1996) cites the many ways this macrosocial contract interacts with the microsocial one among family members. The restructuring of western welfare states since the 1970s has profoundly affected generational relations within families, particularly coupled with a rising life expectancy. Many western welfare states have faced cuts in social expenditure, putting a greater burden on families to provide informal care. Inversely, gender-based care relations within families are in transition, which may affect welfare state social policy. The reduction of women's availability as care-givers is a new reality that needs to be taken into account in social policy.

This chapter addresses family solidarity, conceived as solidarity within the network of family and close relatives, and the informal solidarity contract between family members. A distinction is drawn between two dimensions of intergenerational relations, one at the macrolevel of welfare state provisions related to family care and the other at the microlevel of informal care within the family itself. An interesting question is how the two levels interact with one another. Some empirical results on this interaction are presented. The theme is then positioned in the context of the scientific and societal debate about generations and their interrelations. Evidence is presented on concrete intergenerational solidarity in the form of care for the elderly by the younger generation and attitudes towards this care. Some of the darker sides of family solidarity are addressed as well: the not always positive experiences of care-givers and recipients and the selectivity of family solidarity. In the conclusion the balance is drawn.

MACROSOCIAL AND MICROSOCIAL DIMENSIONS OF FAMILY SOLIDARITY

Most welfare states are based on a silent contract between the generations, with the younger one contributing financially to the care needed by the older one (Walker, 1996). By levying taxes and premiums and by means of social policy, the state provides the material and physical support required by the elderly if they are no longer able to earn a living or care for themselves properly. Compared to the United States and the southern European countries, western and northern European countries have a relatively generous system of pensions and additional partly subsidized state facilities for the elderly such as home care, district nursing, provisions at homes for the disabled and meals delivered at home. So it is not surprising that many old people in western and northern Europe prefer institutional, state care to lasting dependence on their children (de Jong-Gierveld and van Solinge, 1995).

The microsocial and macrosocial dimensions of intergenerational relations are not completely separate. In fact they are interdependent in several ways. Certain features of welfare state social policy for the aged, in particular the ample and easy access to care arrangements, impact the care provided within families. For instance, cuts in state care for the elderly may cause people to turn more to informal care-givers, which means a larger workload for them. Changes in pension amounts can impact the financial and physical dependence of the aged on their family members. These trends are often the unintended side effects of state policy. Another way the state influences microsocial, intrafamilial care arrangements is via the social construction and organization of the traditional family, where women play an important role as informal care-givers. In many western countries, the state is hesitant to interfere too directly with the caring potential of families, fearing as it does that an overly generous supply of state care will reduce the spontaneous care provided within families (Walker, 1996). A paradoxical effect can be detected here: the traditional family ideal is declining rapidly, but at the same time the principle of state non-intervention serves to reinforce traditional family relations.

But the influence also goes the other way around: micro-arrangements are reflected in macrosocial policy, or in the use that is made of macrosocial arrangements (Esping-Andersen, 1999). The nature and quality of relations between parents and their adult children impact the children's willingness to provide care for their parents, and thus the extent to which formal care arrangements need to be called upon. The extent to which adult children and their parents have access to formal, state-based arrangements and facilities will also influence the balance between formal and informal care in a particular family. Financial resources and familiarity with the formal routes to the necessary care and support are some obvious determinants of the access to public care arrangements, and therefore of the actual use that is made of public benefits.

What then is the nature of the relation between the macrosocial and microsocial contract between generations? The idea that a decrease in the care provided by the welfare state will lead to an increase in informal care has been propounded by politicians in periods of structural change in European welfare states: family care as a substitute for state-based care. The substitution thesis may also work the other way around, and is often expressed as a fear: the more the state cares for its citizens, the less its citizens will care for each other. An alternative way to understand the macrosocial and microsocial dimensions of intergenerational relations is the complementarity thesis. It holds that higher levels of formal care go together with higher levels of informal care (see also Knijn in this volume).

Several empirical studies seem to corroborate this (Komter et al., 2000). The findings of the above-mentioned study by Dykstra and de Jong-Gierveld (1997) demonstrate that the most frequent users of informal resources also use formal resources the most. The main focus of the recent book by Arber and Attias-Donfut (2000) is the exchange between adult generations in a framework of the interaction between the public and private domains. They report a study by Künemund and Rein (1999) who used data from a large comparative survey of older people in four Western countries and Japan. The study shows that 'the most important forms of family solidarity with regard to older people take place in those countries where social policies are generous to the welfare of older people' (Arber and Attias-Donfut, 2000, p. 13). The notion that public aid reinforces private aid rather than replacing it is confirmed by these findings. Other research results reported by Attias-Donfut and Arber also show that the rise in public care in recent decades has not resulted in any reduction of informal care-giving by the family. These results are again confirmed in their own study on three-generational families in France based on a representative sample of multi-generational families. The authors conclude:

The complementarity of public and private forms of support has been shown for different categories of transfers. Whether these transfers are for financial help for young adults or care given to the eldest-generation members, the results are the same. In all cases, public benefits increase the recipients' chances of an additional and complementary form of support from members of their family lineage (Arber and Attias-Donfut, 2000, p. 65).

In short, public transfers reshape and sustain family solidarity (see also Kohli, 1999).

In the next section we shift our attention from the macrosocial and microsocial dimensions of the generational contract to the nature of the contract itself.

THE RELATIONS BETWEEN GENERATIONS

Relations between generations have traditionally been a source of great solidarity as well as fierce conflicts. Throughout history members of the younger generation have detested the older generation because of its old-fashioned ideas and beliefs, rigid attitudes and inability to keep pace with the times. The aged, in turn, were faced with a growing emotional distance from the younger generation. Prejudice always flourished in both directions: contemporary youths don't read books any more, they are only interested in watching TV or playing computer games, they do not make any effort whatsoever and are materialistic and egocentric. And some of the reverse stereotypes: old people had better opportunities, they impede the mobility of the young on the labour market by keeping the better jobs occupied and they grow so old that they cause an enormous rise in health care costs, or will do so in the future. These common-sense notions certainly don't give a satisfying answer to the question of whether there is a serious 'generation problem' today, as Karl Mannheim termed it in 1928, and if it exists, how it manifests itself.

An important preliminary question is: what exactly is a generation? Is a generation a historical concept, referring to a certain group of people of about the same age, who define themselves as being the founders of new values, cultural, political and social changes, like the Vietnam generation or the baby boomers? Does the concept merely indicate a macrosociological, demographic category based on the year of birth? Or do we mean the more micro- sociological categories of generations within the context of the family?

The founding father of the generation theory, Karl Mannheim conceived of a generation as a group of contemporaries who share the feeling of belonging to a certain generation. This feeling arises as a consequence of shared experiences of particular social and historical events that have been formative for the course of their lives. It is a shared consciousness and not so much age that determines a generation. An example originating in the demographical approach but containing elements of the historical conception is Becker's typology of generations. Becker (1992) conceives of a generation as an age cohort occupying a particular position in history, and exhibiting similarities at the individual level (life course, values, behaviour) as well as the structural level (magnitude, composition, culture and organization of the generation). The cohort conception of generations has not only been criticized for being static, it has an additional disadvantage, the 'fallacy of cohort-centrism' (White Riley, quoted in Bengtson and Achenbaum, 1993): the tendency to assume that all the members of a cohort will age in the same way.

Yet a different way to conceive of generations has been developed by Kohli (1996), who takes 'welfare' as his point of departure. Paid employment, contributions to the social security system and the extent to which benefits are received are the criteria he uses to distinguish 'welfare generations'. These criteria are obviously related to the life course; as is noted above, significant changes occur in the life experiences of different groups of people at particular stages of their life.

Rather than focusing on welfare, Arber and Attias-Donfut (2000) prefer to speak of a generation as indicating a particular order in the descent of individuals in a family (see also Bengtson, 1993). In their view there are 'no such predetermined groups of generations, since they are determined by the relative position of individuals to their ascendants and descendants within the family's genealogical axis. There is not necessarily a close identity between family generations and welfare generations' (2000, p. 4). Nowadays, for example, it is quite common for parents and children to all be active on the labour market, and in many families there are two generations of retired family members. Although the status of people within family generations and welfare generations may overlap, in many cases the various generational identities do not coincide.

It is interesting to examine how such a dynamic concept of generations is reflected in the concrete practice of help exchange. The exchange of money, goods and services has traditionally been an important aspect of familial solidarity, in particular as expressed in solidarity between generations. Until the era of industrialization the family was the main unit of production and individual survival depended on economic cooperation within the family. Today the economic exchange between family members is no longer a vital precondition for individual survival. Nevertheless, people's well-being still depends largely on the exchange of goods and services with other people. A substantial part of this exchange still occurs within the family. In the past two decades, the family is believed to have lost much of its significance as 'a haven in a heartless world' (Lasch, 1977). As a result of factors like women's increased labour market participation, their greater economic independence, the liberalization of norms and values and the rising divorce rate, the family is said to have lost much of its former cohesion and original significance. Is there any empirical support for these beliefs? The next section discusses some empirical research results on family solidarity.

SOME EMPIRICAL RESEARCH RESULTS

Intergenerational Solidarity: Values and Beliefs

What values do people share concerning intergenerational solidarity? Euro-barometer surveys on public beliefs about the elderly provide a good international overview (Walker, 1996). One question in these surveys concerns the extent to which the respondents agree with the statement that working people have to contribute to a decent living standard for the elderly by paying taxes or other financial contributions. The responses demonstrate a strikingly high level of solidarity; a strong agreement with the statement is noted among 60.1% of the Danes, 45.9% of the British, 45.7% of the Spanish, 42.4% of the Dutch, 41.2% of the Portuguese and 40.7% of the Irish. Somewhat lower percentages are noted in Greece, Italy, Luxembourg, Belgium and Germany, with the lowest percentage of 25.9% noted in France (Walker, 1996).

The Netherlands Interdisciplinary Demographic Institute (NIDI) has investigated beliefs about assistance for the elderly who need care (Dykstra, 1998). A large majority, 93%, thinks the state has the prime responsibility to provide care for elderly people in need of physical or financial assistance. Another 65% are of the opinion that the elderly should first turn to the state if they are in need of care, and only afterwards to their children. Table 8.1 presents an overview of beliefs about solidarity on the part of the young towards the elderly.

A minority of 18% think that, in the event of rising pension costs, the elderly should start paying higher taxes; this belief is shared by younger and older age groups. However, younger people do think the elderly should assume some financial responsibility for the rising costs of health care. Dykstra notes the possibility that prejudice might play a role in the idea that the growing number of older people is a direct cause of the increased costs. This idea is not correct, since the higher costs of health care are due to the rising costs of personnel and new technologies and not to the increasing number of old people in need of care.

When asked their opinion about being entitled to a job in times of economic scarcity, more of the younger than the older respondents think the young and the old should be equally entitled. A relatively large percentage of young people, 59%, are willing to assume some responsibility for elderly people who need care.

Table 8.1.: Beliefs about solidarity of the young towards the elderly, 1997 (percentage 'agree')

	18 - 44	45 - 64	65 - 79
If retirement pension costs rise, the elderly should pay higher taxes	17	20	20
If health care costs keep rising, the elderly should pay their own share	66	49	40
If there are not enough jobs, elderly and young people should be equally entitled to them	81	77	72
If there are more elderly people in need of care, particularly the young should provide more care	59	56	67

Source: Dykstra (1998).

Concrete Behaviour Towards Family

What people think or believe does not always correspond to how they actually behave. It is much easier to say you feel solidarity towards aged people than to actually behave according to that feeling. What picture arises if we examine the concrete care and support given to the elderly? How do care recipients experience that support and what motives underlie the behaviour of the caregivers?

Figures of the 1994 European Community Household Panel show that adult children, particularly women, give a large share of the informal care the elderly receive (Dykstra, 1997). About 10% of all the European adults in the 35–64 group provide unpaid care to members of older generations on a daily basis, i.e. about 14% of the women and 6% of the men. In the Netherlands about 13% of all the adult women, in particular in the 45-54 age group, provide informal care for the elderly, and more than half of them spend more than four hours a day doing so. Under what conditions can the elderly count on support being provided by their adult children? In a recent study, the Netherlands Interdisciplinary Demographic Institute examined this question in a sample of 1,122 Dutch men and women between 55 and 89 who needed care. A distinction was drawn between informal and formal care, and people with and without a partner, whether or not they are officially married, as well as divorced or widowed people were included in the sample. The results are shown in Table 8.2.

Table 8.2: *Sources of help for men and women above the age of 55 who have children and need daily practical help, according to marital history and present partner status (percentages)*

	First marriage		Ever widowed		Ever divorced	
	M	F	M	F	M	F
With partner, receives informal care from:						
Partner	63	63	54	--*	47	73
other members of the household	5	5	3	--*	3	12
children living outside the home	25	25	23	--*	0	15
other family members	4	3	6	--*	3	0
Receives formal care	18	26	20	--*	18	42
Without partner, receives informal care from:						
members of the household	--*	--*	8	7	0	3
children living outside the home	--*	--*	47	53	13	23
other family members	--*	--*	6	11	0	10
Receives formal care	--*	--*	54	50	50	46

* Too few cases

Source: Gierveld and Dykstra (1998).

Elderly people with partners first receive help from their partners. With respect to intergenerational solidarity, it is interesting to observe that 15 - 20% of the elderly who still have a partner do receive help from their children. Children are apparently the second source of help besides partners. Children are the first ones people without a partner rely on if they need help. This applies far more to people whose partner has died than to divorced people. Apparently, divorce has long-term consequences for the relations with children. It is far less automatic for the children of divorced parents to provide informal care and help than for children whose parents are still married. Of all the categories, divorced fathers receive the least support from their children. However, the children from a possible second marriage play a more important role in caring for their once divorced fathers than for their divorced mothers. As to the relation between informal and formal care, the authors conclude that people who do not receive much informal care do not seem to request formal care more frequently (Dykstra and de Jong-Gierveld, 1997). On the contrary, the most frequent users of informal resources are also the largest users of formal resources.

Several studies suggest a relation between social class and ideas about social class and intergenerational solidarity. Kulis (1992) notes certain images pertaining to solidarity and social class: lower-class people are often thought to mainly give each other practical and instrumental help, whereas the middle and higher classes are more apt to exchange emotional and financial support. In a large-scale survey, Kulis examines instrumental, economic and social help and notes that, contrary to the common belief, middle-class parents give their children more instrumental help than lower-class parents and this also applies to financial and social-emotional help. Dutch research on gift giving also shows evidence of a class-bound difference in gift giving patterns, which can be characterized as a 'friends culture' and a 'family culture'. Well-educated people give more gifts to their friends, and less educated people mainly give gifts to their relatives. This is the case with all kinds of gifts, material and nonmaterial, including care and help (Komter and Vollebergh, 1997).

THE DARKER SIDES OF FAMILY SOLIDARITY

Experiences and Motives of Support Givers and Recipients

What are the experiences of help and care recipients and what are the motives of caregivers? An interesting finding is that a high level of intergenerational solidarity does not necessarily coincide with the psychological well-being of aged family members (Mutran and Reitzes, 1984), and in some cases even threatens it (Roberts and Bengtson, 1988). Under certain conditions such as financial pressures, high family solidarity can generate poor mental health due to excessive obligations and too much of a demand on one's time and resources. In a small-scale qualitative study among elderly men and women in London, Gail Wilson (1993) found that intergenerational solidarity is not automatically experienced as something positive. Often, there is a lack of reciprocity (old age limits the ability to return help and care; see also Rossi and Rossi, 1990, who note similar results), causing feelings of dependency. Receiving and accepting help and care is not unproblematic in this case. Moreover, the care may be experienced as a form of control: Is the house kept clean enough? Does one eat regular meals? Younger people often experience the care they give their aged parents as a burden. Many aged respondents in Wilson's study remark that when the young offer a lot of help, 'love declines and duty takes over' (1993, p. 639). Janet Finch notes in her book *Family Obligations and Social Change* (1989) that women's motives for caring for their aged family members may be rooted in a form of 'prescribed altruism', a strongly felt obligation to demonstrate solidarity with aged family members. Inner norms like this kind of obligated intergenerational solidarity are, of course, strongly connected to the gendered division of labour and care still prevalent in our society.

Various studies on aging and the family discuss the possible negative consequences of intergenerational solidarity (Mutran and Reitzes, 1984; Wilson, 1993), how the care-giver's psychological well-being may be threatened (Ryff and Seltzer, 1995; 1996), or the impact stressful events may have on the quality of parent-child relations (Suitor et al., 1995). Family support can be troubled by conflictive aspects of relationships (House et al. 1988; Bengtson, 2001). People may control their relatives or make demands, thus burdening the relationship. As Boszormenyi-Nagy and Spark (1973) argue convincingly, feelings of loyalty, solidarity and mutual trust are dependent on the silent bookkeeping of giving and receiving among family members. This silent bookkeeping may be transmitted from one generation to the next. Parents try to make up for shortcomings in their own upbringing by giving their children what they missed, and children compensate for the imperfections they experienced. In reality, family ties are often a mixture of love and yearning for love, disappointment or anger, feelings of dependency and a desire for autonomy, in short, they are essentially ambivalent (Luescher and Pillemer, 1998). Troubled or ambivalent feelings underlying family ties may be an important cause of a later lack of solidarity, or solidarity of a type characterized by insincerity, insecurity and stress.

In the Netherlands, Ali de Regt (1993) has noted a sense of obligation that many young people have towards their parents. These feelings are often aroused when they visit their parents or help them in the event of illness. As a result of their increased financial resources, parents now care for their children for much longer than in the past, when children went out to work at a much younger age. Former expectations that children will see to the physical and material well-being of their parents have become less compelling, but the new financial dependency of children may contribute to their sense of feeling obliged to their parents. Although affection can play a role in the relationship between parents and their young adult children, these feelings are not automatic and perhaps never were, and are often mixed with forms of 'prescribed altruism'.

There are empirical indications of a gender difference in caring motives: daughters are thought to be more driven by altruistic motives, and sons by feelings of obligation, expectations concerning inheritance and the frequency of existing contacts (Dykstra and de Jong-Gierveld, 1997). More generally, feelings and motives prove to be related to the category of help and care recipients: feelings of moral obligation are predominant if family help is concerned, and help to friends is often accompanied by feelings of affection, regardless of gender (Komter and Vollebergh, 1997).

In general it can be concluded that the nature of contemporary caring relations between generations depend on a subtle balance between reciprocity, affection and obligation.

Selectivity of Family Solidarity

The aim of a Dutch research project on gift giving (Komter and Schuyt, 1993) was to chart the extent and patterns of gift giving in the Netherlands and gain insight into the motives and feelings surrounding the exchange of gifts. The gifts studied included nonmaterial ones such as care and help and material ones such as presents and money. In a secondary analysis of the research data (Komter and Vollebergh, 2002), the focus was on care as one of the most clear-cut indications of solidarity towards other people. In particular, we investigated the relative importance of familial solidarity and solidarity towards friends. We analysed which categories of respondents received the most care or help.

We distinguished several kinds of help or care: incidental help for example with or with odd jobs around the house, help related to daily activities like shopping or gardening or transporting children, emotional support such as sympathy or consolation, and other kinds of support.

Table 8.3 shows that the largest amount of help is given to relatives, then to friends and lastly to parents and children. Note that parents are probably in a numerical minority since a person cannot have more than four parents and parents-in-law, whereas the number of other relatives and friends can be much greater. Table 8.3 also indicates that help and care given to other relatives can be any kind of help, with a somewhat stronger emphasis on incidental help or care. The same applies to friends. Psychological help is mostly given to relatives and friends. The percentage given to parents is far smaller and appears insignificant where children are concerned: this kind of help is presumably considered so obvious that respondents do not even mention it.

Table 8.3.: *Various kinds of help given to various recipients (in number of times help was given and in percentages of total amount of help given to this category).*

Recipient	Incidental: moving, small jobs in the home	Daily help: transport, gardening, shopping	Relational: support, comforting talk	Taking care of children	Other	Total amount
	N %	N %	N %	N %	N %	N
Parents and parents-in-law	29 (24.8)	64 (54.7)	10 (8.6)	2 (1.7)	12 (10)	117
Children	20 (54)	5 (13.5)	-	10 (27)	2 (5)	37
Extended family	54 (32.7)	34 (20.6)	23 (13.9)	39 (23.6)	15 (9.1)	165
Friends	53 (37)	21 (14.7)	29 (20.3)	27 (18.9)	13 (9.1)	143
Total amount	156 (33.8)	124 (26.8)	62 (13.4)	78 (16.9)	42 (9,1)	462

Source: Komter and Vollebergh (2002).

The same probably applies to help given to one's partner, since it is regarded as so natural that it does not even enter the minds of the respondents. For this reason, help or care given to the partner has been omitted from our analysis. This deletion colours our results to some extent, since mentioning help or care automatically entails some connotation of obligation. In cases where help is natural and automatic, the sense of obligation disappears and is no longer perceived. Nevertheless, it can be concluded that parents and other relatives receive more than twice as much help as friends do.

Another finding is that people without children give significantly more help and care than people with children, particularly to their relatives and friends (Komter and Vollebergh, 2002). Two conclusions can be drawn from the results. First, parents and other relatives are overwhelmingly favoured over friends when giving care or help. Second, people with children are less supportive towards their friends and relatives than people without children. Both findings might be interpreted as manifestations of what Salomon (1992) calls philanthropic particularism, an inherent tendency of voluntary initiatives to favour the people one identifies with most. Our study demonstrates that solidarity in the form of care or help has the same selective aspect: members of the primary and extended family receive more care and help than friends. People who have no family relationships are clearly at a disadvantage with respect to day-to-day solidarity in the form of care and help.

THE PARADOX OF FAMILY SOLIDARITY: SOLIDITY AND AMBIVALENCE

Beliefs about extra-familial, state-based intergenerational solidarity generally refer to a high level of solidarity. In the Netherlands as well as many other European countries there is a high consensus about the desirability of working people making a financial contribution, through taxes or otherwise, to a decent standard of living for the elderly. The Dutch grant a major role to the state when it comes to providing for the elderly who need care or help. Most Dutch people think the state is primarily responsible for the care of the aged and children only come second. In day-to-day reality though, concrete care given to family members is still substantially provided by children. The Netherlands is no exception to the general European level of informal care provided to older generations by adult children, particularly women. Despite fears to the contrary, actual family solidarity is still very solid.

Although family care is still provided on a large scale, the motives under-lying the care given to elderly parents and parents-in-law are based more on an inner sense of obligation – a kind of 'prescribed altruism' – than on feelings of affection and identification. Recipients may experience the care they receive as problematic. Their psychological well-being is not always served best when their own children are the caregivers. Their care and help can be felt as a form of control and the diminished reciprocity when the recipient is older can cause feelings of dependency. Reversely, caregivers frequently experience the care as a heavy burden in terms of time and resources.

The concept of family solidarity seems to automatically direct our attention to positive feelings of connectedness and altruistic acts of helping, but we should bear in mind that family ties are fundamentally different from other social ties in that they are given, not chosen. Family solidarity cannot be isolated from the more negative aspects of care given to relatives or from the deeply ambivalent nature of family ties in general. Though bonds between family members can still be solid in terms of the amounts of care and help that continue to be exchanged, family ties may be troubled or conflictive, and can be experienced as a burden.

Another darker side of family solidarity has to do with its selectivity. Informal care and help can be characterized by the restrictions of philanthropic particularism, a preference to care for relatives over other people who might require care. People who do not have any close relatives are clearly at a disadvantage.

REFERENCES

Arber, S., and C. Attias-Donfut (eds) (2000*), The Myth of Generational Conflict: The Family and State in Ageing Societies*, London: Routledge.

Becker, H. (1992), *Generaties en hun kansen* [Generations and their Chances], Amsterdam: Meulenhoff.

Bengtson, V.L. (1993), 'Is the "contract across generations" changing?', in V.L. Bengtson and H. Achenbaum (eds)*, The Changing Contract across Generations*, New York: Aldine de Gruyter, pp. 3 - 25.

Bengtson, V.L. (2001), 'Beyond the nuclear family: The increasing importance of multigenerational bonds'*, Journal of Marriage and the Family,* **63**, 1 - 16.

Bengtson, V.L. and A. Achenbaum (eds) (1993), *The Changing Contract across Generations*, New York: Aldine de Gruyter.

Bengtson, V.L., C. Rosenthal and L. Burton (1990), 'Families and aging. Diversity and heterogeneity', in R. Binstock and L. George (eds), *Handbook of Aging and Social Sciences* (3rd ed), New York: Academic Press, pp. 263 - 87.

Boszormenyi-Nagy, I. and G.M. Spark (1973), *Invisible Loyalties,* New York: Brunner/Mazel.

Dykstra, P. (1998), 'Moet overheid ouderen koesteren? Onze kijk op ouderenzorg [Should the government pamper the elderly?]', *Demos*, **14** (4), 29 - 31.

Dykstra, P., and J. de Jong Gierveld (1997), 'Huwelijksgeschiedenis en informele en formele hulp aan ouderen' [Marital history and informal and formal care to the elderly], *Bevolking en Gezin*, **3**, 35 - 61.

Esping-Andersen, G. (1999), *Social Foundations of Postindustrial Economies*, Oxford: Oxford University Press.

Finch, J. (1989), *Family Obligations and Social Change*, Cambridge: Polity Press.

Gierveld, J. and P. Dykstra (1998), Scheiden doet lijden [Divorce hurts]. *Demos* **14** (1): 1 – 3.

Hareven, T.K. (1995), 'Historical perspectives on the family and aging', in R. Blieszner and V.H. Bedford (eds), *Handbook of Aging and the Family*, Westport, CT: Greenwood Press, pp. 13 – 31.

House, J.S., D. Umberson and K.R. Landis (1988), 'Structures and processes of social support', *Annual Review of Sociology*, **14**, 293 - 318.

Inglehart, R. (1977), *The Silent Revolution: Changing Values and Political Styles among Western Publics*, Princeton, NJ: Princeton University Press.

Jong-Gierveld, J. de, and H. van Solinge (1995), *Ageing and its Consequences for the socio-medical System*, Straatsburg: Council of Europe Press, Population Studies, no. 29.

Kohli, M. (1996), *The Problem of Generations: Family, Economy, Politics*, Collegium Budapest: Public lecture series.

Kohli, M. (1999), 'Private and public transfers between generations: Linking the family and the state', *European Societies*, **1**, 81 - 104.

Komter, A. and K. Schuyt (1993), *Geven in Nederland* [Gift giving in the Netherlands], Amsterdam: Uitgave Dagblad Trouw.

Komter, A. and W. Vollebergh (1997), 'Gift giving and the emotional significance of family and friends', *Journal of Marriage and the Family*, **59**, 747 - 57.

Komter, A. and W. Vollebergh (2002), 'Solidarity in Dutch families: Family ties under strain?', *Journal of Family Issues*, **23** (2), 171 - 189.

Komter, A., J. Burgers and G. Engbersen (2000), *Het cement van de samenleving: Een verkennende studie naar solidariteit en cohesie* [The Cement of Society: An Exploratory Study into Social Solidarity and Cohesion], Amsterdam: Amsterdam University Press.

Kulis, S. (1992), 'Social class and the locus of reciprocity in relationships with adult children', *Journal of Family Issues*, **13**, 482 - 504.

Künemund, H. and M. Rein (1999), 'There is more to receiving than needing: Theoretical arguments and empirical explorations of crowding in and crowding out', *Ageing and Society*, **19**, 93 - 121.

Lasch, C. (1977), *Haven in a Heartless World*, New York: W.W. Norton and Company.

Liefbroer, A. and P. Dykstra (2000), *Levenslopen in verandering. Een studie naar ontwikkelingen in de levenslopen van Nederlanders geboren tussen 1900 en 1970* [Changing Lives: A study on Changes in the Life Course of the Dutch 1900 - 1970 Birth Cohorts.], The Hague: Sdu Publishers.

Luescher, K. and K. Pillemer (1998), 'Intergenerational ambivalence: A new approach to the study of parent-child relations in later life', *Journal of Marriage and the Family*, **60,** 413 - 25.

Mutran, E. and D.C. Reitzes (1984), 'Intergenerational support activities and well-being among the elderly: A convergence of exchange and symbolic interaction perspectives', *American Sociological Review*, **49**, 117 - 130.

Popenoe, D. (1988), *Disturbing the Nest: Family Change and Decline in Modern Societies*, New York: Aldine De Gruyter.

Regt, A. de (1993), *Geld en gezin. Financiële en emotionele relaties tussen gezinsleden* [Money and the Family; Financial and Emotional Relations Between Family Members], Amsterdam: Boom.

Roberts, R.E.L. and V.L. Bengtson (1988), 'Intergenerational cohesion and psychic well-being: Implications over the adult life course', Paper presented at the annual meeting of the American Sociological Association, San Francisco CA, August.

Rossi, A. and P. Rossi (1990), *Of Human Bonding: Parent-child Relations across the Life Course*, New York: Aldine de Gruyter.

Ryff, C.D. and M.M. Seltzer (1995), 'Family relations and individual development in adulthood and aging', in R. Blieszner and V.H. Bedford (eds), *Handbook of Aging and the Family*, Westport, CT: Greenwood Press, pp. 95 – 114.

Ryff, C.D. and M.M. Seltzer (eds) (1996), *The Parental Experience in Midlife*, Chicago: University of Chicago Press.

Sahlins, M. (1972), *Stone Age Economics*, London: Tavistock.

Salomon, L.M. (1992), *America's Nonprofit Sector: A Primer*, New York: The Foundation Center.

Suitor, J.J., K. Pillemer, S. Keeton and J. Robison (1995), 'Aged parents and aging children: Determinants of relationship quality', in R. Blieszner and V.H. Bedford (eds), *Handbook of Aging and the Family*, Westport, CT: Greenwood Press, pp. 223 – 43.

SCP 1999, Sociale en culturele verkenningen [Social and Cultural Explorations], The Hague: Elsevier.

Walker, A. (ed.) (1996*), The New Generational Contract. Intergenerational Relations, Old Age and Welfare*, London: UCL Press.

Wilson, G. (1993), 'Intergenerational solidarity from the point of view of people in advanced old age', in H.A. Becker and P.L. Hermkens (eds), *Solidarity of Generations. Demographic, Economic and Social Change, and its Consequences*, Amsterdam: Thesis, pp. 625 - 43.

9. Kinship Support, Gender and Social Policy in France and Spain

Constanza Tobío

There is a Japanese story about ancient times when the elderly used to be taken to a far away place and left to die. A son took his father to reproduce the ritual, just as the old man had once done with his own father. He left him in the middle of a forest and began to walk but suddenly looked back. He could not endure the sight of the old man and brought him home again. There are several sides to this violation of traditional norms. In the first place, it means there was a surplus to caring for the elderly: adults could afford to do so. As a result, intergenerational transfers have become more complicated. Each generation now receives twice, once from the preceding generation (children are cared for by parents) and once from the succeeding one (the elderly are cared for by their children). And each generation gives twice as adults, taking care of their small children and their elderly parents. A new generational contract based on reciprocity has been established. But the Japanese story does not tell us how things went after the man and his elderly father came home …Who prepared his meals, washed his clothes and kept him company? The generational contract often includes another implicit contract between men and women based on a gendered division of work, as Schultheis (1991) notes. Nor does the story tell us anything about the elderly mother. Even today, Japan has a high suicide rate among elderly widows, which is related to sacrifice as a typical feminine virtue (Andrian, 1991).

Reciprocity means delayed exchange that creates or strengthens social ties. The rationale of the gift underlies it (Mauss, 1950). To give is an obligation, as are to receive and give back. Reciprocity and exchange are different. Exchange implies simultaneity, reducing the social relation between the giver and receiver to a moment, unless the exchange is repeated. Reciprocity basically means there is an obligation to give and a right to receive in the future. The giver and receiver are strongly linked by rights and obligations. Reciprocity also means a certain similarity between what is given and what is received. The obligation to give back relates to the amount received, but it does not have to be exactly the same, as is the case in an exchange.

There has been reciprocity between three generations with a pivot or intermediate generation throughout history, often with direct transfers of money or services between grandparents and grandchildren (Segalen, 1995). Solidarity is a related concept closer to the logic of need linked to citizenship (Attias-Donfut, 1995). Solidarity goes beyond reciprocity, since it does not necessarily include the obligation to give back. In certain cases and at certain moments, a generation can give more than it will receive or receive more than it has given or will give.

Intergenerational relations are being rediscovered nowadays for two reasons. First, the Parsonian nuclear family seems to be much less dominant than it was thought to be in the 1970s and 1980s, and the extended family co-existed in the past with other family models, including nuclear families or lone parent families (Stone, 1977; Todd, 1990; Reher, 1997). Recent research shows the importance of intergenerational relations in Europe beyond the nuclear family and not just in the Mediterranean countries, both in transfers of wealth and in services (Attias-Donfut, 1995; Attias-Donfut and Segalen, 1998; Smith and Drew, 2002; Gregory and Windebank, 2000; Bengtson, 2001; Hagestad, 2000; Trnka, 2000; Tobío, 2001). Second, the family is being rediscovered as one of the pillars of the welfare regime and is no longer overlooked in welfare state literature (Esping-Andersen, 1999; Pérez Díaz et al., 1998). The three pillars, the state, the market and the family, are recognized as such although the analysis of their relation is underdeveloped. In particular, the concept of social care (Daly and Lewis, 1999, 2000), focuses on the specific contents of care as activity, thus transcending particular domains and explicitly focusing on the interaction between the family, the state and the market.

Why have intergenerational relations beyond the nuclear family now emerged as a relevant issue in public debate in Europe? In the first place, there are demographical reasons. Family membership now lasts longer simply because people live longer. Parents and children often share half a century, grandparents and grandchildren three decades (United Nations, 2000). The combination of decreasing fertility and increasing life expectancy is verticalizing family ties and producing what is called the 'beanpole family' (Bengtson et al., 1996). Individuals have fewer brothers, sisters, uncles or aunts but more grandparents or even greatgrandparents for a longer period of time. Normally three or four generations co-exist linked by parent - child relations. The succession of generations is replaced by a superimposition of generations: adult children, or even grandchildren, are often parents themselves (Théry, 1998).

A second reason why intergenerational relations have become an issue has to do with the concern about the capacity of welfare states to respond to the new demands an ageing population will pose in the years to come. In the EU, the percentage of older people has risen since 1960 from 11 to 16%. It is estimated that the population over 65 will have increased from 34 million in 1960 to 69 million by 2010 (European Commission, 2000). Welfare states were based on several implicit premises. One was that retirement was for a short period; another was that women would take care of their dependent family members. Nowadays women are needed as part of the workforce to increase the economic activity of the adult population and broaden the base for social protection systems, but this affects the informal care of the elderly by families, which is still important, especially in Ireland and the Mediterranean countries. Awareness about the family as an important agent of care is now affecting social policy measures based on the combination of private as well as public and formal as well as informal resources with specific forms of support for the main care giver within the family (European Commission, 1999).

This chapter first elaborates on the concept of social care, as it is conceptualized by Daly and Lewis (1999, 2000), to try and specify the contents of intergenerational relations beyond the nuclear family. The chapter then focuses on kinship support as a complement or substitute for social policy. The cases of France and Spain are presented to address the feasibility, limits and contradictions of kinship support in two different social policy contexts.

SOCIAL CARE AND INTERGENERATIONAL RELATIONS

The actual provision of care is the result of a combination of family, state and market resources. These three components are in evidence all over Europe, though the relative significance of each of them can vary considerably. In Germany or northern Europe, the community or voluntary sector also plays a role. Focusing on care means examining the division of work and responsibilities among the family, the state and the market, thus making it possible to analyse the welfare mix in practice. At a macro-level, institutions distribute providing care among them; at a micro-level, individuals give care directly or indirectly within the institutional framework established at the macro-level (Daly and Lewis, 2000). This not only includes the care infrastructure, it also covers the normative dimensions, which can be either explicit or implicit. The normative framework of care is deeply gendered, since it is usually women who bear the ultimate responsibility for caring for their kin. The conceptualization of social care by Daly and Lewis includes change. At the macro-level, change affects the proportions of state, market and family as well as community care; at the micro-level it can mean a different distribution of care activities, a new identity of care givers, different conditions the actual care is given under, or new kinds of relations between care recipients and care givers. Other changes might also take place in the normative dimension of care, affecting the role of women as family providers instead of homemakers as well as the diversification of family typologies with the emergence of new kinds of kinship relations.

The concept of social care is useful in efforts to understand the specific contents of intergenerational relations at the macro- as well as the micro-level. Intergenerational relations and care partly overlap but also exhibit aspects that have no direct relation to each other. Before this issue is addressed, a distinction should be drawn between what generations mean at the micro- and macro-level. Attias-Donfut (1988) and Attias-Donfut and Arber (1999) have thoroughly examined the concept of generation and distinguish five different meanings: demographic cohorts, number of years between the age of parents and children, historical generations, family generations and welfare generations. The last two meanings are useful here. Family generations relate to the lineage between child – parent - grandparent. They can be conceptualized as the 'genealogical rung of the ladder within a family lineage' (Attias-Donfut and Arber, 1999, p. 2). Welfare generations have been described by Kohli (1996) as the effect of the institutionalization of education, work and retirement at different ages: the young (who receive social benefits in the form of education), the adult actives (who provide the basis for social protection) and the elderly (who receive pensions and other benefits). Kohli's typology is incomplete because care is absent but it can easily be introduced. The young should also include children who are cared for through a combination of various resources. In addition, care giving should be considered a dimension of adult and even of retired life. Examining intergenerational relations at the micro-level, it is the family generations that are considered, whereas at the macro-level it is the welfare generations.

At the micro-level there is an intersection between intergenerational relations, intragenerational relations (within the same generation) and care. The intersection of these three concepts is care in the nuclear family, where parents care for their children and spouses care for each other. Beyond the nuclear family there are other care relations between generations. Grandparents who care for their grandchildren are currently one of the main resources families can count on in countries where formal childcare services are underdeveloped and women have rapidly increased their labour force participation, as in southern Europe. Elderly care by adult children, especially middle-aged daughters, has never ceased to be a common resource in most countries with the exception of northern Europe, where state and community care is highly developed (European Commission, 1999). In addition to care, intergenerational relations include other aspects such as personal interaction or money and wealth transfers. In addition to the care provided by the family, individuals have access to care provided by the state or the market.

At the macro-level, the underlying logic is that adults provide care for children and for the elderly. There is a distribution of responsibilities and costs among the state, the family and the market, with the state being the main institution involved. Families contribute through their active members paying taxes, contributing to the social security system, or paying for services in the private sector. The state provides services for children and the elderly or distributes cash to be used by those in need of care to buy it on the market. The private sector offers services to those who can afford to buy them. Care at the macro-level includes dimensions not related to a generational logic, e.g. care for the disabled or health care for everyone regardless of age or generation. On the other hand, the scope of intergenerational relations at the macro-level goes beyond care and includes monetary transfers for children or for the elderly (pensions, allowances, etc.) and services or transfers for the education and training of young people.

The second part of the chapter focuses on care between generations at the micro-level beyond the nuclear family. More precisely, it examines in two social policy contexts (France and Spain) what are probably the two main examples of this situation: grandparents as their grandchildren's care givers, and adult children as their elderly parents' care givers.

CHILDCARE, SOCIAL POLICY AND GRANDMOTHERS

Family and social policy have different histories and meanings in France and Spain. In France the two are closely related in as far as childcare is concerned. There has been a gradual evolution from traditional family policy focused on increasing the low French birth rate and supporting the breadwinner model, to new measures developed since the 1970s to help working mothers by providing collective childcare (Hantrais and Letablier, 1996). The state recognizes that women have the right to choose between being housewives and full-time mothers or remaining on the labour market even with young children, and to be helped in either case. In Spain, family policy has long been taboo since it was associated with the fascist regime's pro-natalist policies of the 1939 - 1975 period. In addition, the Spanish welfare state set up in the 1980s gave priority to other issues like health, education, unemployment or old age pensions. In Spain social benefits for family and children as a percentage of the total social benefits are the lowest in Europe: 1.7% in 1990 and 2% in 1996, and the expenditures on social protection in purchasing power standards per capita are among the lowest: 3160. The figure for France is 5608, which is above the European average (5120). In France social benefits for children are also above the European average but fell slightly between 1990 and 1996 (from 9.3% to 8.7%) (European Commission, 2000).

In France two thirds of the couple households aged 20 - 59 are dual-earner households; the percentage is lower in Spain (43%), but rapidly rising (Eurostat, 2002). In both countries there is a high percentage of women who work full time, even if they are married or live with someone. It is even higher in Spain, where in 83% of the cases both members of the couples work full time; the figure in France is 74%. Female employment has been a fact for quite some time in France. In Spain, it is new but widely accepted as an individual right and a family necessity, since a second family income is often the way to achieve or maintain a standard level of consumption, as various opinion surveys and studies show (Cruz Cantero, 1995; C.I.S., 1999). But employment is largely viewed as a choice for women, and it is still their responsibility to make it compatible with family care and domestic tasks.

In France, the care of children whose mother is employed is based on three main resources: childcare centres, child minders and domestic employees, all of which receive state support. Since the 1980s the number of places in publicly financed childcare centres in France has increased steadily, and 1996 almost 200,000 children, around 9% of the children below 3, attended them (Fagnani, 1998). Data from 1990 show that in the case of mothers who are employed, there is twice the percentage of children in collective childcare (Martin et al., 1999). But childcare centres are not the main kind of childcare in this country. Childminders – 'assistentes maternelles' – are the more commonly used child arrangement, especially among dual-earner families, and are economically supported by a specific allowance created in 1990 (AFEAMA). In addition, there is a specific tax deduction for families who hire a domestic employee to take care of small children. In the 1990s there was a shift in childcare policy from collective systems (childcare centres) to private forms of care supported by the state, as a way to create employment and reduce the cost of childcare. This has been criticized on the following grounds: 1) it favours middle and upper class families who can afford to pay a childminder or a domestic employee, 2) it overlooks issues related to the quality of childcare, 3) in the case of domestic employees it disregards the possible abuse by employers in terms of working conditions (number of working hours, schedules, type of work etc.), 4) it preserves or reinforces the traditional gendered division of labour in care, and 5) there are not enough childcare centres to meet the demand, nor are they evenly distributed among regions and spaces (Fagnani, 1998; Martin et al., 1999).

State support for childcare is far more limited in Spain, even though according to the law[1] the Public Administration is supposed to guarantee that all the care demands for pre-school children are met. In practice, almost all children in the 3 - 5 age group attend educational centres: 91% according to data for the 1999 - 2000 school year (Ministerio de Educación, Cultura y Deporte, 2000). There are no official statistics for the 0-2 age group, but all the indicators show that the demand exceeds the supply.

The other childcare option is paid domestic help. It does not receive any state support with the exception of specific and more limited social security payments that are entirely paid by the employer. Only a minority of families can afford it, though more can if the mothers are employed. Data from the ECFE survey show that in 6% of the cases, domestic help works full time to care for children and do other domestic tasks; in other cases, domestic help is hired to fill in gaps between job and school schedules (Tobío et al., 1998). It is increasingly immigrant workers who do this work, often in irregular situations with no contract or social protection (see also Williams in this volume).

In addition to policies oriented towards dual-earner families, in the French case the state offers some support for parents with at least two children who want to take care of their children themselves (Allocation Parentale d'Education (APE)). This non-meanstested paid parental leave benefit is usually taken by unskilled women. The number of recipients increased rapidly in the late 1990s, reaching more than half a million in 1997. The leave directly influenced female employment rates, which decreased from 1994 to 1997 among the mothers of small children from 69% to 53% (Fagnani, 1998). The APE has been severely criticized – despite its success in terms of take-up rates – about the effects of interrupting employment for several years, reinforcing asymmetrical professional careers within the couple, reinforcing the gendered division of work (Fagnani, 1995) and the social cleavages between highly skilled women who can afford to stay on the labour market and unskilled women who have no choice but to leave their jobs and stay home to care for their children (Daune-Richard, 1994).

Parents who want to stop working for some time to care for their children have no other option in Spain than unpaid parental leaves. A new law to help people combine jobs and family life was passed in 1999.[2] It transposes the EU directives on maternity and paternity leaves (92/85) and parental and emergency leaves (96/34), integrating the previous norms and going beyond them in some aspects. Despite of the law's title it does not include any measures related to reconciling jobs and family life other than leaves, most of them unpaid (De la Villa Gil and López Cumbre, 2000).

Making jobs and family life compatible is a new issue in Spain, which has only recently begun to be constructed as a new social problem the state has to address. In fact the problems combining jobs and family life poses are mainly solved by private, individual and informal strategies that working mothers are developing. The main support they have is the help and solidarity of the preceding generation of women, their own mothers, the majority of whom are and always have been housewives.

Spanish grandmothers are playing the role of substitute mothers, taking care of their grandchildren while their daughters work, and helping with many other domestic tasks. According to data from the ECFE survey, in half the cases (52%) the maternal grandmother takes care of pre-school children (if they live in the same town). In another 44.5% of the cases maternal grandmothers take care of the children when they come home after school, either at their own home or their daughters' home. Often (23%) they prepare meals for their children and grandchildren or take their grandchildren to school and pick them up in the afternoon (22%) (Tobío et al., 1998).

The help of the preceding generation seems to follow a double logic of consanguinity and gender: 1) consanguineous relatives help more, so mothers help more than mothers-in-law, and 2) women help more than men, so mothers help more than fathers and mothers-in-law more than fathers-in-law. But grandfathers' help is highly dependent on grandmothers (their spouses). They are the ones who organize, coordinate tasks and often tell them what to do. Grandfathers who are alone help considerably less.

The help of grandparents is even more important in unusual situations, which in fact are not that unusual. Two thirds of working mothers count on their own mothers if they live in the same town in unusual situations like children's illnesses, school holidays, baby-sitting in the evening when the parents go out or keeping the children for the weekend. Unlike the case with ordinary domestic tasks, grandparents help all working mothers care for children, regardless of their economic and social position.

Despite generous and diversified state childcare facilities, the role of kinship support for small children is still important in France (INSEE, 1993; Gregory and Windebank, 2000; Attias-Donfut and Segalen, 1998). The three-generation survey by Attias-Donfut and Segalen (1998) provides detailed information about the role of grandparents as care givers for their grandchildren; 82% care for their grandchildren on a regular basis (85% of grandmothers and 75% of grandfathers). Socio-economic origin does not make a big difference in the care for grandchildren but it does in the intensity of care. Among the lower socio-economic groups weekly care is much more common than among professionals. Kinship support concentrates on the children and grandchildren who are in greatest need, and is especially intense between inactive grandmothers and active mothers developing a professional career. But what is most surprising is that even employed grandmothers (two out of three interviewees) play an important role taking care of their grandchildren. The generational comparison also has other surprising results. Contrary to what might be expected, care for small grandchildren by grandparents is increasing rather than decreasing. For example, among the older generation, respondents whose children were born between 1930 and 1950, spending school vacations with their grandparents was less common than among the following generation. In the past, grandparents as care givers were a resource for difficult times (war, death of parents, divorce etc.), but they now seem to be a common resource for normal times.

In short, in Spain as well as France grandparents play a relevant role in childcare and this help is transmitted through women, from grandmothers to mothers. It is mainly a women's affair, even if grandfathers do also play a role, as has been observed in other countries (Bloch and Buisson, 1996, 1998; Dench and Ogg, 2001). Something else that is common to both countries is that this kind of kinship support beyond the nuclear family is a new phenomenon related to the massive entrance of women, particularly of mothers, on the labour market. The breadwinner model is based on the nuclear family, which cannot respond to the new needs of dual-earner families. The strength of kinship support in Spain is not an indicator of the persistence of the traditional family but of the rapid changes that are taking place. There are important differences though between France and Spain. In France, the state provides various forms of basic childcare support and grandparents fill all sorts of gaps, especially if mothers are confronted with special difficulties or have demanding jobs. Kinship support complements strong state support. In the Spanish case, intergenerational solidarity is a substitute for the scarce childcare facilities. Grandparents are not just filling gaps; if mothers are employed they are often the main care givers of their grandchildren, a provisional solution for a generation in transition, the first generation of Spanish working mothers.

SOCIAL POLICY AND CARE FOR THE ELDERLY

Parallel to the increasing concern about the aging of the population, there was an intense social debate in France in the 1980s and 1990s on the dependent elderly. Several reports were presented and discussed in parliament but did not ultimately generate legislation until 1994 when a new flexible benefit for the dependent elderly was introduced based on hired home help. As in the case of childcare policy, concern about unemployment was also implicit. In 1996, another law was passed on long term-care insurance that promoted care within the family and stressed coordination between the sectors involved in care for the elderly (formal care, local councils, family, private sector etc.) (European Commission, 1999). The main allowance created by this law was the 'Prestation spécifique dépendence' (PSD), a payment for the carer even if they are a relative as long as they are not a spouse. It was means-tested and over a certain income it could be recovered from the inheritance (Martin, 2001).

By the year 2000, the PSD covered 140,000 dependent persons, but it was still only 15% of those in need of some help and 20% of the severely dependent. The new allowance only affected a minority of the elderly people in need of help, those with a low income or severely dependant, but not the majority of the cases (Martin, 2001). Paying the care givers was one of the main specificities of the French experience. The aim was to improve their work conditions as well as the social perception of caring as a job. After four years, the outcome was not very clear, as Martin points out. Care givers continue to be mainly women (99%), even if they are not part of the family but work for a salary. The increase in the number of jobs has been moderate, but what seems to have happened is that jobs in the grey economy have emerged and have turned into real jobs in the formal economy. Many of them are short part-time jobs that do not usually yield an acceptable income. The new allowance seems to be part of a complex patchwork by families to buy a few hours of home help for the elderly, which often do not fit well into a work schedule. There are also two sides to the situation of informal family care givers, often middle-aged daughters or daughters-in-law paid by PSD. Though the payments acknowledge and value the work they do, it is not easy for care givers to simultaneously be relatives and employees; these are two logics that sometimes conflict. If the care giver is paid, the family system of rights and obligations is redefined, often creating tension.

In 1994, half a million elderly people were living in public institutions, 6% of the French population over 65 (Martin et al., 1999). This is higher than the European average (5%) and much higher than the figure for Spain, 3% (Guillemard, 1992). The total number of dependent people was estimated to be 1.5 million, so most frail elderly people live in their homes and are helped by their relatives, i.e. the women in the family or other people. As in France, a majority of Spanish elderly people live by themselves. This is something new in this country, and is related to the economic autonomy acquired in the last twenty years through improved old-age pensions. The percentage of those who live in their children's homes and are thus dependent on them in some way is very small until age 75 (around 3%) but rises to 27% after 80 (normally if they are alone and in need of help) (Ministerio de Asuntos Sociales, 1996).

The French three-generation survey mentioned above shows that more than one in three members of the intermediate or pivot generation regularly help their elderly parents with basic everyday activities. This help is even more important among grandparents who also help their grandchildren. All in all, around 16% of the men and 33% of the women in the intermediate generation bear heavy care responsibilities. Among grandparents, the percentages that care for at least one parent are very high: 30% of the grandfathers and 44% of the grandmothers (Attias-Donfut and Segalen, 1998).

In Spain informal family care is the norm for the elderly who cannot care for themselves. An estimated 700,000 people provide at least 50 hours a week of care for the elderly, and most of them are women.[3] The main care giver can be a daughter (40%), another relative (20.5%), a spouse (10%), a worker hired by the family (10%), or a son (6%). Only in 3.5% of the cases is care for the elderly mainly provided by social services (3.5%) (Méndez, 2002). The social profile of the care givers is very specific: 84% are women, 50% are in the 45 - 64 age group, 62% are poorly educated (primary school or less) and 75% do not have a paid job. Of the men, 45% are retired and of the women, 60% are housewives (Ministerio de Asuntos Sociales, 1995).

Opinions and attitudes on who should take care of the elderly can be contradictory, probably as a reflection of the period of transition Spain is in nowadays. Nine out of ten care givers consider it a moral obligation to do what they do, but five out of ten think the state should do it. When asked about the kind of help the state should provide, 61% mention a salary for the care giver, 14% help in the home, 5% promote the voluntary sector for these tasks and 4% cite a reduced number of working hours (Ministerio de Asuntos Sociales, 1995).

In the period when the PSD was implemented in France, it was severely criticized on various grounds, mainly the limited number of recipients who could benefit from it. A new law began to be discussed in 2000 and was finally passed in 2001 and implemented in 2002. It was presented as a shift from a social assistance to a public solidarity perspective in old age policy. The objective is universal coverage for the entire dependent population through a new allowance to pay for care givers called 'allocation personalisé d'autonomie' (APA). The number of elderly persons receiving support is expected to rise from 140,000 to 800,000 (Blanchard, 2001).

In Spain, a few things happened in the 1990s that affected social policy on the elderly. There is some awareness and concern at the national as well as the regional and local levels about the increasing demand for care for the elderly and the decreasing number of women available as care givers. There are plans to increase the number of places at collective residences and there has been some debate about the public-private mix and some initiatives in this sense.[4] The dominant perspective seems to be to help families so they can continue taking care of the elderly at home, but there are serious doubts about the feasibility of this option. For example, the leitmotiv of the Regional Plan for the Elderly of Madrid is 'Aging at home', but what is offered is a very limited number of services for very low income families to make care easier, such as home help for a few hours, day centres, tele-assistance or training for care givers (Consejería de Sanidad y Servicios Sociales de la Comunidad de Madrid, 1999). Another service that is part of the current approach to care for the elderly is 'let care givers take a breath' or 'care for care givers'. It is conceived as a break for informal family care givers who work long hours. A professional care giver replaces them for several hours a week or every two weeks, so they can have some time for themselves.

So to summarize, in France there is a combination of high levels of kinship support and high levels of social protection. However, as Martin et al. (1999) note, the state has not tried to withdraw or reduce expenditure in childcare or care for the elderly although a trend towards privatization can be observed in the way services are provided. But what is new in French public debate and policy alike is that intergenerational relations are recognized as key actors in the provision of care.

In Spain intergenerational solidarity has been and still is a substitute for scarce social policy towards small children and the elderly. Beyond the nuclear family, the role of grandparents as care givers for their grandchildren and of middle-aged women as care givers for their elderly parents is responding to new needs related to women who work outside the home and to the ageing of the population. But in a European perspective, Spanish female activity is still low, as is the percentage of elderly people in the population. The care need on the part of both these groups will thus increase considerably, and it is uncertain whether middle-aged women will continue to be as available as care givers as they have been until now.

CONCLUSION

Intergenerational relations are increasingly a subject of interest from an academic as well as a policy perspective. Contrary to what was generally thought not so long ago, intergenerational relations are not disappearing in the developed countries, in fact they are playing a more important role than several decades ago. The implicit welfare state presumptions can no longer be sustained. The women of the family can no longer bear the sole or even the main responsibility as care givers (and care is no longer their main responsibility). For a wide range of reasons – objective and subjective ones, related to economics or to the construction of a new desired identity – women's involvement in paid work is now the norm. However, the number of years people now live after they retire or as the elderly is increasing rapidly. The combination of retirement at an earlier age[5] and a higher life expectancy increases the number of years retired or elderly people live, thus creating a greater demand for care.

Intergenerational relations seem to have become more important in countries with high as well as low levels of social protection towards the family and the elderly. In France, a majority of grandparents take care of their grandchildren as a complement to more formal systems of childcare. Care for the elderly is often based on the family and there is strong support provided by the state. Kinship support for small children and elderly people is important as a complement to the state, not a substitute for it.

The case of Spain is different. Intergenerational relations play a fundamental role in a transition period with more and more working women and scarce public childcare services. The first generation of active women is receiving support from the last generation of housewives, their own mothers who are available and willing to help their daughters become workers. Between grandmothers and mothers, beyond reciprocity, there is solidarity. Grandmothers are giving more than they will receive, having cared for their children and now for their grandchildren. Without the help of the preceding generation of women, many mothers who are now on the labour market would not have been able to continue their jobs once they had children. But grandmothers as a childcare resource raise several issues. First, to what extent is this desirable or adequate from the child's or the grandmother's perspective? Second, to what extent will the next generation of grandmothers (the current generation of working mothers) be equally willing to care for their grandchildren in as intense a way? The elderly in Spain are also cared for by the family, normally by adult inactive middle-aged daughters, often grandmothers themselves, with very limited support from the state.

In the near future, demands for childcare and care for the elderly will no doubt increase significantly. At the same time a new group of retired people in good mental and physical health is emerging. They are already retired but not yet in need of care themselves. They are the perfect candidates as providers of kinship support. Their role as care givers will probably increase. However, the extent to which this is desirable or acceptable should be a matter of public debate, as should how to complement this kind of resource with other resources from the state, the market or the community. Another issue of debate should be the unequal contract between men and women underlying the appeal to intergenerational reciprocity or solidarity.

NOTES

1. Ley 1/1990 de 3 de octubre Orgánica General del Sistema Educativo.
2. Ley 39/1999, de 5 de noviembre, para promover la conciliación de la vida familiar y laboral de las personas trabajadoras.
3. Data presented by Héctor Maravall, former Director General of Social Services, *El País*, 6 June 2002.
4. For example, through regional governments and the founding of public banks like Caja Madrid or La Caixa de Pensions.
5. Even if this is now changing and the postponement of retirement is increasingly encouraged through multifarious policies, as a recent report from the European Commission (2002) shows.

REFERENCES

Andrian, J. (1991), 'Le suicide', *Autrement*, **124**, 47 - 54.

Attias-Donfut, C. (1988), *Sociologie des générations. L'empreinte du temps*, Paris: Presses Universitaires de France.

Attias-Donfut, C. (1995) (ed.), *Les solidarités entre générations. Vieillesse, familles, état*, Paris: Nathan.

Attias-Donfut, C. and M. Segalen (eds) (1998), *Grands-Parents. La famille à travers les générations*, Paris: Odile Jacob.

Attias-Donfut, C. and S. Arber (1999), 'Equity and solidarity across the generations', in S. Arber and C. Attias-Donfut (eds), *The Myth of Generational Conflict. The family and state in ageing societies*, London and New York: Routledge, pp. 1 - 21.

Bengtson, V.L. (2001), 'Beyond the nuclear family: the increasing importance of multigenerational bonds', *Journal of Marriage and Family*, **63**, 1 - 16.

Bengtson, V.L., T. Rosenthal, C. and D.L. Burton (1996), 'Paradoxes of families and ageing' in Robert H. Binstock (ed.), *Handbook of Ageing and the Social Sciences*, San Diego, California: Academic Press, pp. 254 - 82.

Blanchard, S. (2001), 'L'allocation personalisé d'autonomie doit changer le quotidien des personnes âgées', *Le Monde*, 30 December, p. 6.

Bloch, F. and M. Buisson (1996), *Faire garder ou garder les enfants: une affaire de femmes*, Paris: Ministère de Logement, Direction de l'Habitat et de la Construction.

Bloch, F. and M. Buissone (1998), *La garde des enfants, une histoire des femmes*, Paris: L'Harmattan.

C.I.S. (1999), 'Los jóvenes de hoy', *Boletín Datos de Opinión*, 19.

Consejería de Servicios Sociales de la Comunidad de Madrid (1999), *Plan de Mayores*, Madrid: Comunidad de Madrid.

Cruz Cantero, P. (1995), *Percepción Social de la Familia en España*, Madrid: Centro de Investigaciones Sociológicas.

Daly, M. and J. Lewis (1999), 'Introduction. conceptualising social care in the context of welfare state restructuring', in J. Lewis (ed.), *Gender, Social Care and Welfare State Restructuring in Europe*, Aldershot: Ashgate, pp. 1 - 24.

Daly, M. and Lewis, J. (2000), 'The concept of social care and the analysis of contemporary welfare states', *The British Journal of Sociology*, **51**, 2, 281 - 298.

Daune-Richard, A.M. (1994), 'A social policy perspective on work, employment and the family in France, the United Kingdom and Sweden', in M.T. Letablier and L. Hantrais (eds), *The Family-Employment Relation*, Cross National Research Papers, Loughborough University, pp. 68 - 79.

De la Villa Gil, L.E. and L. López Cumbre, (2000), 'Adaptación de la legislación española a la Directiva 96/34/CE sobre permiso parental', *Revista del Ministerio de Trabajo y Asuntos Sociales*, Número extraordinario sobre Conciliación de la Vida Familiar y Laboral, pp. 41 - 69.

Dench, G. and J. Ogg (2001), 'Grands-parents par la fille, grands-parents par le fils' in C. Attias-Donfut and M. Segalen (eds), *Le siècle des grands-parents. Une génération phare, ici et ailleurs*, Paris: Autrement, pp. 187 - 199.

Esping-Andersen, G. (1999), *Social Foundations of Postindustrial Economies*, Oxford: Oxford University Press.

European Commission (1999), *Social protection for dependency in old age in the 15 EU Member States and Norway*, Luxembourg.

European Commission (2000), *The Social Situation in the European Union*, Luxembourg.

European Commission (2002), 'Informe de la Comisión al Consejo, al Parlamento Europeo, al Comité económico y Social y al Comité de las Regiones sobre el Aumento de la tasa de población activa y fomento de la prolongación de la vida activa', COM 9 24.01.2002, Brussels.

Eurostat (2002), 'Women and men reconciling work and family life', *Statistics in Focus*, **3**, 9, 1 - 8.

Fagnani, J. (1995), 'L'allocation parentale d'éducation: effets pervers et ambigüités d'une prestation', *Droit Social*, **3**, 287 - 95.

Fagnani, J. (1998), 'Helping mothers to combine paid and unpaid work-or fighting unemployment? The ambiguities of French family policy', *Community, Work and Family*, **1**, 3, 297 - 312.

Gregory, A. and J. Windebank (2000), *Women's Work in Britain and France. Practice, Theory and Policy*, London: Macmillan Press.

Guillemard, A.M. (1992), *Análisis de las políticas de vejez en Europa*, Madrid: Ministerio de Asuntos Sociales.

Hagestad, G.O. (2000), 'Adult intergenerational relations', in *Generations and Gender Programme. Exploring future research and data collection options,* New York and Geneva: United Nations, pp. 125 - 43.

Hantrais, L. and M.T. Letablier (1996), *Families and Family Policies in Europe,* London and New York: Longman.

INSEE (1993), *La Société Française-Données Sociales,* Paris.

Kohli, M. (1996), *The Problem of Generations: Family, Economy, Politics,* Budapest: Public Lecture Series.

Martin, C. (2001), 'Les politiques de prise en charge des personnes âgées dépendantes', *Travail, Genre et Societés,* 6, 83 - 103.

Martin, C., A. Math and E. Renaudat (1999), 'Caring for very young children and dependent elderly people in France: Towards a commodification of social care?', in J. Lewis (ed.) *Gender, Social Care and Welfare State Restructuring in Europe,* Aldershot: Ashgate, pp. 139 - 74.

Mauss, M. (1950), *Sociologie et Anthropologie,* Paris: Presses Universitaires de France (original publication 1923).

Méndez, R. (2002), 'Los servicios sociales sólo atienden al 7% de los discapacitados que necesitan ayuda', *El País,* 6 June, p. 26.

Ministerio de Asuntos Sociales (1995), *Cuidados en la vejez. El apoyo informal,* Madrid.

Ministerio de Asuntos Sociales (1996), *Las personas mayores en España. Perfiles. Reciprocidad familiar,* Madrid.

Ministerio de Educación, Cultura y Deporte (2000), *Estadísticas de la Educación,* www.mec.es/estadistica.

Pérez Díaz, V., E. Chuliá and M.B. Alvárez (1998), *Familia y sistema de bienestar. La experiencia española con el paro, las pensiones, la sanidad y la educación,* Madrid: Argentaria.

Reher, D.S. (1997), *Perspectives on the Family, in Spain, Past and Present,* Oxford: Clarendon Press.

Schultheis, F. (1991), 'Affaires de famille-affaires d'état: des visions et des divisions interculturelles d'une réflexion sociologique', in F. de Singly and F. Schultheis (eds), *Affaires de famille, affaires d'Etat,* Nancy: Colloque Franco-Allemand, pp. 7 - 22.

Segalen, M. (1995), 'Continuités et discontinuités familiales: approche socio-historique du lien intergénérationnel', in C. Attias-Donfut (ed.), *Les solidarités entre générations. Vieillesse, familles, état,* Paris: Nathan, pp. 27 - 40.

Smith, P. and L. Drew (2002), 'Grandparenthood', in M.H. Bornstein (ed.), *Handbook of Parenting, Vol 3: Being and Becoming a Parent* (2nd ed), London: Lawrence Erlbaum, pp. 141 - 172.

Stone, L. (1977), *The Family: Sex and Marriage in England, 1500 - 1800,* London: Weidenfeld and Nicolson.

Théry, I. (1998), *Couple, filiation et parenté aujourd'hui,* Paris: Odile Jacob.

Tobío, C. (2001), 'En Espagne, la "abuela" au secours des mères actives', in C. Attias-Donfut and M. Segalen (eds), *Le siècle des grands-parents. Une génération
phare, ici et ailleurs*, Paris: Autrement, pp. 102 - 115.

Tobío, C., C. Fernández, A. Juan and S. Agulló (1998), 'Análisis cuantitativo de las
estrategias de compatibilización familia-empleo en España'. Madrid: Programa
Sectorial de Estudios de las Mujeres y el Género, Departamento de Humani-
dades, Ciencia Política y Sociología/Instituto de la Mujer. (Research Report.)

Todd, E. (1990), *L'invention de l'Europe*, Paris: Seuil.

Trnka, S. (2000), *Family Issues between Gender and Generations*, Luxembourg:
European Commission.

United Nations (2000), Generations and Gender Programme. Exploring Future Research and Data Collection Options, New York and Geneva.

10. 'What are Children for?': Reciprocity and Solidarity between Parents and Children [1]

Ilona Ostner

The twentieth century was heralded as the 'century of the child' (Key [1902], 1992). Children – female and male alike – were to be recognized as individuals in their own right, and no longer seen and treated as subject to their parents' wishes or their parents' economic assets (Therborn, 1993). Parents developed new relations with their children, and birth rates steadily declined. The new focus on the quality and not the quantity, the mere number of children, and on children's rights was accompanied by a steadily decreasing family size, and sometimes even reluctance to have any children at all. The decreasing family size and the emphasis on the quality of children explain why from the start the twenty-first century has put children at the top of the political agenda.

Many Western societies, especially in northern and western Europe, have developed policies to facilitate family building and mitigate the costs of having children. So far these policies have only marginally increased birth rates if at all, but they have once again changed the status of children, this time from 'private' to 'public goods'. In addition, they have impacted relations between children and their parents, altering the scope if not the nature of familial obligations. Parents have been relieved from some of the costs of having children, often by 'de-familializing' the family, i.e. through services such as childcare or care for the elderly provided by the state or market. Care services have 'individualized' children in relation to their parents and mothers in relation to their children and their children's fathers, and transformed filial and parental obligations, and thus the ideas and practices of reciprocity – give and take – and solidarity within the family.

Numerous former familial obligations have been shifted to the societal level and transformed into obligations towards society as a whole. These obligations are to be met through market-related activities like paying taxes or social security premiums or tuition fees for the regular or for special skills. Obviously, 'individualizing' children by way of 'de-familialization' and '*Vergesellschaftung*' of rights and obligations are two sides of the same coin. If reciprocity – give and take within families – is shifted from the family to the societal level, it becomes more abstract and thus more precarious and conditional in highly individualized and consequently heterogeneous societies. So why have children? What are children for? If they are increasingly transformed into public goods, why should we care? And what about parents? Who should care for whom and why? What is left of familial reciprocity and solidarity?

The following does not answer these questions but focuses on the dialectics of children's individualization and the accompanying transformation of give and take within the family. I explain the concepts of 'reciprocity' and 'solidarity' and how they can be related to family issues. By addressing the questions 'Why have children?' and 'What are children for?' historically and sociologically, I present a brief history of the changing status of children in relation to their parents and society as a whole, changes which impact children's and their families' responsibilities to society. I then argue that children and their families have become means to market ends, e.g. a function of the labour market. This becomes clear as I analyse the recent debates on declining birth rates and the way children are framed in terms of costs: costs children impose on their parents' (especially women's) budgets, time and opportunities. European welfare states have aimed to ease these burdens to rational actors, albeit in different ways. The differences are however slowly disappearing.[2] As stipulated in the Amsterdam Treaty, European Union member states have agreed to boost employment, increase the employability of every working age person (including mothers) and combat non-employment and unemployment. The subsequent increase in the number of dual-earner households helps cope with the costs of having children. The employability strategy consists in part of measures to better balance jobs and family life. A closer look reveals the extent to which women (like men) and their children have increasingly become economic assets and the elderly a liability for society. This is also a double-edged change with regard to reciprocity and solidarity within families.

RECIPROCITY VERSUS SOLIDARITY

Reciprocity refers to the norms and practices of give and take that do not follow the principle of equivalence, although something is expected back, at least in the long run. An extended time horizon and the iteration of social interaction are constitutive elements of reciprocity. People have to belong to an entity (group, organization, society) that remains relatively stable over time if they are to be able to reiterate interaction and thus reciprocate. Since reciprocity is contingent – something is expected to be given back but might not be – it requires trust. Trust is enhanced if people repeatedly and preferably visibly interact, which necessitates the continuity of situations where individuals meet each other again (Axelrod, 1984). While reciprocity is a universal norm and practice which keeps societies going (Gouldner, 1984; 1996), our highly individualized societies have restricted opportunities for iterative face-to-face give and take, thereby making it more difficult to control whether people reciprocate. As a result, collectively provided goods can be easily consumed 'by defection', i.e. not giving anything back or not doing so appropriately.

Unlike the case with reciprocity, there is no convention for defining 'solidarity' – a word that is moreover alien to many languages (including English). Solidarity is either used as a synonym for reciprocal acts within groups – a usage that comes close to the original French meaning (Latin 'solidum' as a mutual good) – or to emphasize the togetherness of people engaged in solidaristic actions. The definitions can be seen as a continuum going from 'reciprocal altruism' to cases where people need help or receive a gift but will never be willing or able to reciprocate. In a strict idealtypical sense, solidarity should be limited to 'non-reciprocal giving' (Nell-Breuning, 1957; Hondrich and Koch-Arzberger, 1992). According to this definition, in reality there are only rare instances of solidarity. However scarce, they inform the very specific nature of non-reciprocal acts and their preconditions, and this knowledge helps us study the family as sphere of solidarity.

Most of the solidaristic incidents in history flourished among people with shared socio-cultural roots and socio-economic experiences, though a similar background or lifelong destiny hardly sufficed to regularly generate solidaristic action. And if it did emerge, it usually served strategic ends. People in similar situations facing similar risks join forces to achieve important collective ends. This type of collective action is primarily based on reciprocal altruism. Many workers' past and present solidaristic actions were at the crossroads of Emile Durkheim's 'mechanical' and 'organic' solidarity. They were based on *Gemeinschaft*-like elements, e.g. social homogeneity with regard to origin, vocational training and skills, and the effects of growing social differentiation (*Vergesellschaftung*) that constitute modern Western society.

Social policies have traditionally implied reciprocity. Solidarity (as implied in non-reciprocal gifts) is ostensibly a kind of redistribution incorporated into contribution-based social insurance and tax-financed social security. The fact is often overlooked though that private insurance also regularly presupposes redistribution, e.g. if people contributed but will not receive appropriately back. One can say what the privately insured get back is at least a feeling of security and that in essence that is what private insurance is strategically for. In any case, due to institutionalized redistribution (solidarity), some groups or people will be 'net' recipients of collective action – and get more than they have paid in (Ullrich, 2000).

The reasons for accepting or rejecting redistribution can be equally strategic and normative in the case of private as well as 'social' insurance against risks. Utilitarians and achievement-oriented individuals tend to resent 'net' recipients (who they feel unduly got a gift). There is little or no resentment towards legitimate 'net' recipients, small children being the prototypical example, albeit only since very recently and by no means universally (Ullrich, 2000). As regards the elderly, notions of reciprocity once again emerge more explicitly, e.g. as regards a well-deserved retirement pension. Indeed, the idea and reality of having contributed to a private or social insurance fund has so far nourished the idea of a deserving work-free old age. As is noted below, even in the case of children, solidarity is not fully free of charge.

What is noted more generally on instances of solidaristic action thus also applies to the specific case of social policies. Homogeneity of interests, values and resources makes it easier for group members to accept some members being 'net' recipients. Historically, solidaristic forms of social security became more inclusive and went beyond their original particularism (parochial interpretation of membership) if they were founded on the idea of imagined communities / commonalities. Common risks like old age disability have helped extend provisions for 'people like us' to the needy. In reality, however, highly redistributive social policies that produce numerous 'net' recipients have so far done best in socially homogeneous societies that allowed for what I call 'universalized particularism'. This in turn suggests that heterogeneous societies tend to more strictly control or minimize the 'net' receipt of benefits. In fact, much of the new welfare state politics is more about 'recalibrating' give and take to minimize undue net gains than about retrenchment.

Since societies in general and welfare states in particular rely on reciprocity, they try to control and enhance reciprocal acts. Solidarity is a very ambitious moral guideline and practice based on many premises that cannot readily be confirmed. Apparently, we feel or practice solidarity more readily for people we love or feel close to and more reluctantly, if at all, for strangers. In the first instance, strangers are a prototypical example of my strict definition of solidarity: a gift relation beyond reciprocity. All societies have rules for dealing with and giving to strangers. They assume, first, that everyone is sometimes a stranger and hence in a situation where it could be hard to give back what has been given. Second, they assume that by definition, strangers will not stay and if they do, they will sooner or later become like us (and no longer be strangers) and reciprocate (Simmel 1908, 1983).

Does this suggest that couples and families are the original site for solidarity and solidaristic action? Historically, they were not, at least not primarily. Families hardly went beyond reciprocity. Parents gave strategically to their children, and wanted nothing back that had not been given before. Needy family members were often treated like strangers and expected to leave or die once they became a continuing burden. This does not mean loving and caring families did not exist; they did (Ehmer and Gutschner, 2000). Families were the last resort for sick or frail elderly people who could no longer make a living, and they often cared for their grandchildren. We do not know yet whether they did so driven by 'freely given love' or an established norm of filial or parental love. Summarizing the findings of recent historical studies, Ehmer (2000) maintains though that norms (including the norm of parental and filial love) probably shaped generational ties more than economic assets and inheritance rules.

It was not until the twentieth century, however, and especially in Western societies, that an ever-increasing number of families could first start to fully build upon and enjoy non-strategic relations with their members. Solidarity flourishes best in loving relations where people treat each other as values in themselves and not as means to strategic ends. This is what the modern family, in contrast to the traditional family, is essentially about. Unfortunately, modern families are notorious for falling short of this potential. These are reasons why more and more people refrain from lasting relationships, even with children, and why the state has come in and changed parental and filial obligations. Parents are still expected to care for their children, but in some countries they also have to care for grown-ups, be it with increasing help from society. There is ample evidence though that society no longer expects children to help their needy parents by providing either cash or through care. So why become a parent and 'What are children for'?

DEAR FAMILIES: THE CHANGING STATUS OF CHILDREN AND THEIR PARENTS

The fertility rate has been dramatically declining everywhere over the past forty years. The social change has been most striking in 'familialist' countries like Spain, Italy or Japan, where people heavily rely on the members of their families' obligation to take lifelong care of each other. The number of children, however, has also fallen below the reproduction rate in welfare states that praise themselves for their 'family-friendly' policies. Women and men postpone having children, and a growing number of them will not have children at all. Often childlessness is not a matter of choice. Yet many people choose not to have a child. There are numerous explanations for this social change, but very few of them are satisfactory, since most of them assume a simple causal relationship. Many comparative welfare state scholars immediately link welfare state care services for families to women's inclination to have children. The argument was first introduced and elaborated upon by Esping-Andersen (1996; 1999). Mary Daly's (2000) approach, in contrast, rejects simple causalities. Her fine balance of factors explaining differences in women's labour market participation also applies to differences in fertility rates or attitudes towards childcare outside the home. A multitude of factors is needed to explain why fertility rates hardly differ between the 'family-friendly' French and Scandinavian and the 'liberal' (Anglo-American) welfare states that provide neither universal childcare facilities nor universal child benefits. Attitudes do not neatly fit welfare state typologies. British and German mothers are more sceptical about state services than French or Scandinavian ones and consequently prefer 'mother-like' (surrogate) forms of childcare, e.g. day care mothers, to state provision. Looking at French and German women's attitudes towards childcare outside the home, Fagnani (2002) notes the hard choices confronting women in 'conservative' or 'familialist' welfare states like Germany. In her empirical study, Sims-Schouten (2000) studied British, Finnish and Greek parents' attitudes towards the role of the state and perceptions of the quality of childcare provided by the state. The Finnish interviewees did not question the role of the state nor did they mention the quality of care, which was such an important issue for British and German parents. Needless to say, attitudes differed and still differ in formerly socialist East Germany. Former East German mothers take a shorter parental leave and are less apt to work part-time than their former West German counterparts. A lower percentage of East than West German mothers and fathers think public or full-time childcare will harm small children, although very few argue for full-time childcare outside the home for newborn babies or children under the age of two (Datenreport, 2002). Attitudes, as we know, also express the need to avoid cognitive inconsistencies, which means they adapt to circumstances. In any case, societies obviously differ with regard to what they think should be left to the family.

Although childcare facilities are far more more limited in Britain than Germany, Britain has a higher fertility rate than Germany. Is having children only an option for people with poor career expectations or for those who are so well off they can afford childminders who will run the household and take care of the children while they are at work? The Taylors (2001) pose this question, and also note that Edwardian style families with nannies, gardeners and cleaners have re-appeared over the last ten years, a trend that is not restricted to Britain (see also Williams in this volume).

There are many reasons why having children seems counterintuitive. The standard argument revolves around the changing economic role of children. Industrialization and corresponding social differentiation separated households and economic activity and thus redefined the roles of family members including children. The male breadwinner slowly emerged. Mechanical solidarity no longer tied family members together. Frail elderly people who could not contribute to their own living traditionally meant a burden to their children that was hardly compensated by a strict sense of obligation. After the expanding restrictions on child labour, the child also emerged as a matter of cost and a growing burden for wage dependents. Historian Hendrick (1994) chronologically enumerates the various kinds of status British society and in particular public policies have conferred on children since the mid-19th century: from the child who worked full-time to the one who increasingly worked part-time, combining paid work, school and help at home, to the schoolchild and since the late 20th century the child endowed with rights, the 'citizen-child'. The incremental expansion of Children's Acts, banning child and restricting youth labour – early measures of 'decommodification' without compensatory measures in the beginning – stimulated the changes in children's status. Paid work outside the home, as Hendrick maintains, contributed to the social status and value of children in the family. Their status no longer solely depended on their families'. Wage work and school hours structured children's daily lives and were perceived by many social welfare experts a perfect way to fight deviance and destitution on the part of working parents' children.

After the final abolition of child labour, the child emerged as 'family child'. The state and employers now increasingly compensated the costs parents had to bear for their children. Family wages began to rise, as did the social security benefits for wives and children derived from the breadwinner. Often employers paid part of the family-related benefits. Children became economically irrelevant if not costly, and their non-economic emotional value rose and seemingly made up for the financial burdens. Their status changed again. According to economists, children have become consumer commodities and a matter of preference or public goods who constitute a serious collective problem. If others consume the gains of having children while their parents still incur all the losses, only altruists can be expected to mother or father a child. Since altruists are rare, the birth rate will inevitably further decline. Huinink (2001; 1995) distinguishes two arguments put forward by economists. The first draws upon Becker (1981), who recognizes the possible existence of non-economic (e.g. emotional) utility components of the 'consumer commodity child', so that it still makes sense to invest in having children. The second argument was developed by Coleman (1990) who maintains that children have turned into mere public goods in modern societies, and that no rational actor was seriously interested in investing cash and care in raising children. Children thus constitute a collective action problem. Some people, i.e irrational ones, still raise children at their own expense, others (childless ones) free-ride. Family policies are increasingly based on the latter argument.

Obviously, the reasons for declining birth rates go beyond the usual suspects like 'feeding child-bearing into the system of cost-accounting' or 'prizing choice and autonomy over all other human capacities', as Laurie and Matthew Taylor (2001, p. 23) nicely put it. The authors identify various features of the modern world that undermine the traditional reasons for having children, all of which have to do with what I like to call a 'break with continuity' and the erosion of parental expertise and authority. First, the Taylors remind us that in a meritocracy based on individual achievement, children can no longer be referred to in terms of 'descendants'. We hardly give our children the first names of our parents, brothers or sisters to underline the family's continuity. Nor do the names we choose bear any normative meaning or message for our children that are conveyed from one generation to the next. It has been a sociological truism that children in modern societies do not follow in their parents' footsteps, but pursue their own vocation. Status and position are no longer transmitted but are achieved by each child and generation anew. Nor are children the natural heirs to parental norms and morality. Parents do not provide a master script for the next generation. The numerous contingencies of modern life make it difficult for them to see their children climb the social ladder. Happiness, not social mobility is what parents now wish for their offspring.

Discontinuity and the devaluation of parental expertise have been also expanded by two other factors: outside forces like rapidly changing new technologies that cut parents and even more so grandparents off from their children's type of knowledge and, in addition, the dynamics of modern living arrangements. An increasing number of children experience the separation and sometimes repeated re-partnering of their parents. Grandparents, like their daughters and sons, are confronted with a mix of new family members, including social as well as biological offspring. Post-modern grandparents and grandchildren try hard to preserve their ties, ignoring the turbulence their grown-up sons and daughters and their parents cause by their personal choices. While the contingencies of modern partnering have multiplied the conceivable generational relations and increased the number of family members who can provide support, very little research has been conducted on the quality of relations between biological and social family members.[3] How members of post-modern extended families deal with each other seems to depend on their beliefs and the quality of experienced interactions.

In traditional societies, familial obligations had to be defended. Today commitments are still strong but contingent. Few would openly expect and rely on them. Aside from assets, there seems to be little for children to inherit or for women and men to pass on. Continuity no longer binds generations and drives family building. Factors like the experience and anticipation of discontinuity, the erosion of parental authority and the contingency of filial commitment have, as Laurie and Matthew Taylor put it (2001, p. 23), 'invalidated the traditional reasons for having children and thereby opened the door to the type of calculus' said to have permeated private decisions and public discussions. If families had become a matter of cost evaluation only, this would indeed impact reciprocity and solidarity.

However, two reservations must be considered. First, ideas of continuity like passing on one's name, status and expertise might have been limited to propertied families and their male members in the past.[4] To a certain extent, perhaps they were merely a substitute for men who could not mother children. Up until very recently, bearing children constituted a fatal risk to women's lives, hence the very real experience of discontinuity. Universal access to technologically advanced medical treatment and contraception converted pregnancy into a matter of low risk and choice; opportunities for educational attainment and professional careers devaluated the skills of a housewife and mother that were previously passed from mother to daughter. New women emerged who, for a short while in the twentieth century, became role models for their daughters pursuing a career. The idea of continuity might have entered here, be it limited to daughters. But what was said, in general, about contingent commitments and low expectations also applies to generational ties between women. Another reservation concerns the norm and reality of generational reciprocity. There is still ample reciprocity, even solidarity. This is especially true with regard to the continuous give and take between biological parents and their children and grandchildren. Recent German empirical studies confirm that generational reciprocity is still strong if the focus is on the 'multi-local' or modified extended family (Bien, 2000). Ties are robust and support is frequently given, although expectations are low. Most parents do not expect their children to be supporters of first resort in the event of continuing need.[5] The elderly prefer to help themselves, if possible, and they do so increasingly with the help of the state. (Helping oneself includes caring for one's spouse or partner in need.) The emphasis on self-reliance does not imply however that children do not feel obliged to help their parents and provide support. According to historian Sieder (1997), who studied generational ties in Austria and Germany, the younger generation more easily divorces a partner than a parent. Obligations are still strongly felt, especially by daughters. While the younger generation cares for the older one, the older generation significantly and continuously helps the younger one with cash if not care as long as they live, and through a last will and testament after they die (Motel and Szydlik, 1999; Szydlik, 1999). Forms of support have changed as well. In Germany or Austria, today's devoted and loving daughter will be her parents' care manager and try to find the best care package offered by the statutory long-term care insurance for them (Dallinger, 1993).

Are strong filial and parental obligations a leftover from the past? Would it be more rational to pay taxes and have the state take care of children and the elderly? Or abstain from having children at all, thus foregoing any chance of having caring children in one's old age? These questions overlook the new quality of personal relationship that was promoted by the changing status of children and parents and that neither the market nor the state can offer. Liberated from economic considerations, women and men enjoy love and intimacy shared with their partners and children. These intimate relationships provide the sole opportunity for non-strategic or communicative action (Habermas, 1973) and hence the affirmation of one's authenticity (Günther, 2001). Loving adults and parents and children as well treat the other as a value in itself, at any rate not primarily as a means towards strategic ends. Even people who are sceptical about idealizing personal relations must admit that these differ from what markets and state agencies expect. Most people still fall in love and will continue to do so and invest in their love by trying to cope with the many crises, and invest in having children (Huinink, 2001). However, it might suffice to have and love only one child, perhaps a second, if loving parents think it is nice for their child to have a companion and ally.

Love implies solidarity and even sacrifice. This is why, strictly speaking, ideas and norms of partnership and love do not go well together. Being a good partner requires a fair division of domestic labour and equal mutual support for both partners' jobs. To summarize, it requires strict reciprocity if not equivalence of give and take, i.e. compliance with public as well as market – not private – virtues (Koppetsch, 2001). Love, however, indulges what partnership norms denigrate as a violation of fairness and individual autonomy and even view as exploitation. Parents increasingly perceive and invest in their children as 'expansion of their own selves' (Huinink, 2001). Children are expected to develop in such a way as to match or accomplish their parents' selves. Like partnership, the idea of children as private goods or values and non-economic utilities opens the door to strategic thinking and a very restricted notion of reciprocity and continuity.

In the twentieth century families became 'dear' in every sense of the word. For some people it might have turned into a matter of cost calculation, but most people mainly still perceive the family as an entity that entails two relationships and patterns of love, with an adult couple on the one hand and children on the other. Both relationships are ambiguous and open to tension, and they do not easily coincide (Tyrell, 2001). Intimate spousal relations specialize in love and happiness and are based on daily face-to-face contact and physical interaction. Their closeness does not tolerate much third party intervention. Conflicts, even violent ones, can easily arise in this type of setting and can often only be avoided by a fictional consensus. Since love and parental relations follow different logics, children are usually the ones who suffer and lose out due to parental conflicts. Ambiguities make love and personal communication fail, parents split up, or women and men refrain from having any children at all. New ideas like partnership have entered the family, but no matter how positive they might be from a citizen's perspective, they do not combine well with love and solidarity.

There are any number of reasons not to have children, most of them non-economic (Burkart, 1994). Public discourses and policies, however, have thus far been largely linked to economic cost-of-children explanations for the low fertility rates. Many of them favour de-familialization, i.e. providing more public care services to relieve families from filial and parental obligations. It is argued that they lower the opportunity costs for women to have children and jobs at the same time. This rationale obviously overlooks the specific complexity of spousal and parental relations. It also overlooks the fact that economic resources and better work and family arrangements are still not enough to motivate women and men to have children. Parents still want to promise their children a good future. Whether or not they will want to have children thus depends on how women and men evaluate what the future will bring for their children (Huinink, 1995; Ostner, 2001). Money and services provided by society are only part of the future. Discourses do matter here. Focusing on the economic costs of having a family and the negative aspects of family life will deter people who are already reluctant and calculating. However it is the financial burdens and family failures that have been mostly publicized, at least in Germany.

DE-FAMILIALIZATION – A NEW DEAL BETWEEN FAMILIES AND SOCIETY?

The family has been often criticized. Only naive functionalists assume that families function as expected. At present, however, critics of the family identify multiple family failures. The solution to much of the dysfunction that has been proposed requires significant de-familialization – reduced family obligations to care for one's own children and elderly family members – to safeguard the family. Elites wedded to power make assumptions about the family and family practices – often with little reference to the empirical experiences of children or their parents – and design policy proposals. These assumptions and proposals easily enter public debates and agendas and imprint themselves on policies to restructure western welfare states. OECD and European Commission experts see the family primarily if not exclusively as a function of the labour market. This holds true even in cases where experts care about declining fertility rates, persistent gender inequality in unpaid care or deficient early childhood education. Unsurprisingly, children enter assumptions and proposals as costs or as opportunities that should either be reduced or taken (Ostner, 2002).

German sociologists and politicians, including conservative ones, maintain that the family has lost out due to continuity and change alike. On the one hand they argue that families have not changed enough, especially in their attitudes towards their children. Families are said to have remained non-democratic, authoritarian or indifferent, which makes it difficult for their children to adjust to an increasingly complex world (Schneider, 2002). Since families divorce, reorganize and divorce again, they can no longer provide the stability and security children need to learn how to cope with increased work expectations (BMFSFJ, 2002). As a consequence, mothers' and fathers' contributions to their children and to wider society are seen as decreasing. It is also argued that families do no better than other providers such as childcare centres, since the quality of family achievements depends so much on such factors as the quality of the attachment between children and their parents and the quality of the parents' relationship, personality, social class and circumstances (Schneider, 2002). This relatively negative assessment of family efforts becomes more salient if it is combined with other family failures like declining birth rates, low female labour market participation and children's poverty. In addition, families seem to no longer appropriately teach their children. Politicians argue in favour of public early childhood education. In sum, the diagnosis of German politicians and sociologists mirrors what was described earlier as a break with continuity and the erosion of parental expertise and authority.

The solution that has been proposed to deal with the numerous family failures is both paradoxical and radical. It requires de-familialization to safeguard the family that is by definition reduced to 'any living arrangement with children'.[6] Obviously, the new definition cuts off the second generational aspect, the relation between adult children and their elderly parents. The present focus is on young children. If people are to have more children, far-reaching de-familialization is called for. Measures that allow for better work and family life arrangements are to harmonize gender roles and enhance positive attitudes towards the family (Huinink, 2002; BMFSFJ, 2002). Liberating families, mostly women, from family obligations will not only increase women's employment, it will increase the birth rate.

De-familialization has so far focused on highly qualified women. They are said to especially experience the opportunity costs of having children and child care at home. Huinink speaks of 'structural constraints' and 'structural familialism' that keep women from having a career equal to their male counterparts as opposed to 'cultural constraints' and 'cultural familialism' that still makes women have children and fully care for them. Although the emphasis is on highly qualified women whose resources (skills, labour, children) are needed and can be made available via de-familialization, 'cultural familialism' – the quality of loving relationships in the intimacy of the private sphere – has in itself been questioned. Why do women still care for their children at home? Why don't they work?[7] Or why should mothers work? One answer is given by the OECD:

> The main policy concern addressed is that of encouraging a higher participation by mothers in paid employment. This is important to maintain their labour market skills, to ensure adequate resources for families and women living by themselves, and to make further progress towards gender equity. In addition, the skills of mothers will be increasingly needed in the labour market as the population of working age in most OECD countries begins to shrink. The chapter notes the probable relevance of the work/family relationship to fertility – the low fertility rates seen in most OECD countries will exacerbate shortfalls in labour supply if they continue (2001, p. 29ff).

De-familializing measures that aim to increase the employment of all mothers, including happy non-working and unskilled ones, are seen as family-friendly. These women, argues the OECD, 'may become detached from the labour market and be unable to make a successful entry, or re-entry, later in life' (ibid, p.154).

Since most EU countries pursue a part-time strategy for increasing women's labour market participation and many mothers prefer part-time work, it should at least be continuous. Germany has adopted this strategy and redesigned institutions and redefined institutional rules to increase incentives for mothers to continue to work part-time. Policies to boost employability and fight poverty by enhancing the transition of one-earner to dual-earner-households and strategies to ensure the supply of human capital have merged in de-familializing policies. Put in a more provocative way: the family has become a function of the labour market; children have become opportunity costs for families, and public, in fact economic assets for society.

In the course of reforms following the de-familialization path, generational reciprocity has been shifted from the familial to the societal level. One may speak of '*Vergesellschaftung*' or of give and take between children and parents. Social rights are to be matched by social obligations that citizens

owe society. Women and men of working age, including parents, are expected to be employed, pay taxes and contribute to social security. Children
enter the school system earlier than ever. In turn, society offers services to
citizen mothers, citizen fathers and citizen children, which are paid by taxes
and premiums, to help them meet the expectations of an increasingly open
and competitive market economy. Obligations are first towards society, and
in reality towards market needs. Entitlements, above all, pertain to employability. Is the care of frail elderly people thus left to their families? Pensions
are declining, old-age income security is rapidly eroding for low wage-
earners and growing numbers of the flexibly employed. Many frail elderly
people may become economically and socially vulnerable again, public social
care arrangements notwithstanding. Who will take care of them and be their
public advocates if not their children?

Filial and parental obligations are still strongly felt, and give and take still
flourish between children and parents. The state and society, however, have
increasingly come to provide for children and the elderly based on the idea of
a public contract between the generations. German sociologists call the reciprocal give and take of cash and care within families the 'private' or 'small'
generational contract. Citizens' support for public measures, often redistributive ones, is often explained by their familiarity with the first contract,
the give and take in extended families (Kohli, 1993). Unsurprisingly, familialist welfare states have so far provided generous old-age pensions, especially compared with public expenditure for children. But these provisions
have been severely attacked (see Esping-Andersen et al., 2001).

One might argue that, since the private and public generational contracts
intertwine, sooner or later any change in private or public commitment will
feed back. Optimists stress the quality of personal relationships that most
people continue to seek and enjoy, all the tension notwithstanding. If children
have loving parents, if their mothers and fathers visibly and lovingly care
about or even provide care for their own parents, they may support policies to
care for those in need, however costly. Pessimists allude to the limited time
budgets of employed mothers and fathers and increasingly of children as
well. More importantly, they allude to increasingly strategic attitudes towards
others that are needed to survive competitive environments. While sociologists like Martin Kohli maintain that vital family ties have so far supported
redistributive policies favouring the elderly, there are very few theoretical
accounts that elaborate the conditions for this type of support in the future.

NOTES

1. I took the title from the article 'What are children for?' by Laurie and Matthew Taylor, in *Prospect* magazine, June 2001. I am also indebted to a collection of articles edited by Huinink, Strohmeier and Wagner (2001) in *Solidarität in Partnerschaft und Familie* ('Solidarity in partnership and family'). I thank the editors Trudie Knijn and Aafke Komter and the participants of the Amsterdam meeting for their helpful comments.

2.. While even 'familialist' EU welfare states are rapidly moving towards dual earning or as Jane Lewis (2001) calls it the 'adult worker model', this model comes in many forms. Most married or partnered women work part-time, and often short hours.

3. Ehmer (2000) emphasises that 'family' and 'affiliation' are socio-cultural, not biological or genetic categories. This is clear in the case of adoption – adopting a child instead of having a biological one – a practice widespread in many cultures (including Germany where children immediately gain citizenship rights regardless of notorious *ius sanguinis* based membership rules by being adopted). Behavioural biologists (Paul, 1998; Skamel and Voland, 2000) also stress the role of the context for explaining parental (even maternal) as well as non-biological group members' often caring attitudes towards children.

4. I am grateful to Jane Lewis, who formulated this argument at the Amsterdam meeting where I presented a draft version of the article.

5. This contradicts the laws of 'familialist' countries (including Germany), stipulating that children have to provide cash for their needy parents all their lives and vice versa. Germany has recently started to deviate from this rule, though: neither poor pensioners nor lone mothers of children below the age three have to first rely on cash from their children or parents before they are eligible for social assistance.

6. In the 2002 federal election campaign, all the political parties converged in defining the family as any living arrangement with children: 'Familie ist wo Kinder sind' ('Family is where children are'). The Christian Democrats supported this stance more ambivalently though, but for strategic reasons.

7. One might easily turn the question around and ask: Why should they work? And more specifically: Why should unskilled mothers work? Poor mothers and in general poor families have only recently gained some rights and opportunities to take care of their own children. This has in turn imprinted on their attitudes and practices, something which should not be deplored.

REFERENCES

Axelrod, R. (1984), *The Evolution of Cooperation*, New York: Basic Books.

Becker, G. (1981), *A Treatise on the Family*, Cambridge: Harvard Univerity Press.

Bien, W. (2000), 'Die multilokale Familie. Beziehungen zwischen den Generationen am Beispiel von Deutschland', in J. Ehmer and P. Gutschner (eds), *Das Alter im Spiel der Generationen*, Wien-Köln-Weimar: Böhlau, pp. 193 - 209.

BMFSFJ (2002), *Elfter Kinder- und Jugendbericht. Bericht über die Lebenssituation junger Menschen und die Leistungen der Kinder- und Jugendhilfe in Deutschland*, Bonn: Bundesministerium für Familie, Senioren, Frauen und Jugend.

Burkart, G. (1994), *Die Entscheidung zur Elternschaft*, Stuttgart: Enke.

Coleman, J.S. (1990), *Foundations of Social Theory*, Cambridge: Harvard University Press.

Dallinger, U. (1993), 'Die Pflege alter Eltern – Balanceakt zwischen Normerfüllung und Individualisierungschancen im weiblichen Lebenslauf', *Sozialer Fortschritt* **42**, 110 - 113.

Daly, M. (2000), 'A fine balance: women's labour market participation in International Comparison', in F.W. Scharpf and V.A. Schmidt (eds), *Welfare and Work in the Open Economy*, Vol. II, Oxford: Oxford University Press, pp. 467 - 511.

Datenreport (2002), *Datenreport 2002*, edited by the Bundeszentrale für Politische Bildung, Bonn: Bundeszentrale für Politische Bildung.

Ehmer, J. (2000), 'Alter und Generationsbeziehungen im Spannungsfeld von öffentlichem und privaten Leben', in J. Ehmer and P. Gutschner (eds), *Das Alter im Spiel der Generationen*, Wien-Köln-Weimar: Böhlau, pp. 15 - 48.

Ehmer, J. and P. Gutschner (eds) (2000), *Das Alter im Spiel der Generationen*. Wien-Köln-Weimar: Böhlau.

Esping-Andersen, G. (1996), 'Welfare states without work: the impasse of labour shedding and familialism in continental European social policy', in G. Esping-Andersen (ed.), *Welfare States in Transition. National Adaptations in Global Economies*, London: Sage, pp. 66 - 87.

Esping-Andersen, G. (1999), *Social Foundations of Post-industrial Economies*, Oxford: Oxford University Press.

Esping-Andersen, G, D. Gallie, A. Hemerijck and J. Myles (2001), *A New Welfare Architecture for Europe?*, Report to the Belgian Presidency of the EU, Brussels: CEC.

Fagnani, J. (2002), 'Why do French women have more children than German women? Family policies and attitudes towards child care outside the home', *Community, Work & Family*, **5** (1), 103 - 119.

Gouldner, A.W. (1984), *Reziprozität und Autonomie. Ausgewählte Aufsätze*, edited by E. Weingarten and H. Ebbinghaus, Frankfurt a.M.: Suhrkamp.

Gouldner, A.W. (1996), 'The norm of reciprocity', in A. Komter (ed.), *The Gift: An Interdisciplinary Perspective*, Amsterdam: Amsterdam University Press, pp. 39 - 48.

Günther, T. (2001), 'Zwischen Rationalisierung und Kolonisierung der Lebenswelt. Zum familiensoziologischen Gehalt von Habermas' "Theorie des kommunikativen Handelns"', in J. Huinink, K.P. Strohmeier and M. Wagner (eds), *Solidarität in Partnerschaft und Familie*, Würzburg: Ergon, pp. 65 - 83.

Habermas, J. (1973), *Legitimationsprobleme im Spatkapitalismus*, Frankfurt: Suhrkamp.

Hendrick, H. (1994), *Child Welfare in England 1872 - 1989*, London: Routledge.

Hondrich, K.O. and C. Koch-Arzberger (1992), *Solidarität in der modernen Gesellschaft*, Frankfurt a.M.: Fischer TB.

Huinink, J. (1995), *Warum noch Familie? Zur Attraktivität von Partnerschaft und Elternschaft in unserer Gesellschaft*, Frankfurt a.M.: Campus.

Huinink, J. (2001), 'Entscheidungs- und Vereinbarkeitsprobleme bei der Wahl familialer Lebensformen', in J. Huinink, K.P. Strohmeier and M. Wagner (eds), *Solidarität in Partnerschaft und Familie*, Würzburg: Ergon, pp. 145 - 65.

Huinink, J. (2002), Polarisierung der Familienentwicklung in europäischen Ländern im Vergleich', in N.F. Schneider and H. Matthias-Bleck (eds), *Elternschaft heute. Gesellschaftliche Rahmenbedingungen und individuelle Gestaltungsaufgaben* (Zeitschrift für Familienforschung. Sonderheft 2), Opladen: Leske + Budrich, pp. 49 - 73.

Huinink, J., K.P. Strohmeier and M. Wagner (eds) (2001), *Solidarität in Partnerschaft und Familie*, Würzburg: Ergon.

Key, E. ([1902)]1992), *Das Jahrhundert des Kindes*, Weinheim and Basel: Beltz.

Kohli, M. (1993), 'Generationenbeziehungen auf dem Arbeitsmarkt – Die Erwerbsbeteiligung der Älteren in alternden Gesellschaften', in K. Lüscher and F. Schultheis (eds), *Generationsbeziehungen in 'postmodernen' Gesellschaften. Analysen zum Verhältnis von Individuum, Familie, Staat und Gesellschaft*, Konstanz: Universitätsverlag, 383 - 401.

Koppetsch, C. (2001), 'Die Pflicht zur Liebe und das Geschenk der Partnerschaft: Paradoxien in der Praxis von Paarbeziehungen', in J. Huinink, K.P. Strohmeier and M. Wagner (eds), *Solidarität in Partnerschaft und Familie*, Würzburg: Ergon, pp. 219 - 39.

Lewis, J. (2001), 'The decline of the male breadwinner model: implications for work and care', *Social Politics*, **8** (2), 152 - 169.

Motel, A. and M. Szydlik (1999), 'Private Transfers zwischen den Generationen', *Zeitschrift für Soziologie*, **28** (1), 3 - 22.

Nell-Breuning, O. von (1957), 'Solidarität und Subsidiarität im Raume von Sozialpolitik und Sozialreform', in E. Boettcher (ed.), *Sozialpolitik und Sozialreform*, Tübingen: Mohr, pp. 213 - 26.

OECD (2001), 'Balancing work and family life: helping parents into paid employment', in OECD (ed.), *Employment Outlook*, Paris: OECD, pp. 89 - 166.

Ostner, I. (2001), 'Régimes de protection sociale, taux d'activité des femmes et famille', in C. Daniel and B. Palier (eds), *La protection sociale en Europe. Le temps de réformes*, Paris: MIRE/DREES, pp. 153 - 68.

Ostner, I. (2002), 'Am Kind vorbei – Ideen und Interessen in der jüngeren Familienpolitik', *Zeitschrift für Soziologie der Erziehung und Sozialization*, **22** (3), 247 - 66.

Paul, A. (1998), *Von Affen und Menschen. Verhaltensbiologie der Primaten*, Darmstadt: Wissenschaftliche Buchgesellschaft.

Schneider, N.F. (2002), 'Elternschaft heute. Gesellschaftliche Rahmenbedingungen und individuelle Gestaltungsaufgaben – Einführende Betrachtungen', in N.F. Schneider and H. Matthias-Bleck (eds), *Elternschaft heute. Gesellschaftliche Rahmenbedingungen und individuelle Gestaltungsaufgaben,* (Zeitschrift für Familienforschung. Sonderheft 2), Opladen: Leske + Budrich, pp. 9 - 21.

Sieder, R. 1997), 'Freisetzung und Bindung. Eine Fallstudie zu aktuellen Dynamiken im Ehe- und Familienleben', in J. Ehmer et al. (eds), *Historische Familienforschung. Ergebnisse und Kontroversen*, Frankfurt a.M.: Suhrkamp, pp. 220 - 53.

Simmel, G. ([1908] 1983), *Soziologie*, Berlin: Duncker and Humblot.

Sims-Schouten, W. (2000), 'Child care services and parents' attitudes in England, Finland and Greece', in A.A. Pfenning and T. Bahle (eds), *Families and Family Policies in Europe: Comparative Perspectives*, Frankfurt a. M.: Lang, pp. 270 - 88.

Skamel, U. and E. Voland (2000), 'Vom ewigen Kampf der Geschlechter zu Solidarität in Partnerschaft und Familie', in J. Ehmer and P. Gutschner (eds), *Das Alter im Spiel der Generationen*, Wien-Köln-Weimar: Böhlau, pp. 85 - 102.

Szydlik, M. (1999), 'Erben in der Bundesrepublik Deutschland. Zum Verhältnis von familialer Solidarität und sozialer Ungleichheit', *Kölner Zeitschrift für Soziologie und Sozialpsychologie,* **51** (1), 80 - 104.

Taylor, L. and M. Taylor (2001), 'What are children for?', *Prospect Magazine*, June 2001, 22 – 6.

Therborn, G. (1993), 'The politics of childhood: the rights of children in modern times. A comparative study of Western nations', in F.F. Castles (ed.), *Families of Nations,* Aldershot: Ashgate, pp. 241 - 291.

Tyrell, H. (2001), 'Das konflikttheoretische Defizit der Familiensoziologie', in J. Huinink, K.P. Strohmeier and M. Wagner (eds), *Solidarität in Partnerschaft und Familie*, Würzburg: Ergon, pp. 43 - 63.

Ullrich, C.G., (2000), *Solidarität im Sozialversicherungsstaat. Die Akzeptanz des Sozialversicherungsprinzips in der Gesetzlichen Krankenversicherung*, Frankfurt a.M.: Campus.

11. Post-Industrial Families: New Forms of Bonding?

Arnlaug Leira

Across Western Europe, the moral and material basis of post-industrial families is now the subject of discussion. A weakening of marriage as the basis for family formation, an increase in the divorce rate and growing employment among women are all indicative of a fragmentation of the safety net family and kin once provided and demonstrate how the family's capacity to provide welfare and care can no longer be taken for granted. In this setting, it is no wonder the relation between the family and the welfare state is high up on the political agenda: a yearning for a revival of family values, morals and duties is commonly voiced. At the same time, there are increasing demands for the defamilialization of family obligations as welfare states are denounced for failing to meet the welfare and social service needs of the population (Saraceno, 1997).[1]

Different forms of the welfare state support different family forms, and the boundaries between the welfare state and the family are drawn up differently (Leira, 1994; Millar and Warman, 1996; Esping-Andersen, 1999). Since the 1970s and 1980s, social reproduction in the Nordic welfare states has been depicted as going public (Hernes, 1984), but in Southern Europe the impact of familialistic ideology is still evident in welfare legislation and family law (e.g. Saraceno, 1994; Esping-Andersen, 1996). In other words, the debate on the rights and responsibilities that being part of a family entails should make it clear how the relation between the welfare state and the family is defined, and what family relationships the state aims to influence, strengthen or uphold.

Terms like family responsibilities or family obligations generally have at least three connotations: 1) the common normative assumptions in a society concerning what family members ought to do for one another, 2) what they actually do, and 3) the prescriptions defined in legislation and public policy (Finch, 1989; Leira, 1996).   This chapter focuses on family obligations, re-

sponsibilities and duties in the latter sense, as formally constructed and politically institutionalized. I present a brief overview of family obligations in
Western Europe as stipulated in family and welfare legislation, and then turn
to Scandinavia, where the expansion of the welfare state has been interpreted
as producing a defamilialization of responsibilities (Esping-Andersen, 1999).[2]
Important as they may be, I contend that de-familializing processes do not
give the full Scandinavian picture; there is a more complicated story to family policies. In the 1990s, some reforms promoted defamilialization but others
supported a familialization and refamilialization of care and welfare. Family
policies were even aimed at creating new forms of bonding, illustrated well
in reforms supporting relationships between fathers and their children. Examining the politicization of parental responsibilities, in concluding I devote
special attention to the adoption and use of childcare-related reforms and
discuss the gendered outcomes.

WHO IS FAMILY?

Family law and welfare legislation identifies who is and who is not 'family';
it defines who is included and who is excluded from the rights and obligations related to being family and articulates the contents of formal family-
related rights and responsibilities. In a legal sense, who belongs to a family is
defined by descent and adoption or marriage, and in some countries by formal agreements on non-marital (sometimes homosexual) partnerships. In
some countries, family and welfare legislation refers primarily to the nuclear
family, though in others it may include the extended family as well. As formally defined, family duties refer to relations within and between generations. Often gender-neutral in their formulation, family obligations circum-
scribe a division of labour and responsibilities between women and men as
partners/spouses, mothers and fathers, sons and daughters, and obligations to
family have different implications for women and men (e.g. Saraceno, 1997).
    What family duties are about, their scope and content, varies across West-
ern Europe (see e.g. Millar and Warman, 1995; Hantrais and Letablier, 1996;
Gauthier, 1996). Heading from the south of Europe to the north, what is
meant by formal family obligations decreases from a wide set of family relationships to one that only includes a limited set. In the Mediterranean region,
family obligations refer to spouses and their dependent children and may also
include members of the extended family. In some countries such as France,
The Netherlands and the UK, family obligations are mainly restricted to the
nuclear family, while in the Nordic countries formal family obligations are
minimal and state care is generally individualized (Millar and Warman,
1996). The variation also illustrates whether state care is considered second

to family care or vice versa, when it comes to providing for relatives who can not fully provide for themselves. In the Mediterranean region, the state is considered second to the family, thus demonstrating the familialistic ideology at work (Banfield, 1958; Saraceno, 1994; Esping-Andersen 1999). In the Nordic countries the family is defined in several respects as second to the welfare state, the family is depicted as 'going public' and the welfare state is referred to as a 'caring state', terms invoking positive as well as negative connotations (Hernes, 1984, 1987; Jensen, 1990).

Differences between welfare states in terms of family arrangements are demonstrated in an analysis of reproduction policies by Anttonen and Sipilä (1996), who focus on the state-family division of responsibility for the care of very young children and the elderly. Highlighting social reproduction, traditionally a family responsibility, the authors underscore the considerable public investment in social care, particularly in Sweden, Finland and Denmark. The welfare states with limited provisions include Germany, Greece and Spain, and the medium providers include France, Italy, the UK, The Netherlands and Norway. Indeed, classifications of welfare states based on studies of reproduction policies do not necessarily correspond to those focused on the social rights of the wage-earner (e.g. Saraceno, 1997; Gornick et al., 1998). Interestingly, a number of these studies generate classifications that differ from the seminal regime typology by Esping-Andersen (1990), classifying the Scandinavian states as social democratic, Great Britain and Ireland among the liberal, and Italy, France, Germany among others as belonging to the conservative welfare state regime.

Returning to the relation between the state and the family, Esping-Andersen (1999) finds that his tripartite typology of welfare states largely based on the arrangement between the welfare state and the labour market still holds; the degree of de-familialization adds to the distinctions between different types of welfare state regimes. 'A familialistic welfare regime is (..) one that assigns a maximum of welfare obligations to the household' (1999, p. 45). A defamilializing regime '(..) is one which seeks to unburden the household and diminish individuals' welfare dependence on kinship' (p. 51). Hence, in Esping Andersen's analysis, the conservative welfare states, especially the Mediterranean welfare states, are the more familialistic, while the liberal and social democratic ones have opted for de-familializing, the liberal ones by using market provided services and the social democratic ones by developing state-funded services (Esping-Andersen, 1999, p. 85; see also Korpi, 2000).

FROM INDUSTRIALISM TO POST-INDUSTRIALISM: FAMILY MODELS

In Scandinavia, the shift from the gender-differentiated nuclear family to the dual earners started in the 1950s, first in Finland, then in Sweden and Denmark, and lastly in Norway. Social research has captured the change in family forms in different models: one model presumes a specialization of the roles of the mother and the father, another views the mother as the second or junior provider, and a third projects shared societal roles for the parents. In a condensed form, the three models convey important interpretations of family and family values in Western societies and reflect the influence of different cultural and political traditions. In the first model, known in social analysis particularly from the work of Talcott Parsons (1955), work and the family are combined via a differentiation of the roles of the mother and the father as homemaker/carer and economic provider. Potential conflicts of interest are defined away by assuming the domestication of women to be natural, leaving the role of breadwinner to the male head of household. The second model includes the sequential, secondary employment of mothers. Acknowledging that women's employment was rising, Myrdal and Klein (1956) outlined and advocated a family form where mothers take on more of the economic provider responsibilities in periods when paid work does not conflict with maternal duties. Thus, the domestication of women is denaturalized and the male breadwinner privilege loosened. A very different arrangement is the one presented by Liljeström (1978) as the shared roles model. Presuming that mothers and fathers are both capable of being employed and of taking care of children, this is an early identification of a dual-earner, care-sharing family, and a family model that has proved highly controversial.

A common presumption of the models is that parents cooperate with respect to economic provision and to family-related domestic work and care, although in very different ways. The first two models focus on a differentiation by gender, ascribing the main breadwinner responsibilities to the husband/father and the homemaking and caring to his mate, the mother/housewife. The third model, however, intimates a more equal sharing of tasks, a de-differentiation. Any recent empirical survey of family forms in Scandinavia would include all three models. Since the 1970s, however, the dual-earner family is numerically predominant among parents of young children. This does not necessarily mean that the influence of the gender-differentiated family model is a thing of the past, although it has been reduced. As normative statements on 'good' motherhood, fatherhood and childhood, the three models are indicative of conflicting social norms and political interests when it comes to the policy response to different family forms. What happens to the division of labour if the parents split up, the models do not foretell. Family policy reforms now increasingly underline the responsibilities of both parents to care and provide for their children even if the couple relationship has ended.

Although more indirectly, Liljeström's study reflects an approach to families, and especially to parenthood, work and the state, that has had a profound impact on Scandinavian societies. All able-bodied adults are expected to be able to provide economically for themselves and their children by working for wages. Full employment includes the commodification of women's labour. Accordingly, marriage and the family have become less important as economic provider institutions for women. Paid work enables the economic provider aspects of motherhood. It also furthers the contribution of mothers to the common good via their payment of taxes. Public funding of services for the ill, the frail elderly and children promotes women's gainful employment and serves to maintain the institutional welfare state developed in the Nordic countries. In the jargon of the 1970s, social reproduction was going public, an interpretation later integrated in Hernes's (1987) outline of the woman-friendly potentialities of the Nordic welfare state, and in Esping-Andersen's analysis of the defamilializing welfare state. Hernes (1984) also uses the term 'public family' to specify the transfer of responsibility for care provision from the family to the state and local government. In this process, individual needs are redefined to form a basis for social rights, and the public provision of services adds to the repertoire of economic benefits available as of right. Hence the responsibility of the state and local government has increased with the decrease of the responsibility of the family.

DE-FAMILIALIZING WELFARE STATES?

In the Nordic region, welfare state expansion in the fields of education, public health, welfare and social care has meant a profound redrawing of the boundaries between the state and the family. Formal obligations are restricted to the nuclear family. Spouses are under a reciprocal obligation to support and care for each other as long as the marriage lasts, but cohabiting partners are not. Family policies are very much about parents and their dependent children. Formally, the responsibility for the care of dependent adults and the frail elderly lies with the state and local authorities. This does not mean that the welfare state has completely replaced the help of the family; families are still highly important as care providers for the elderly, often in cooperation with public or market-based services (e.g. national reports in Millar and Warman, 1995; Lingsom, 1997; Szebehely, 1998).[3]

Although by no means underestimating the differences in the formal obligations to the family in Western Europe, the Millar and Warman classification does seem to exaggerate the dilution of formal duties to the family in the Nordic countries, indicating that individualism reigns supreme and families have been freed of the responsibility to care and provide for the well-being of their members. In Scandinavia, however, an individualization of rights is accompanied by policy measures aimed at reinforcing some family relationships. In particular, the Millar and Warman analysis underplays the significance of one set of family responsibilities, i.e. of parents for their dependent children. As in other European countries, these responsibilities generally include a dual set of duties to provide for the child materially and to nurture, care, rear and foster the child. In addition, parents have a responsibility and a right to make decisions concerning the child in personal matters. The state and local authorities share the responsibility with the parents to provide care for children. In fact the care of children is commonly regarded as a 'joint venture' between parents and the state. The state contributes to the costs of raising children via family allowances and funds of various forms of childcare. Subsequently, over time, state intervention has redesigned the parental obligation to provide materially for children as well as the responsibility to raise, nurture and care for them. But this does not mean that parental responsibility has gone; it has attained new dimensions. As a social institution, the family is changing, but the image of the individual who has been set free from family responsibilities does require some qualification.

NEW FAMILY FORMS

Two of the processes generating family change and adding to the debate on family policy reform deserve special mention: one is the weakening of marriage as the legitimate basis for family formation, and the other is the rise in women's labour market participation and the decline of the male breadwinner norm. Indeed, the changing gender balance of employment is taken as a characteristic of post-industrial labour markets, and the dual-earner family as the model family of post-industrialism (Esping-Andersen, 1996). However, it should be noted that the impact of these processes varies from one European region to the other, welfare states differ in their response, and the processes have affected women and men in different ways.

In recent decades the Nordic countries have witnessed a weakening of marriage, as is illustrated by the growing numbers of couples who live together without being married and of extramarital births, and the high divorce rates and increase in non-married couples breaking-up. Cohabitation without marriage is especially popular among young people, though it is not exclusive to them. It is not always clear what norms and obligations sustain consensual, extra-contractual family arrangements that are not covered by formal agreements between the partners. With the exception of legislating for the right of homosexual partnerships, the Nordic authorities have not been in any hurry to legislate for adults who want to live together without being married (e.g. Koch-Nielsen, 1996; Bjørnberg and Eydal, 1995; Anttonen et al., 1995; Leira 1996). The rapid privatization of heterosexual partnership and cohabitation has however made parenthood more of a public concern. Just as marriage is becoming less important in signifying family formation, biological parenthood or blood relations are becoming more important. In the mid-1990s about half the children born in Denmark, Norway and Sweden were born to parents who were not married (Jensen, 1999, p. 8), and the protection of the parent-child relationship has become increasingly important in policy reform. From the 1970s onwards, Nordic family policies have emphasized that parental obligations are an ongoing concern. Regardless of decisions made by the parents about their couple relationship, parenthood is forever.

Following the rise in extramarital births, the identification of the biological father is being given a higher priority. This is advocated as a support for children in knowing both their parents, and as a means of strengthening the relationship between the father and the child. Whatever the formal or informal relationship between the parents, whether they are married or not and whether or not they have ever lived with the child, parents are under the obligation to provide and care for their children. As in several countries in Europe, the Nordic countries have introduced policy reforms to protect the relationship between children and the biological parent who does not live with them after a parental break-up, separation or divorce (see e.g. national reports in Millar and Warman, 1995). Cohabiting parents split up far more often than married parents, and the percentage of children whose parents break-up or get a divorce is rising. An increasing number of children spend parts of their childhood living with only one parent, and an increasing number of parents, especially mothers, experience periods when they are the main or lone parent.

When parents split up, the economic provider obligations of the parent who leaves still apply to married and unmarried parents, and to some extent the obligation to pay child support has been reinforced. The rights of biological parents to care for their children even if they don't live in the same house have been expanded. These measures appear to have been motivated by a mixture of economic and moral reasons: to maintain the obligations of parents who live elsewhere to provide for their children, to lessen the public expense on child support, and to maintain the right of the child and the non-residing parent to keep a relationship going.[4]

According to Jensen (1999), it is the changes in parenthood more than in partnership that have been the central elements in the family changes in Europe. She notes a shrinking of fatherhood due to decreased fertility in

Southern Europe, family dissolution in the Northern countries and a combination of the two trends in Eastern Europe (see also Kotowska in this volume). However, as noted, even if more parents split up, in Scandinavia the formal rights of the child to maintain a relationship with both parents have been strengthened.

THE PARTIAL DECLINE OF THE MALE BREADWINNER NORM

Changes in parenthood are also highly visible among mothers in Western Europe. In a period of labour market restructuring and spells of high unemployment, the economic activity rates of women and mothers exhibit a long-term increase. In this respect, welfare states are gradually converging. An OECD report (1994) indicates a vast transformation of the social order: the gender-differentiated nuclear family no longer serves to support the general employment contract based on the male breadwinner, dual-parent family. A feminization of the labour force has come to characterize the post-industrial labour markets, and among parents with young children, dual earners are now the dominant family form.

The structural incompatibility between the labour market and the family increasingly prompts questions on the welfare state's response to new family forms, particularly employed mothers and dual-earners. Which family models (if any) should welfare states facilitate, how and why? For example, should the welfare state support families where the mother goes out to work and bears more of the breadwinner responsibilities, or should it support families where the mother stays home and depends economically on her husband or partner as provider? Indeed, the post-industrial family, characterized by the decline of the male breadwinner norm, is regarded by some as necessitating the intervention of the welfare state to harmonize work and family obligations (Esping-Andersen, 1996). However, since the shift from the single-earner to the dual-earner family has often preceded policy reform, this is far from the general experience (see e.g. Leira, 1992; Lewis, 1993; EC Childcare Network, 1996; Drew et al., 1998).

In the 1990s, women's employment rates approached those of men in Scandinavia. Ever since the 1960s the employment rates of the mothers of pre-schoolers had rapidly increased and they remained high at 70 - 80% in the 1990s. By and large though, mothers and fathers did not enter the labour market on equal terms; the Nordic labour markets are characterized by strong sex segregation and part-time work is widespread, especially among Norwegian and Swedish mothers. However, as the gender balance of employment shifted and the economic provider aspects of motherhood became more pronounced, the call for public support of childcare was put on the political agenda. Increasingly, policy reforms have addressed the issue of combining work and family. Public day care for children was promoted to facilitate the employment of mothers and as being advantageous for children. Access to high-quality state-funded childcare is even sometimes presented as a child's democratic right. The 1970s also witnessed a broadening of the welfare state approach to working parents: childcare in the Scandinavian welfare states was redesigned as being an interest common to both parents and the state. Policies aimed at combining work and family targeted fathers as well as mothers. The concept of the caring father was politically institutionalized and the familializing of fathers was put on the political agenda well before it became a policy issue in other countries. Familializing reforms were added to state-funded de-familialized childcare services, as witnessed in the expansion of parental leave legislation and prolongation of the leave period. Parental leave legislation illustrates the welfare state policies promoting new forms of fatherhood. Importantly, the mother no longer has the sole right to care for a newborn child, the father is also entitled to paid leave for infant care.

CHILDCARE AS A SOCIAL RIGHT: FAMILY CHANGE AND POLICY REFORM

In recent decades in Scandinavia, the concept of childcare has been expanded from its central element of being a parental obligation to children, and now includes the parent's right to make legitimate claims on the state. In this respect, the welfare state is not generally regarded as undermining the moral obligations of parents, but as supporting the parent - child relationship. The reconceptualization of childcare is of special interest, I argue, illustrating as it does how care-related rights may entail the familialization as well as the de-familialization of childcare and the commodification as well as the decommodification of the parent as carer. Parents' acceptance and use of their entitlements also demonstrate gendered outcomes of reforms that are in principle gender-neutral entitlements.

The childcare-related policies that are of special relevance to working parents include benefits in cash and kind related to services, time and money. The three sets of policies mentioned here include the state sponsoring of childcare services, the expansion of paid parental leave, and the legislation of cash benefits for childcare. Roughly speaking, these policies may be linked to the three family models mentioned above: cash benefits for parental childcare schemes encourage the gender-differentiated family, childcare services facilitate the employment of mothers and the dual-earner model, and parental leave legislation further encourages dual-earning and care-sharing parenthood.

If state-funded childcare services are universally provided or parents are entitled to claim such services, access to publicly funded day care for children becomes a social right. Part of the care for children is de-familialized and the responsibility is collectivized. All the Nordic governments aim to make publicly funded childcare available for all the children whose parents want it, promoting universal access in an egalitarian tradition. Access to state-funded services is formally established as a social right in Finland, where local authorities are under the obligation to provide a place in state-funded childcare if the parents do not want to claim a cash grant for childcare. Denmark and Sweden are close to universal provisions for parents who wish to have their children in publicly funded childcare facilities, and Norway is planning for full coverage of the demand by 2005. State-sponsored services supplement care provided at home and have been instrumental in allowing both parents to engage in paid employment. Since the option for fathers not to participate in care for children has clearly been widely accepted, the public provision of childcare has been interpreted as especially important for facilitating the economic provider aspects of motherhood. Assisted by state-funded childcare, large numbers of women have been 'liberated' from their full-time caring responsibilities and have entered the labour market. Gaining access to paid work, they now have the opportunity to establish and maintain an independent household (Orloff, 1993) and provide economically for themselves and their children even if they and their husband or partner split up. Childcare-related entitlements are also about familializing and re-familializing, establishing the right of working parents to be the principal carers for their children. Scandinavian parental leave legislation has instituted the right to give priority to children's care over the demands of a job. If parental leaves entitle parents to wage compensation, there is a de-commodification of labour (Esping-Andersen, 1990). Parental leave legislation supports the carer aspects of the parenthood of fathers as well as mothers, while retaining their job security. Throughout Scandinavia, most employed parents are entitled to a paid leave of absence following the birth of a child. In the late 1990s, Sweden offered the longest period of paid leave, 450 days, and Denmark the shortest, 28 weeks. The entitlement is partly for individual leave and partly for leave to be used according to parental discretion. All the countries reserve part of the leave for the mother as maternity leave, and they all offer fathers the right to some days off after the birth of a child (paternity leave or daddy days). Furthermore, in the 1990s all the countries, Finland excepted, reserved special periods of the leave (daddy quota) for fathers on a use-or-lose basis. What remains of the total leave period can be used at the discretion of the parents. In the Nordic countries, parental leave and daddy quota are considered to be in everyone's best interest; they give the father and child an opportunity for early bonding and establishing a relationship, and they further gender equality at home and at work (Leira, 1998). These policy reforms, especially the fathers' quota, are striking examples of state intervention not only in the general employment framework applied in the public and private sector labour market, but also in the internal organization of the family. What is more, they favour the familialization of fathers.

At the birth of a child, most eligible mothers and fathers take up some paid leave. The individual right of fathers to some days of leave after a child is born is widely used, but the earmarking of more of the total leave for fathers has met with a mixed reception. In Norway, the special period reserved as daddy leave or fathers' quota was an instant success. Despite its being interpreted as encouraging father care via gentle force, it is taken up by 70 - 80% of the eligible fathers. In Sweden, however, the fathers' quota has not made much of a difference in the fathers' use of the leave. The entitlement of parents to choose how to split the greater part of the leave has hardly been used by fathers anywhere except Sweden. So the fact that many fathers take some leave does not mean fathers are great leave-consumers; fathers or parents do not opt for long periods of fathercare. In 2000, Danish, Finnish and Norwegian fathers used less than 10% of the paid leave, and Swedish fathers 13% (NORD 2001, Table 50, p. 114).

Further support for the re-familialization of childcare is witnessed by the introduction of cash benefits for childcare, reforms that were hotly debated in the 1990s. An arrangement of this kind was legislated in Sweden in the early 1990s, but withdrawn shortly afterwards. In Finland and Norway, cash grant plans have been instituted as an entitlement of families who do not use state-funded childcare for their young children. The cash benefit may be used to support parental care at home or for extra-parental, private childcare arrangements. Unlike the fathers' quota of the parental leave, the cash grant is not an incentive for recruiting the parent of the underrepresented sex into childcare. Argued as a support for familialized care of young children and parental choice with respect to childcare, the cash grant was widely viewed as targeting mothercare, not fathercare. Not surprisingly, it is largely mothers who take advantage of the grants, and only a few fathers take on the main caring responsibilities during the cash benefit period (Salmi and Lammi-Taskula, 1999; Baklien et al., 2001). Accepted by non-employed mothers, the cash grant may be interpreted as a commodification of childcare offering a symbolic childcare payment. Accepted by an employed mother who prolongs her leave of absence from salaried work, the grant represents a decommodification but not a salary to live on. In either case, the underlying assumption is that someone who is not the cash recipient has the main responsibility for providing for the family.

The three reforms also illustrate variations in the relation between family change and policy reform. For example, family change may precede policy reform, and policy reform may be instituted to induce family change or to reduce or postpone family change. As is the case elsewhere in Western Europe, in the Nordic region the transformation of motherhood initiated by mothers entering formal employment and the state funding of childcare services were not synchronized from the start. The transformation of motherhood preceded policy reform. Over time, however, state funding of childcare has facilitated the earner aspects of motherhood and made mothers more equal to fathers as economic providers.

Policy reforms promoting familialized father care for infants were introduced well before any mass demand was registered on the part of fathers or male-dominated organizations. Legislation for parental leave was influenced by and contributed to the cultural redefinition of men and masculinity at the end of the twentieth century, including new images of fathers as carers. Cash grants for childcare demonstrate that traditional family values are still important. Advocated as promoting parental choice regarding familialized or defamilialized childcare, the reforms did not target fathercare; instead they were interpreted as supporting the gender-differentiated nuclear family, a family form in decline in Scandinavia since the late 1960s.

PARENTAL CHOICE - NEW FORMS OF BONDING?

Since the 1970s, Scandinavian families have been moving beyond the model family of industrialism, but towards what? Relations between the welfare state, the labour market and the family have been profoundly transformed, as have intrafamily relations. Critics of these trends argue that state-funded individualism and autonomy will undermine family solidarity and moral obligations (Wolfe, 1989; see also Beck, 1992). But this is not the whole story. It is difficult to disagree with observations concerning greater fluidity, pluralism and diversity in family arrangements, but in a general sense relations between the genders and generations in families have become more egalitarian, less authoritarian (e.g. Hernes, 1987; Giddens, 1992).

The ongoing transformation of motherhood, fatherhood and childhood generated by the diversification of family forms and the mass entry of mothers on the labour market has revived the interest in family values as highlighted in discussions on the responsibility for children's care. In the Nordic region, family policy reforms of various kinds have been put forward as ways that the parent-child relationship can be fostered, nurtured or supported. Support for familialized care of young children is regarded as important in this respect, especially for establishing an early relationship between fathers and their children. Institutionalization of the right of fathers to leaves of absence from work has allowed men to participate in the care of their children starting at birth. Including fathers among those as entitled to care, even earmarking periods of the parental leave for fathers, has obviously made it easier for fathers to take the leave, thus facilitating negotiations in the workplace and with their partners at home.

The extent to which childcare-related reforms have created new forms of bonding is not an issue, but it does remain an open empirical question. What is important is that legislation has created new opportunities for exercising fatherhood and motherhood. However, granting parents the right to claim childcare-related services and benefits does not entail an obligation to make use of them. The acceptance and use by fathers and mothers of the parental leave and cash grant for childcare are indicative of gendered outcomes of reforms that are in principle given a gender-neutral formulation as parental choice. In all the Scandinavian countries, most fathers take some days of leave when a baby is born or is still very young. In this sense, fathers have been turning home to their children, which is important. While it may be argued that the entitlement to daddy leave promotes the familialization of fathers and most fathers do make use of the options for fathercare, it is also evident that legislation offers parents much more scope in how to share the leave than is actually accepted or used (see also Bruning and Plantenga, 1999). Parental leave legislation has opened up new ways of 'doing' fatherhood, but the potential for change it entails is far from fully developed or utilized. Apparently, a small dose of fathercare is fine and is all most fathers use. What remains of the leave is almost by definition for the mothers.

The unequal response of fathers and mothers to parental leave or cash benefits is a reminder that mothers and fathers pursue different combinations of work and parenthood and make different investments in their families. Caring is an important element in social and cultural norms on good motherhood, but might be less emphasized in the interpretation of good fatherhood. The different responses of mothers and fathers also illustrate the limits to choice in a context where the labour market is strongly segregated by sex, and parental obligations remain gendered, be it less so than a generation earlier.

It should also be noted that several studies caution against taking the use of leave as the only indicator of fathers' involvement with their children, since fathers' working hours may allow them to spend ample time with their children without making much use of the leave (e.g. Carlsen, 1993). Scandinavian studies indicate considerable differences between how men respond to fatherhood. In Norway and Sweden, time budget analyses show that fathers now spend more time with their children than fathers did twenty or thirty years ago. Small-scale studies report cases where fathers are the main carers, and others report parents who share the care for young children. The different ways mothers and fathers arrange for paid work and childcare indicate an increasing polarization among post-industrial families in how work and family are reconciled, with mothers and fathers opting for a dual-earner, care-sharing family at one end, and families with a traditional division of labour at the other.

Promoting the familializing of fathers via parental choice with respect to leave (as parental leave or leave linked to cash grants for childcare) has not proved successful, however. It has not resulted in gender equality with respect to time spent with children, but rather in a predominance of mothercare over father care. In all four Scandinavian countries, one main effect of parental choice with respect to care-related reforms is the prolonged decommodification of mothers and the familializing of maternal care for the very young.

NOTES

1. This chapter draws upon work done for my book *Working Parents and Welfare States*, Cambridge University Press, 2002.
2. The terms Scandinavia and the Nordic countries are sometimes used synonymously. Often, however, Scandinavia refers to Denmark, Norway and Sweden, whereas the Nordic countries also include Finland and Iceland. I draw upon data from four of the Nordic countries (Iceland is not included), and use the terms Scandinavia or Nordic countries interchangeably
3. For example, the Norwegian Ministry of Social Affairs acknowledged the importance of family as follows: 'If family members did for each other only what was prescribed in legislation, the public expenses for social insurance and social assistance would explode, and the provision of caring break down' (*Fornyelse av velferdsstaten 1996*, p. 23).
4. The gender-neutral terminology obscures the reality that if their parents break up, most children live with their mother.

REFERENCES

Anttonen, A. and J. Sipilä (1996), 'European social care services: is it possible to identify models?', *Journal of European Social Policy*, 6 (2), 87 - 100.
Anttonen, A., H. Forsberg and R.Huhtanen (1995), 'Family obligations in Finland', in J. Millar and A. Warman (eds), *Defining Family Obligations in Europe*, Bath, University of Bath, Social Policy Papers no. 23, pp. 65 - 86.
Baklien, B., A.L. Ellingsæter and L. Gulbrandsen (2001), *Evaluering av kontantstøtteordningen* (Cash Benefits for Childcare-An Evaluation), Oslo, Norges Forskningsråd.
Banfield, E. (1958), *The Moral Basis of a Backward Society*, New York: The Free Press.

Beck, U. (1992), *Risk Society: Towards a New Modernity*, London: Sage Publications.

Bjørnberg, U. and G. Eydal (1995), 'Family obligations in Sweden', in J.Millar and A. Warman (eds), *Defining Family Obligations in Europe*, Bath: University of Bath, Social Policy Papers no. 23, pp. 359 - 78.

Bruning, G. and J. Plantenga (1999), 'Parental leave and equal opportunities: experiences in eight European countries', *Journal of European Social Policy*, **9** (3),195 - 209.

Carlsen, S. 1993. 'Men's utilization of paternity leave and parental leave schemes', in S. Carlsen and J. Elm Larsen (eds), *The Equality Dilemma: Reconciling Working Life and Family Life*, Copenhagen: Danish Equal Status Council, pp. 79 - 90.

Drew, E., R. Emerek and E. Mahon (eds) (1998), *Women, Work and the Family in Europe*, London and New York: Routledge.

Esping-Andersen, G. (1990), *The Three Worlds of Welfare Capitalism*, Cambridge: Polity Press.

Esping-Andersen, G. (1996), 'After the golden age? Welfare state dilemmas in a global economy', in G. Esping-Andersen (ed.), *Welfare States in Transition. National Adaptations in Global Economics*, London: Sage Publications, pp. 1 - 31.

Esping-Andersen, G. (1999), *Social Foundations of Postindustrial Economies*, Oxford: Oxford University Press.

European Commission Childcare Network (1996), *A Review of Services For Young Children in the European Union 1990 - 1995*, Brussels: European Commission. Equal Opportunities Unit.

Finch, J. (1989), *Family Obligations and Social Change*, Cambridge: Polity Press.

Gauthier, A.H. (1996), *The State and the Family: A Comparative Analysis of Family Policies in Industrial Countries*, Oxford: Clarendon.

Giddens, A. (1992), *The Transformation of Intimacy*, Cambridge: Polity Press.

Gornick, J.C., M.C. Meyers and K.E. Ross (1998), 'Public policies and the employment of mothers: a cross-national study', *Social Science Quarterly*, **79** (1), 35 - 54.

Hantrais, L. and M.T. Letablier (1996), *Families and Family Policies in Europe*, London and New York: Longman.

Hernes, H.M. (1984), 'Women and the welfare state. The transition from private to public dependence', in H. Holter (ed.), *Patriarchy in a Welfare Society*, Oslo: Universitetsforlaget, pp. 26 - 45.

Hernes, H.M. (1987), *Welfare States and Woman Power*, Oslo: Norwegian University Press.

Jensen, A.M. (1999), 'Partners and parents in Europe: a gender divide', in A. Leira et al. (eds), *Family Change: Practices, Policies, and Values*, Comparative Social Research, vol. 18, Stamford, Conn.: JAI Press, pp. 1 - 29.

Jensen, K., (1990), 'Omsorgsideologi i endring' (Changing the Ideology of Care), in K. Jensen (ed.), *Moderne omsorgsbilder* (Modern Images of Care), Oslo: Ad Notam/Gyldendal, pp. 10 - 31.

Koch-Nielsen, I. (1996), *Family Obligations in Denmark*, Copenhagen: The Danish National Institute of Social Research.

Korpi, W. (2000), 'Faces of inequality: gender, class and patterns of inequalities in different types of welfare states', *Social Politics*, **7** (2), 127 - 91.

Leira, A. (1992), *Welfare States and Working Mothers. The Scandinavian Experience*, Cambridge: Cambridge University Press.

Leira, A. (1994), 'Combining work and family', in P. Brown and R. Crompton (eds), *A New Europe: Economic Restructuring and Social Change*, London: UCL Press, pp. 86 – 107.

Leira, A. (1996), *Parents, Children and the State. Family Obligations in Norway*, Oslo: Institute for Social Research.

Leira, A. (1998), 'Caring as social right: cash for child care and daddy leave', *Social Politics*, **5** (3), 362 - 78.

Leira, A. (2002), *Working Parents and the Welfare State*, Cambridge: Cambridge University Press.

Lewis, J. (ed.) (1993), *Women and Social Policies in Europe*, Aldershot, UK and Brookfield US: Edward Elgar.

Liljeström, R. (1978), 'Sweden', in S.B. Kamerman and A.J. Kahn (eds), *Family Policy. Government and Families in Fourteen Countries*, New York: Columbia University Press, pp. 19 - 48.

Lingsom, S. (1997), *The Substitution Issue*, Oslo: NOVA.

Millar, J. and A. Warman (eds) (1995), *Defining Family Obligations in Europe*, Bath: University of Bath, Social Policy Papers no. 23.

Millar, J and A. Warman (1996), *Family Obligations in Europe*, London: Family Policy Studies Centre.

Myrdal, A. and V. Klein (1956), *Women's Two Roles*, London: Routledge and Kegan Paul.

NORD (2001), *Nordic Statistical Yearbook* 2001: 1, Copenhagen: Nordic Council of Ministers.

OECD (1994), *Women and Structural Change. New Perspectives*, Paris: OECD.

Orloff, A.S. (1993), 'Gender and the social rights of citizenship', *American Sociological Review*, **58** (3), 303 - 329.

Parsons, T. (1955), 'The American family: its relations to personality and the social structure', in T. Parsons and R.F. Bales (eds), *Family Socialization and Interaction Process*, Glencoe, Illinois, The Free Press, pp. 3 - 33.

Salmi, M. and J. Lammi-Taskula (1999), 'Parental leave in Finland', in P. Moss and F. Deven (eds), *Parental Leave: Progress or Pitfall*, Brussels, NIDI/CBGS Publications, pp. 85 - 121.

Saraceno, C. (1994), 'The ambivalent familism of the Italian welfare state', *Social Politics*, **1** (1), 32 - 59.

Saraceno, C. (1997), 'Family change, family policies and the restructuring of welfare', in *Family, Market and Community. Equity and Efficiency in Social Policy*. OECD Social Policy Studies no. 21. Paris, OECD, pp. 81 - 100.

Szebehely, M. (1998), 'Changing divisions of carework: caring for children and frail elderly people in Sweden', in J. Lewis (ed.), *Gender and the Restructuring of Social Care in Europe*, Cheltenham, UK and Northampton, MA, USA: Edward Elgar, pp. 257 - 283.

Wolfe, A. (1989), *Whose Keeper? Social Science and Moral Obligation*, Berkeley: University of California Press.

12. Trends in Women's Employment, Domestic Service, and Female Migration: Changing and Competing Patterns of Solidarity

Fiona Williams

This chapter aims to make a link between changing patterns of solidarity at the local level within families and households and issues of global solidarity between richer and poorer nations. More specifically, the chapter looks at some of the processes involved in the increased use of (private and sometimes migrant) domestic/care work in those countries where there has been an increase in mothers' employment. Women's increased economic activity is thus placed in the context of three changing phenomena: the rapid increase in outsourcing of household services, patterns of international migration, and changing welfare regimes. This generates a number of questions. First, in so far as the activities entailed in maintaining family bonds, such as caring for children and older frail relatives, providing meals and general house- and kin-keeping, have traditionally, within a male-breadwinner system, been assumed to be largely women's responsibility, then how do women (and men) seek to maintain these bonds when they are in paid work? Second, how far are the conflicts created by the unequal sexual division of care in the home, the continuing male model of working time and conditions, and the limited responses of changing welfare regimes, being resolved through the use of privately hired domestic help? And third, why is this happening, and why is it that in some of the major European cities this waged domestic labour (referred to here as 'domestic service') is largely undertaken by migrant and racialized minority women?

In exploring these questions the chapter proposes that privately hired domestic help mediates the lack of time and capacity experienced by full-time working women in the West and the poverty and limited opportunities faced by those women who provide domestic services. In particular, it is suggested that such help facilitates, for better-off families in the West, new expressions of solidarity between the sexes and generations that place a value on the closeness and 'quality' of intimate/family relationships, whilst straining at the family solidarities of domestic service providers. At the same time, practices associated with both the use and provision of these services allow the continuation of traditionally gendered responsibilities.[1] In its turn, the premium placed on 'quality' relationships legitimizes the private hiring of such help. However, this also takes place within a context in which public provision is shifting from services to cash (to buy in services) or not meeting adequately the needs of working parents, and this leads to the use of temporary, low paid and sometimes undocumented migrant women workers to provide household services. This raises the question of the solidarities that exist between and within different groups of women, and the exploitative nature of the interdependence between richer and poorer women and richer and poorer nations.

The chapter starts with a theoretical note about the way in which disciplinary boundaries operate around research on female migration, care and welfare regimes. The following section documents the rise of employment in household services in Europe and, in particular, the private employment of paid (sometimes migrant) domestic labour. The reasons for this rise are then discussed in terms of three changing factors: the way women (and men) reconcile work and care; the response of welfare regimes to this; and patterns of migration and migration regimes.[2] The conclusion discusses the implications of these changes for our understanding of patterns of macro- and micro-solidarities and the relationship between the two.

MAPPING DOMESTIC SERVICE

The mapping and documentation of domestic service, and its relation to migration and/or globalization, has been gathering pace over the last decade, conducted mainly by feminists in geography, sociology and international relations (Enloe, 1989; Sassen, 1991; Gregson and Lowe, 1994; Heyzer et al., 1994; Phizacklea and Anderson, 1997; Phizacklea, 1998; Kofman et al., 2000; Anderson, 1997, 2000; Pettman, 2000; Collini and Lutz, 2000; Hochschild, 2000; Parrenas, 2001). With one or two exceptions (e.g. Kofman et al., 2000), these accounts and analyses of the geo-political inequalities of gender, 'race' and class relations caught up in the changing patterns of women's work make few connections to the welfare regimes in which women live or emigrate from. One the other hand, in those increasingly sophisticated feminist analyses of care, gender and welfare regimes, there is little analytical space provided for these international relationships to be explored. The conceptual gap here is, as I have argued before (Williams, 1995), a critical understanding of the significance of 'nation' in relation to welfare. In other words, welfare citizenship and welfare practices, in general, and unpaid and paid care practices and provision, in particular, are subject to the changing internal and external boundaries of the 'nation'. The internal refers to the nation-imaginary, and how this influences the (multi) cultural frame through which care practices and provision are constituted. But there are also transnational issues associated with the external boundaries of the nation, such as 'diasporas of care' where families care across continents (Ackers, 1998; Chamberlain, 1998). Another aspect is the 'global care chain' (Hochschild, 2000) where female migrant workers move from poorer countries to provide domestic service for individuals and families in richer countries. These external dimensions also include the formal recruitment of migrant labour to fill gaps in the mixed economy of social and health care (Glover et al., 2001).

DOMESTIC SERVICE IN LOCAL AND GLOBAL CONTEXT

The increased demand for waged domestic labour (cleaning, caring, or both) is evident in many European countries and can be seen as part of a more general increase in the employment of people in household services over the last ten to twenty years. In other words, tasks which might have earlier been carried out in the home by family members – childcare, care of older people, domestic cleaning and laundering, catering, and household maintenance and gardening – are now being provided in part by private, public and voluntary individuals and organizations.

In terms of domestic service, in the UK four billion pounds was being spent on domestic service in private households by 1996, four times as much as ten years previously (Mintel, 1997, cited in Anderson, 1997). In the early 1990s, 30 to 40% of dual career households employed waged domestic labour of some sort. In 2002 it was estimated that about 50,000 young women from abroad were working as 'au pairs' (nannies) in the UK (Addley, 2002). In Spain by 1997 there were over 600,000 domestic workers; in France 900,000 people belonged to the federation of employers of domestic labour, and in Germany the number of employers was estimated to be between 700,000 and one million (Anderson, 1997). However, while all of these figures register increases in the use of domestic labour, most of them are likely to be significant underestimates since, by its very nature, private domestic work is often undeclared by both homestate[3] women and migrant women, whether as employers or employees, because of rules attached to immigration, to benefit entitlements, to tax, or to national insurance.[4] A European Foundation study has estimated that in Europe 50 to 80% of domestic service work is undeclared (Cancedda, 2001).

Although the focus of this paper is on migrant women and domestic service, it is not only migrant women or women from racialized groups who take up domestic service, although this varies across countries. In Britain and France, much domestic service is done by homestate white women with migrant women concentrated in the metropolitan area. Gregson and Lowe (1994) found that in the early 1990s, outside the South East of England, cleaning was the province of older working-class women supplementing their pension and younger women on state benefits, whilst younger women with childcare qualifications who could find no other work normally undertook childcare. This contrasts with Greece, Spain and Germany where domestic service is *less* likely to be undertaken by homestate women, and, if it is, it is restricted to very old or very young workers (Anderson, 1997). However, statistics here present difficulties because of compounding minority ethnic categories with migrant workers. For example, in assessing the characteristics of domestic workers, the European Foundation reports that, in the Netherlands, ethnic minority workers in cleaning services represent 12 to 20% with 8% in private households, in Finland, 11% of home helps belong to linguistic minorities (5% are Swedish speakers), in Italy, 28% registered cleaners are non-EU citizens (and in Rome they are 70.5%), and in Spain, 32% domestic service workers are non-EU, and in France, 14.3% immigrants work in personal services (compared with 7.9% total economically active population) (Cancedda, 2001). There is, nevertheless, in all of these countries, an increase of migrant women, documented and undocumented, employed in domestic service.

Migrant domestic service is not only the privilege of Western countries. There have been significant legal and illegal flows within South and South East Asia – from SriLanka, Java and the Phillipines to Malaysia, Hong Kong and Bahrain and Saudi Arabia, as well as illegal movement from Burma and Bangladesh to Pakistan (Heyzer et al., 1994). In Singapore, for example, there is a tradition of women migrating into domestic service; however, by the 1970s these were mainly drawn from poorer homestate women. With the economic upturn, however, these women were drawn into other paid work and migrant workers were recruited into domestic work. By 1984 10% of all households had a migrant domestic worker in Singapore (Pettman, 2000). In addition, temporary migrant workers move between Central, Nothern and Eastern European countries.

However, the distinction noted above between cleaning and caring for homestate women does not operate in the same way for the work of migrant women:

> It includes all the work of the household: cooking, cleaning, shopping, washing, sewing, serving at table, ironing, and may be extended to cover gardening, chopping wood, washing cars, feeding, walking and caring for pets, performing intimate (but not necessarily sexual) services....care of children, the disabled, the elderly (Anderson, 1997, p. 38).

The key distinction for migrant domestic workers, Anderson points out, was not between caring and cleaning, but between 'live-in' and 'live-out', and this is influenced by a further distinction as to whether a migrant was documented or undocumented.[5]

WHY AN INCREASE IN DOMESTIC SERVICE?

In relation to the demand for domestic service, there are four generally accepted reasons for this increase: women's increased economic activity and the difficulties in combining paid work and domestic responsibilities; increased geographical mobility and loss of family support; an entrenched and unequal sexual division of labour in the home; and inadequacies in public provisions for care of young and older people. Allied to this are socially and culturally constructed preferences for privatized, home-based care, as well as policies that promote the buying in of services. In relation to the supply and availability of particular forms of 'flexible' labour, the dynamics revolve around migration patterns and migration regimes, and gendered and racialized hierarchies of labour. The complexity of factors involves changes in the opportunities and constraints both for those women who use domestic service and those who provide it. In this chapter I focus mainly on migrant domestic workers on the 'supply' side, rather than homestate women, although this is an equally important issue (Ungerson, 2000). From the perspective of women who use domestic service, it is not simply a consequence of their involvement in paid employment, it is also the nature of that work. Gregson and Lowe's study in Britain found that it was families in which both partners had full-time professional and/or managerial jobs that decided to employ private domestic help. From the 1980s women's entry into an increasing number of professions grew. Furthermore, many of these jobs are structured organizationally to the times and career patterns of a male (breadwinning and home-serviced) worker (Gregson and Lowe, 1994). What the female employer buys is 'quality time' outside of working time, which is not satisfied by spending such extra-curricular time in labour-intensive domestic work. Interestingly, given that economically active women now spend *more* time with their children in Britain than did their largely non-economically active mothers in the 1960s and 1970s (Gershuny, 2000), then one might speculate that the trade-off for employing a cleaner is to gain quality time with children. Domestic service is a way of resolving a work-rich, cash-rich, but time-poor situation for working mothers/women. However, in some ways, domestic service workers (especially live-in) may have even more work and less time, as well as much less cash, than their employers. Also, it is not only women who are time-poor who employ other women; there are some time-rich women and men for whom having domestic service buys in greater leisure time.

Mobility and the Chains of Care

Women's increased involvement in professional and managerial jobs combined with similar commitment from a partner also involves greater geographical mobility, and, with that, less recourse to other kin for childcare support (grandmothers also increasingly have paid work commitments). This is particularly important in those countries where women have depended upon extended family networks for care support, whether out of tradition, choice or necessity. Of course, mobility of a different sort pervades the life of a migrant worker. Rather than moving her family to find work, she moves herself to find work and leaves her family to be cared for by kin – usually a sister or mother. The consequence is that professional women in the developed regions may reconcile the difficulties of combining motherhood, domestic labour and full-time work by buying in the labour of other women to allow them time with their families. The migrant mother may 'buy-in' (through remittances sent home) a relative to care for her children but, in doing so, she forfeits time with her family. Yet both women are part of the same chain. It is this that Arlie Hochschild has called the 'global care chain' (Hochschild, 2000; Parrenas, 2001). Based on the experience of the United States, Hochschild estimates that half of the legal migrants to the US are women aged between twenty-five and thirty who have migrated in order to support their families back home. The global care chain involves the displacement of mothers caring for their own children: the aunt or grandmother who looks after the migrant worker's children and the migrant worker who looks after the professional woman's children. The dynamic is not only, she suggests, about the globalization of women's labour but the 'globalization of love'.

Gender Divisions within the Home

Both ends of this care chain also demonstrate entrenched assumptions about women's responsibilities in the home. If the increase in domestic service is about new opportunities in women's lives, it is also about unchanging constraints. These include men's lack of involvement in sharing domestic tasks and care in the home, as well as the structures of paid work that perpetuate such a lack of involvement. Gregson and Lowe's study of the use of domestic service in Britain found that amongst middle class dual earner families who employed cleaners, the division of labour did not remain totally unreconstructed, rather, there was a sharing of certain tasks (such as cooking, shopping, the school run) but a relegation of the most labour-intensive tasks (cleaning, ironing) to the female management of paid, and female, domestic labour. At the other end of the chain, Pearson demonstrates that in many developing regions where women's labour force participation has increased, this has not been matched by any shifts in the gender division of labour in the home (Pearson, 2000). Other trends, such as the incorporation of food and fabric production, are more significant. These both create paid work for women whilst enabling women to combine paid work with unpaid domestic responsibilities. In addition, women have become more likely to become either the breadwinner partner, or lone parent breadwinner, in addition to keeping their domestic responsibilities. And it is this situation that begins to account, in part, for the increases in female migration. Before looking at the question of migration, there is one further important factor, and that is the relationship between public provisions for the care of old and young, increased female labour participation and the use of private domestic service.

Public Provision and European Welfare Regimes

In much of the research on domestic service, and the increased involvement of migrant women in domestic service, there is a correlation given between this increase and a withdrawal of, or failure to provide, public services for children and older people (Anderson, 2000). Kofman et al. (2000) push this analysis a little further by trying to connect the use of domestic service, and migrant domestic service, to welfare regimes:

> The reliance of conservative and liberal regimes on unpaid domestic labour has provided new spaces for migrant labour. Italy and Spain have seen major migrations of female service workers. The employment of household labour has allowed Italian women to avoid upsetting the gender balance within the home because working women do not have to make demands on their partners to increase their share of domestic tasks (Tacoli, 1999, p.117). Migrant labour is increasingly employed in this way in Britain (Anderson, 1997). In Germany, on the other hand, the female labour force has brought a polarization between full-time childless women workers and full-time mothers (Anderson and Phizacklea, 1997).

> The proportion of working mothers remains smaller with a correspondingly lower demand for migrant domestic workers. The prevalence of the dual-income family and publicly funded childcare in social democratic regimes has meant there has been less room for migrants either within the formal labour market or as domestic workers (Kofman et al., 2000, pp. 143 - 4).

These observations, drawn mainly from studies of women migrants, are important and provide a different set of calculations in the emerging policy developments on both 'welfare to work' and 'work/life balance'. They also call up questions about gaps in current provisions for working households, as well as issues to do with state institutionalization of particularly exploitative forms of labour to fill those gaps.

How significant is the use of nannies in Britain to meet the childcare needs of working mothers? Recent statistics on the arrangements for childcare used by working mothers (full-time and part-time) in Britain only show between 2 and 4% using nannies or unregistered childminders (although around 20% would ideally choose a daily or live-in nanny from the formal childcare options) (Bryson et al., 2000). How far can we lay the increased use of domestic service in the form of cleaning and ironing at the door of the welfare state and the decline in public provisions, for most welfare states have not in the past included universal provision of home helps for working mothers? Also, how is it that France, with its much greater public provision of nurseries, also shows an increased use of domestic service? The main reason Anderson found was the mismatch between provision and women's working patterns. Almost four fifths of the requests for childcare at one agency in Paris that she studied were for children under two and for after school care where little other provision exists (Anderson, 2000).

A further relevant factor is the increasing provision in Europe of cash payments, tax credits or tax incentives to pay childminders, relatives or domestic helps, or parents/ mothers themselves, for their services. The move to payments, direct or otherwise is part of one of the key changes in the shape of European welfare states over the past decade (Daly and Lewis, 2000). But there are also links between this and international migration. In 2002 in the UK, on the same day as the government announced increased tax credits for working parents to use approved childcare in their own home, it also extended its scheme from 16 to 22 non-EU countries (almost all Eastern Europe) to allow nannies aged 17 - 27 to work in the UK.[6] Recent research by Ungerson (2002) on direct payments to older care users in Europe demonstrates how particular migration regimes and forms of regulation influence patterns of employment of migrant women as home carers by older people.

CHALLENGES AND CHANGES TO FAMILIAL OBLIGATIONS

These issues point up the complexities in the use and experience of domestic service. Although, officially, domestic work is defined in terms of cleaning, washing, ironing and cooking (ILO, 1990), as mentioned earlier, the distinctions between cleaning and caring work, which also often pertain to homestate domestic workers in Britain, do not tally with the experiences of migrant domestic workers:

> When I asked them what they did, workers frequently responded 'everything': 'We have to do everything, do the garden, clean the garage, clean the car, take the goats out for work, the children, there is nothing we are not told to do' (Irene, a Sri Lanken, working in Athens, quoted in Anderson, 2000, p.15).

In some cases, this *is* acknowledged officially. For example, in 1998 the UK government stipulated that non-nationals coming into Britain to take up domestic service had to demonstrate they had responsibilities which went beyond the ILO's definition to include caring responsibilities for a sick, old or disabled person (cited in Anderson, 2000). 'Domestic service' particularly when undertaken by migrant workers (and possibly also minority ethnic homestate women) covers a multitude of responsibilities that may well include a significant amount of caring for which there is no available or suitable public provision. Furthermore, how individual employers perceive domestic service may position workers in a 'no-man's-land' (so to speak) between being an employee and 'family'. In their British study, Gregson and Lowe (1994) analyse how combined relations of 'false kinship' and waged labour characterize, in different ways, the employment by female partners of nannies and cleaners. In differing degrees, all parties may go along with the construction of false kinship ('just one of the family'), but for different reasons. For example, for the employees it explains better their work practices, for employers, it may justify better their employment practices. However, the experiences of migrant domestic workers recounted by Anderson, are more at odds with their employers' perceptions:

> The problem is, they don't treat me as a slave or anything. The problem is they treat me as family. I think being a family you stay in the family. I say, if you are in the family you should be there from morning to night (Emma, Philipina working in Paris, quoted in Anderson, 2000: p. 44).

In fact, being considered to be 'one of the family' is also an important part of what various writers see as a reconciliation by (working) mothers of being employed outside the home and unable to care for their own children, but believing that mother-care, or home-care, is the most appropriate form of care (see Gregson and Lowe, 1994). There are a number of different ways we might interpret this in relation to the changing relations between the sexes and the generations. One way would be to see in this traditionally gendered ideas of who should care for children. Research on the 'gendered moral rationalities' of mothers in the UK taking up paid work shows that preferences for mother-substitution for childcare is prevalent although it is not wholesale (Duncan et al., forthcoming). Class, occupation and ethnicity mediate such preferences. In the main it is white working-class mothers and African Caribbean mothers (middle and working class) who feel this way.

A second explanation might, as indicated above, be in terms of the unsatisfactory experiences with public provision. To support this, as far as Britain is concerned, two large-scale surveys demonstrate that the majority of mothers preferred informal childcare by someone who would look after children in the same way as the parents, preferably partner or grandparent (Bryson et al., 2000). Thus the construction of the choice of nannies for those who could afford them could be seen as the part of this continuum of preference for informal care and is influenced by dominant national and local discourses on what constitutes appropriate childcare. These discourses are also influenced by the choices that have been available to working mothers, in other words, by the provision of a particular welfare/care regime. Thus, it is not surprising that in Britain, a welfare regime with a post-war history of relatively small and targeted provision in day care for the under 5s, many mothers have greater trust in informal childcare arrangements. by partners or grandparents than in formal provision (Bryson et al., 2000). By contrast, in France with a history of public provision, domestic service fills gaps in that provision, whereas, in Southern European welfare regimes built on traditional practices of familial obligations (Millar and Warman, 1996) and middle-class use of domestic help, it is the intensification of the private employment of domestic workers which resolves work/ care tensions for employed mothers.

Employment of domestic service workers for either cleaning or caring is also a way of coping with an ongoing and unequal sexual division of domestic commitments. Research shows that while men have a greater involvement in domestic work, women still have overall responsibility for organizing and managing domestic life, including the work of women whom they may employ (Sullivan, 1997). Similarly, the resistance of work organizations to change to fit with the demands of home life also suggests that women who are in full- time occupations organized around a 'male worker model' will not have the time to maintain the familial obligations that they and others might expect of them without delegating some of it elsewhere.

An additional interpretation for the increase in domestic service may lie in the changing nature of partnering and parenting, especially changing expectations around closeness, sharing and emotional intimacy. Much of the empirical work on family practices in Britain does not go as far as to support the theoretical propositions of Giddens (1992) that intimate relationships have become individualized to the extent that emotional satisfaction is the all or nothing of people's commitment to a relationship. However, the practices of discussion, reflexivity and negotiation do seem to be given higher value (Smart and Neale, 1999; Ribbens-McCarthy et al., 2000; Crow, 2002), even although, as Duncan and colleagues point out, negotiating and sharing household tasks may be based on traditional assumptions about what men and women should do (Duncan et al., 2003). In relation to parenting, recent studies demonstrate that parents and young people in Britain have strong ideals about democratic, equal relationships, 'friendships' or 'companionships' based on negotiated and open communication (Langford et al., 2001). The demand for 'quality time' may not only have emerged in the subjective assessment of what matters in close family relationships, but also as a result of the demands increasingly placed on parents to be effective and responsible for the development of their children into knowledge-acquiring, self-regulating adults. The point here is that in a situation where a value is placed on quality of interaction within families, for those time-poor mothers who can afford it, the delegation of household tasks to allow for this may be one factor behind the decision to use domestic service. Whilst not denying that the basis of the employer/ employee relationship is open to exploitation, and that one women's privilege is at another woman's expense, this idea would qualify Anderson's interpretation in her study of migrant domestic workers. This is that the employing women are buying into the privilege of a male form of 'care as emotion freed from labour' (Anderson, 2000, p. 87), although for some women of the class used to having servants, this may be the case. For some women, this pattern, common traditionally amongst those classes used to having servants, may be the case.

All this provides possible reasons for the way domestic service may mediate both changing and unchanging relationships within families. However, this does not answer why the increase has been in migrant workers. In other words, what is the relationship between (different) women's employment, the sexual division of labour, changing welfare/care regimes, especially in relation to policies for old and young, prevailing discourses and practices of care, *and* migration regimes?

MIGRATION REGIMES AND DOMESTIC SERVICE

It is now widely acknowledged that the increased feminization of migration is one of the major changes in recent patterns of migration (Castles and Miller, 1998), even though this may underplay the element of continuity in female migration. Migration has also accelerated recently through national and ethnic conflicts resulting in greater numbers of refugees and asylum seekers. But the growth of casual and short-term labour as well as greater tourist activity also plays a part. In addition, migration has diversified to include skilled, professional as well as unskilled workers, and this applies to women as well as men. Women also migrate for different reasons, not only, as is often assumed, to join their husbands as part of family reunification opportunities. For many, migration provides economic opportunities to provide for their families. According to the IMF, at the beginning of the 1990s, remittances sent home by migrant workers were 65 billion dollars, some 20 billion more than official overseas global aid programmes (Travis, 2000). It also may provide the chance to escape a violent marriage or oppressive regimes that disallow divorce or hold divorcées in contempt. In many countries migrant workers fill the jobs that homestate workers do not want or have not the skills for. Work opportunities have increasingly been created by the movement of multinational firms into the major cities of the world 'global cities' (Sassen, 1991). It is towards these that migrants gravitate. In her analysis of work and wages in London, Bruegel (1999) found that high land values lead to attempts to cut labour costs, creating low paid jobs that homestate workers will not take, and which then become open to migrant workers. At the same time, multinationals also attract higher paid elite workers whose consumption practices depend upon labour-intensive services – restaurants, laundries and private domestic services. Bruegel found that male and female workers constitute both elite and low paid service workers, but the differences lay in the latter's minority ethnic or migrant status (although a small minority of migrant women workers are also part of the elite labour force). Only 41% of UK-born women occupy personal service jobs in London, compared with 64% for the rest of the country. Wage differentials are widening along class, gender and racialized lines, and it is this matrix into which female migrant workers step.

However, migration regimes and their impact upon women has also channelled women into particular forms of work. For undocumented women migrants the privacy afforded by live-in domestic work makes it particularly attractive, as well as providing the possibility of earning money to pay back loans built up in the course of migrating without having to incur housing costs, or to immediately be proficient in a new language. These advantages also render live-in domestic workers vulnerable to exploitation as many high-profile cases of migrant housemaids imprisoned, raped and tortured have demonstrated. In addition many migration regimes operate their family reunification policies on a 'male breadwinner model' in which the conditions of reunification stipulate the economic dependency of the new migrant on her partner. In many cases this may be financially impossible. Further, following the moral panic around asylum-seekers, some countries, such as Britain, have withdrawn cash benefits and provide instead food vouchers. It is these conditions of economic stringency and unwanted dependency that make the grey economy of private domestic service attractive.

Whilst these migration policies effectively criminalize those un-documented workers who seek domestic work, it is also apparent from some states that have intermittently regularized the existence of migrant workers in domestic service, that such workers meet a need for work not filled by homestate workers. Many countries both vilify but depend upon migrant workers. Italy has regularized undocumented domestic workers several times since 1986. Migrant women, mainly from the Philippines and North Africa, have occupied domestic service jobs in Italy since the late 1960s when homestate women became less interested in live-in domestic posts. However, in spite of constraints placed upon migrant domestic workers (not allowed to take up hourly paid work; tied to an individual employer), this only made them more attractive to Italian employers. Between 1986 and 1988 the Italian government stopped issuing work permits and provided an 'amnesty' for undocumented migrants. During this time, 118,000 non-EU citizens received a work permit. This happened again in 1990, regularizing, in the main, Philipino domestic workers. Acts passed in 1990 and 1991 facilitated the employment of non-Italian citizens as domestic workers. In 1995, regularization took a new turn in making employers liable to a prison sentence if they hired illegal immigrants, but also offering amnesty to those who had resided for more than four months, so long as the employed paid their social insurance contributions. In spite of difficulties in policing this, almost quarter of a million migrants received work permits by 1996 (Kofman et al., 2000).

It is not only that migrant workers are not in a position to demand the wages of homestate workers that makes them attractive to employers. Often women working as domestic workers are overqualified for their work. Many migrant women who have qualified as nurses find themselves working as care assistants or domestic workers. One study found that half of those Filipinas interviewed in Italy had a college education. Filipinas working with children in Italy carry the added advantage of being able to teach them to speak English, although these skills are never acknowledged financially (Kofman et al., 2000).

In Anderson's study she found that live-in migrant domestic workers were preferred because they had developed caring skills through the experience of having had their own children, yet did not have any of the demands the presence of their own children might make, such as taking time off for children's sickness. Employment agencies often represented this separation of the migrant worker from her own family as a bonus for the employer as she would redirect her emotional energy to the employer's children. This situation also helps to create the double bind of 'false kinship', as mentioned above, where the migrant worker becomes 'one of the family'. In short, undocumented workers are flexible, cheap, do not have to be given contracts, nor their National Insurance paid: they provide value for money and are not constrained by their own family commitments. Not only does this give rise to possible exploitation, but also it may position the employer as the one who is 'doing a favour'. These conditions also make employees vulnerable to racism. Anderson also found that racist stereotypes and hierarchies underpinned recruitment and treatment of domestic workers, and these were reinforced by levels of pay and by placement agencies. Black Africans were at the bottom of the hierarchy with Filipinas at the top. But particular stereotypes operate in different countries, with Ukrainians for example, being less favoured in Greece.

Migration regimes in different countries also construct different geographical patterns of migration. Thus, in Germany, where citizenship is based upon the law of blood, Poles, as *Aussiedler* (having German descent), do not need a visa to live in Germany for up to three months. However, they are not allowed to work. This means that Polish women will often work, illegally, as domestic workers in private households renewing their residence visa by spending some time in Berlin and some time in neighbouring western Poland. However, by the same principle of blood law, Ukrainians cannot entry Germany without a visa, so it is they who are employed as domestic workers by Polish women to look after their families while they are away. The presence of Ukrainians in Poland is because, like the Poles, they focus upon Germany as the place to earn good money. Unlike the Poles, they cannot get in without a visa, and if they do try, they are caught and sent (by an agreement negotiated with the EU) to Poland. It is in Poland that they find alternative employment in domestic work (Anderson, 2000).

In so far as the employment of migrant domestic service provides employing families with very low cost caring and cleaning, there is also the issue of the costs saved by the state in encouraging women workers to find their own, privatized, solutions to their child/elder care needs. These are filled by workers whose own skills have been developed at no cost to the state in which they work, and whose dependants incur no added costs of healthcare or education. Indeed, these workers' own access to services to meet their own welfare needs may be severely circumscribed by the vulnerability of their status, and by the low priority given to specialist services for migrants and refugees. Further, if and when such workers achieve legal status, they may find that they take on a new role as 'mediators' between their own communities and the formal welfare services (see Kofman et al., 2000). Indeed, it is a feature of migrant workers' lives that new organizations of solidarity have developed to defend and advance their rights in both migration and work.[7]

CONCLUSION

This chapter has linked together the relationship between welfare regimes (and care), migration regimes (and citizenship) and women's increased participation in paid work, and has pointed to issues for future research. Mothers' increased employment creates problems for the emotional, social and physical maintenance of parent and partner relationships. Many of those women who earn enough are choosing to buy in certain caring and cleaning services in order to buy back time in which to carry out their remaining responsibilities. This problem of sustaining 'family solidarity' is exacerbated in situations where men's involvement in household and emotional labour has shifted only slightly, and where places of work continue to be organized according to a male working time model. As a result of this, the outsourcing of all forms of household services has increased in most European countries. At the same time, policies for the care of the young and older people in a number of countries are placing the onus on care users and parents to buy in their own care providers through, for example, direct cash payments or tax credits. In other countries provisions for working parents are still limited. In addition, particular cultural preferences for mother-substitute care, and shifts in the meaning of parenting and partnering which place a premium on the quality of emotional interaction, influence the strategy of better-off mothers reconciling work and care tensions through the buying in of domestic services of cleaning and childcare.

If these shifts point to the changing contours of 'home' and the blurring of public and private, then this picture is incomplete without a gendered understanding of migration flows and migration regimes. For many women in Eastern Europe, parts of Latin America, of Africa and South East Asia, there are different pressures which also strain at family cohesion and lead to the strategy women of moving across countries or continents to find work to support their families. Increased restrictions placed on women migrants to support themselves makes attractive the 'grey' economy of work in the home. It is here that the dissolution of the boundaries of the 'home' and of the 'homeland' meets. When migrant women workers (or poorer homestate women) step into this confluence, it is their labour that is crucial in keeping together the threatened framework of solidarities of genders and generations.

NOTES

1. To talk of 'gendered responsibilities' within the home might appear to assume that all households include two adults, male and female. It should be acknowledged that this is not the case and that 'families' are diversely constituted in terms of numbers and sex and of adults, and presence of children. Nevertheless, for an exploratory chapter such as this, it is not possible to account for intra-familial differences. Any future research along these lines would have to take these into account.

2. This chapter has benefited particularly from two excellent analyses, based upon empirical research, of female migrants in Europe, by Bridget Anderson (1997, 2000) and Eleanore Kofman, Annie Phizacklea, Parvati Raghuram and Rosemary Sales (2000).

3. I have used the word 'homestate' to mean women who are settled citizens of a country, whatever their ethnic origin.

4. Being 'undeclared' for migrant workers does not mean they are illegal.

5. Working with or without a work permit.

6. They must do 25 hours' childcare or light housework and two evenings' babysitting for £45 a week, a room and the opportunity to learn English.

7. Anderson (2000, chapter 6) documents the development of the campaign group, Kalayaan, and the self-help group, Waling-Waling, as key organizations in the UK (see also Heyzer et al., 1994, Chapter 8, and Williams, 2003).

REFERENCES

Ackers, L. (1998), *Shifting Spaces: Women, Citizenship and Migration within the European Union*, Bristol: Polity Press.

Addley, E. (2002), 'Not quite Mary Poppins', *the Guardian G2*, 28.11.02: 2 - 3.

Anderson, B. (1997), 'Servants and slaves: Europe's domestic workers', *Race and Class*, **39** (1), 37 - 49.

Anderson, B. (2000), *Doing the Dirty Work*, London: Zed Press.

Browne, A. (2001), 'Abused, threatened, trapped – Britain's foreign slave nurses', *The Observer*, London, 27th May, p.5.

Bruegel, I. (1999), 'Globalization, feminization and pay inequalities in London and the UK', in J. Gregory, R. Sales and A. Hegewisch (eds), *Women, Work and Equality: The Challenge of Equal Pay*, Basingstoke: Macmillan, pp.73 - 93.

Bryson, C., T. Budd, J. Lewis and G. Elam (2000), *Women's Attitudes to Combining Paid Work and Family Life*, London: The Women's Unit, Cabinet Office.

Cancedda, A. (ed.) (2001), *Employment in Household Services*, Dublin: The European Foundation for the Improvement of Living and Working Conditions.

Castles, S. and M. Miller (1998), *The Age of Migration*, Basingstoke: Macmillan.

Chamberlain, M. (ed.) (1998), *Caribbean Migration: Globalised Identities*, London: Routledge.

Collini, M. and H. Lutz (2000), 'Gender, migration and social inequalities', in S. Duncan and B. Pfau-Effinger (eds), *Gender, Economy and Culture in the EU*, London: Routledge, pp. 143 - 69.

Crow, G. (2002), *Social Solidarities: Theories, Identities and Social Change*, Buckingham: Open University Press.

Daly, M. and J. Lewis (2000), 'The Concept of social care and the analysis of contemporary welfare states', *British Journal of Sociology*, **52** (2), 281 - 98.

Duncan, S., R. Edwards, T. Reynolds and P. Alldred (2003) 'Paid work, partnering and childcare: values and theories', *Work, Employment and Society*, **17** (2), 309 – 30.

Enloe, C. (1989), *Beaches, Bananas and Bases*, London: Pandora Press.

Gershuny, J. (2000), *Changing Times: Work and Leisure in Post-Industrial Society*, Oxford: Oxford University Press.

Giddens, A. (1992), *The Transformation of Intimacy*, Polity Press: Cambridge.

Glover, S., C. Gott, A. Loizillon, J. Porter, R. Price, S. Spencer, V. Srinivasan and C. Willis (2001), *Migration: an Economic and Social Analysis*, RDS Occasional Paper 67, London: Home Office.

Gregson, N. and M. Lowe (1994), *Servicing the Middle Classes: Class, Gender and Waged Labour in Contemporary Britain*, London: Routledge.

Heyzer, N., G. Lycklama à Nijeholt and N. Weekaroon (1994), *The Trade in Domestic Workers: Causes, Mechanisms and Consequences of International Migration*, London: Zed Books.

Hochschild, A. (2000), 'The nanny chain', *American Prospect*, 3 Jan.

ILO (International Labour Organisation) (1990), *International Standard Classification of Occupations*, Geneva:ILO.

Kofman, E., A. Phizacklea, P. Raghuram and R. Sales (2000), *Gender and International Migration in Europe: Employment, Welfare and Politics*, London: Routledge.

Langford, W., C. Lewis, Y. Solomon and J. Warin (2001), *Family Understandings*, London: Family Policy Studies Centre.

Millar, J. and A. Warman (1996), *Family Obligations in Europe*, London: Family Policy Studies Centre/JRF.

Office for National Statistics (2000), *Labour Market Trends*, **108**, London: ONS.

Parrenas, R. (2001), *Servants of Globalization*, Stanford, US: Stanford University Press.

Pearson, R. (2000), 'All change? Men, women and reproductive work in the global economy', *The European Journal of Development Research*, **12** (2), 219 - 36.

Pettman, J. (2000), 'Women on the move: Globalisation and labour migration from south and south East Asian states', *Global Society*, **12** (3), 389 - 403.

Phizacklea, A. (1998), 'Migration and gobalization: A feminist perspective', in K. Koser and H. Lutz (eds), *The New Migration in Europe*, London: Macmillan, pp. 21 - 38.

Phizacklea, A. and B. Anderson (1997), *Migrant Domestic Workers: A European Perspective*, Brussels: European Commission Equal Opportunities Unit.

Ribbens-McCarthy, J., R. Edwards and V. Gillies (2000), 'Moral tales of the child and the adult: Contemporary family lives under changing circumstances', *Sociology*, **34** (4), 785 - 803.

Sassen, S. (1991), *The Global City: New York, London, Tokyo*, Princeton: Princeton University Press.

Smart, C. and B. Neale (1999), *Family Fragments?*, Cambridge: Polity Press.

Sullivan, O. (1997), ' Time waits for no (wo)man: An investigation into the gendered experience of domestic time', *Sociology*, **31** (2), 221 - 39.

Tacoli, C. (1999), 'Just like one of the family', in J. Gregory, R. Sales and A. Hegewisch (eds), *Women, Work and Equality: the Challenge of Equal Pay*, Basingstoke: Macmillan.

Travis, A. (2000), 'Open the door', *the Guardian*: London, 20 June.

Ungerson, C. (2000), 'Thinking about the production and consumption of long-term care in Britain: Does gender still matter', *Journal of Social Policy*, **29** (4), 623 - 44.

Ungerson, C. (2002), 'Cash and care: Whose independence?', Paper given at the *6th Global Conference on Ageing*, Perth, Western Australia, October, 2002.

Williams, F. (1995), 'Race/ethnicity, gender and class in welfare states: A framework for comparative analysis', *Social Politics*, **2** (1), 127 - 59.

Williams, F. (2003),'Contesting "race" and gender in the European Union: a multi-layered recognition struggle', in B. Hobson (ed.), *Recognition Struggles and Social Movements: Contested Power, Identity and Agency*, Cambridge: Cambridge University Press.

Index